Six Sigma Measures and Formulas

Keep this Cheat Sheet on hand when making your calculations!

Measures of Variation Location

For a collection of data or measurements $(x_1, x_2, ..., x_n)$:

- **Mode.** The most frequently observed data or measurement value (the peak)
- **Median.** The value which half the data or measurements are below and half are above
- **Mean (average).** $\bar{x} = \dfrac{\Sigma x_i}{n}$

Shifting between short-term and long-term sigma score

- $Z_{LT} = Z_{ST} - 1.5$
- $Z_{ST} = Z_{LT} + 1.5$

Capability Indices

- $C_P = \dfrac{USL - LSL}{6\sigma_{ST}}$
- $C_{PK} = \min\left(\dfrac{USL - \bar{x}}{3\sigma_{ST}}, \dfrac{\bar{x} - LSL}{3\sigma_{ST}}\right)$
- $P_P = \dfrac{USL - LSL}{6\sigma_{LT}}$
- $P_{PK} = \min\left(\dfrac{USL - \bar{x}}{3\sigma_{LT}}, \dfrac{\bar{x} - LSL}{3\sigma_{LT}}\right)$

Sigma (Z) Score

$$= \dfrac{|SL - \bar{x}|}{\sigma_{ST}}$$

Sigma (Z) Score ↔ Defects Per Million Opportunities (*DPMO*)			
Z	DPMO	Z	DPMO
0.0	933,193	3.5	22,750
0.5	841,345	4.0	6,210
1.0	691,462	4.5	1,350
1.5	500,000	5.0	233
2.0	308,538	5.5	32
2.5	158,655	6.0	3.4
3.0	66,807		

Measures of Variation Spread

For a collection of data or measurements $(x_1, x_2, ..., x_n)$

- **Range:** $R = x_{MAX} - x_{MIN}$
- **Variance:** $\sigma^2 = \dfrac{\Sigma(x_i - \bar{x})^2}{n - 1}$
- **Standard Deviation:** $\sigma = \sqrt{\dfrac{\Sigma(x_i - \bar{x})^2}{n - 1}}$
- **Long-term Standard Deviation:** $\sigma_{LT} = \sqrt{\dfrac{\Sigma(x_i - \bar{x})^2}{n - 1}}$
- **Short-term Standard Deviation:** $\sigma_{ST} = \dfrac{\Sigma R_i}{1.128(n - 1)}$

  where R_i is the range between each sequential pair of data points or measurements.

Coefficient of Determination

$$R^2 = \dfrac{\sum_{i=1}^{n}\left(\hat{y} - \bar{y}\right)^2}{\sum_{i=1}^{n}\left(y_i - \bar{y}\right)^2}$$

Simple Linear Regression

That is, fitting a line to a set of (x, y) data:

- Model: $\hat{y} = \beta_0 + \beta_1 x + \varepsilon$
- Parameters: $\beta_1 = \dfrac{\sum_{i=1}^{n}(x_i - \bar{x}) y_i}{\sum_{i=1}^{n}(x_i - \bar{x})^2}$
- $\beta_0 = \bar{y} - \beta_1 \bar{x}$

Proportion Defective Chart p

- $p_i = \dfrac{d_i}{n_i}$ where d_i is the number of inspected items found to be defective. The number of items inspected n_i doesn't have to be the same for each sample.
- $\bar{p} = \dfrac{d_1 + d_2 + \cdots + d_k}{n_1 + n_2 + \cdots + n_k}$
- $UCL_i = \bar{p} + 3\sqrt{\dfrac{\bar{p}(1 - \bar{p})}{n_i}}$
- $LCL_i = \bar{p} - 3\sqrt{\dfrac{\bar{p}(1 - \bar{p})}{n_i}}$

Six Sigma Workbook For Dummies®

Confidence Intervals

- Confidence interval for mean (μ), when sample size (n) is greater than 30: $\mu = \overline{x} \pm Z \dfrac{s}{\sqrt{n}}$

- Confidence interval for mean (μ), when sample size (n) is less than 30: $\mu = \overline{x} \pm t \dfrac{s}{\sqrt{n}}$

- Confidence interval for standard deviations (σ):

$$\sigma = \left[\sqrt{\dfrac{(n-1)s^2}{\chi^2_{\text{LOWER}}}}, \sqrt{\dfrac{(n-1)s^2}{\chi^2_{\text{UPPER}}}}\right]$$

- Confidence interval for the ratio of two variances:

$$\dfrac{\sigma_1^2}{\sigma_2^2} = \left[\dfrac{1}{F(c=n_2, r=n_1)}\dfrac{s_1^2}{s_2^2}, F(c=n_1, r=n_2)\dfrac{s_1^2}{s_2^2}\right]$$

- Confidence interval for a proportion:

$$p = \dfrac{y}{n} \pm Z\sqrt{\dfrac{(y/n)(1-y/n)}{n}}$$

- Confidence interval for the difference between two proportions:

$$\dfrac{y_1}{n_1} - \dfrac{y_2}{n_2} \pm Z\sqrt{\dfrac{(y_1/n_1)(1-y_1/n_1)}{n_1} + \dfrac{(y_2/n_2)(1-y_2/n_2)}{n_2}}$$

Individuals and Moving Range 1-MR

Individuals chart

- $\overline{X} = \dfrac{1}{k}(x_1 + x_2 + \cdots + x_k)$ where k is the number of points you are charting.
- $\text{UCL}_x = \overline{X} + 2.659\overline{\text{MR}}$
- $\text{LCL}_x = \overline{X} - 2.659\overline{\text{MR}}$

Moving Range chart

- $\text{MR}_i = |x_i - x_{i-1}|$
- $\overline{\text{MR}} = \dfrac{1}{k-1}(\text{MR}_2 + \text{MR}_3 + \cdots + \text{MR}_k)$ where k is the number of points you are charting.
- $\text{UCL}_{\text{MR}} = 3.267\overline{\text{MR}}$
- $\text{LCL}_{\text{MR}} = 0$

Correlation Coefficient

$$r = \dfrac{1}{n-1}\sum_{i=1}^{n}\left(\dfrac{x_i - \overline{x}}{\sigma_x}\right)\left(\dfrac{y_i - \overline{y}}{\sigma_y}\right)$$

2^k Factorial Experiments

- Main Effects: $E_i = \dfrac{1}{2^{k-1}}\sum_{j=1}^{2^k} c_{i,j}y_j$

- Interaction Effects:

$$E_{ab\cdots z} = \dfrac{1}{2^{k-1}}\sum_{j=1}^{2^k}\left(c_{a,j} \times c_{b,j} \times \cdots \times c_{z,j}\right)y_j$$

- $Y = f(X)$ equation parameters: $\beta_{ab\cdots z} = \dfrac{1}{2}E_{ab\cdots z}$

Averages and Ranges Chart $\overline{X}$-R:

Ranges chart

- $R_i = \max(x_1, x_2, \ldots, x_n) - \min(x_1, x_2, \ldots x_n)$
- $\overline{R} = \dfrac{1}{k}(R_1 + R_2 + \cdots + R_k)$ where k is the number of subgroups you are charting.
- $\text{UCL}_R = D_4\overline{R}$
- $\text{LCL}_R = D_3\overline{R}$

Averages chart

- $\overline{X}_i = \dfrac{1}{n}(x_1 + x_2 + \cdots + x_n)$ where n is the number of measurements in each sample subgroup.
- $\overline{\overline{X}} = \dfrac{1}{k}(\overline{X}_1 + \overline{X}_2 + \cdots + \overline{X}_k)$ where k is the number of subgroups you are charting.
- $\text{UCL}_x = \overline{\overline{X}} + A_2\overline{R}$
- $\text{LCL}_x = \overline{\overline{X}} - A_2\overline{R}$ where the formula parameters A_2, D_3, and D_4 depend on the size of your sample subgroup (n).

Defects Per Unit Chart u

- $u_i = \dfrac{D_i}{n_i}$ where D_i is the number of defects found in the inspection of the units in the sample. The number of units inspected n_i doesn't have to be the same for each sample.

- $\overline{u} = \dfrac{D_1 + D_2 + \cdots + D_k}{n_1 + n_2 + \cdots + n_k}$

- $\text{UCL}_i = \overline{u} + 3\sqrt{\dfrac{\overline{u}}{n_i}}$

- $\text{LCL}_i = \overline{p} - 3\sqrt{\dfrac{\overline{u}}{n_i}}$

For Dummies: Bestselling Book Series for Beginners

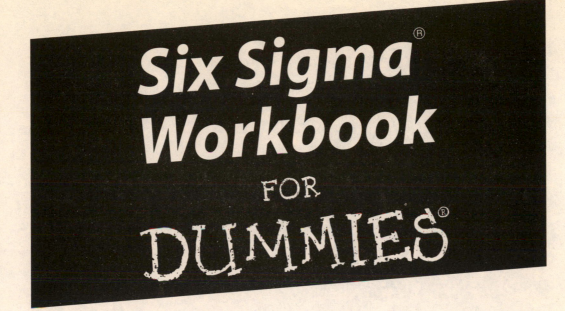

Six Sigma® Workbook

FOR DUMMIES®

Six Sigma® Workbook

FOR DUMMIES®

by Craig Gygi
Bruce Williams
Terry Gustafson

WILEY

Wiley Publishing, Inc.

Six Sigma® Workbook For Dummies®

Published by
Wiley Publishing, Inc.
111 River St.
Hoboken, NJ 07030-5774
www.wiley.com

For general information on our other products and services, please contact our Customer Care Department within the U.S. at 800-762-2974, outside the U.S. at 317-572-3993, or fax 317-572-4002.

For technical support, please visit www.wiley.com/techsupport.

Wiley also publishes its books in a variety of electronic formats. Some content that appears in print may not be available in electronic books.

Library of Congress Control Number: 2006927762

ISBN-13: 978-0-470-04519-0

ISBN-10: 0-470-04519-1

Manufactured in the United States of America

10 9 8 7 6 5 4 3 2

1O/QV/QZ/QW/IN

WILEY

About the Authors

Craig Kent Gygi began studying and applying the elements of Six Sigma well before they were formalized into today's renowned breakthrough method. As an engineering graduate student at Brigham Young University in the early 1990s, he integrated these then-unorganized improvement techniques into his research and coaching of student product development teams. Upon beginning his career in 1994 at Motorola's Advanced Manufacturing Research Lab in Florida, he was formally introduced to the just-formalizing Six Sigma method. It resonated deeply with his previous findings. From that time, Craig has applied, taught, and led Six Sigma in all his endeavors, including management and technical capacities at Motorola, Iomega, and General Atomics.

In 1998, Craig founded TolStack, Inc., to develop commercial Six Sigma software tools. He also worked for several years as a technical colleague of Dr. Mikel J. Harry, the original consultant of Six Sigma, co-developing and teaching new advances in its theory and application. In 2002, Craig co-founded Savvi International, into which TolStack merged. Savvi provides solutions for business performance improvement using Six Sigma, Lean, and Business Process Management techniques. Craig acted as the director of Savvi's products, service, and tools. Today, Craig works with companies in the USA and internationally to integrate Six Sigma practices directly into their core operations.

A Master Black Belt, Craig has wielded Six Sigma techniques now for over 13 years, spanning projects from design to manufacturing to business management. He is also an expert teacher, having instructed and mentored at all levels of Six Sigma, from executives to White Belts.

Bruce David Williams has been fascinated with complex systems since the launch of Sputnik on his third birthday. With undergraduate degrees from the University of Colorado in Physics and Astrophysics, he entered a career in aerospace systems, where he first encountered Six Sigma after Motorola won the inaugural Baldridge Award in 1988. Later, with graduate degrees in technical management and computer science from Johns Hopkins University and Colorado, and as a member of the Hubble Telescope development team, he was intrigued by how breakdowns in the smallest components could lead to colossal system failures. He entered the Six Sigma industry for good in the mid-1990s when he founded a software company to pursue product life-cycle traceability.

Bruce has since been founder and CEO of two Six Sigma research and technology firms, and is now Chairman and CEO of Savvi International, a provider of solutions for business performance improvement using Six Sigma, Lean, and Business Process Management techniques. He resides in the highly-variable environment of the desert foothills of North Scottsdale, Arizona, with his wife, two children, and a normal distribution of dogs, cats, birds, and horses.

Terry James Gustafson comes out of the world of business and finance, and brings a practical and entrepreneurial perspective to Six Sigma. After an undergraduate degree in finance from Baldwin-Wallace, and an MBA degree from Kent State, he began his career in the field of accounting with KPMG Peat Marwick in 1969, and advanced to a Partner position in auditing. After leaving public accounting in 1990, Terry helped found, build, and operate a series of technology-based entrepreneurial ventures, including venture-backed companies as well as a public company.

In 2002, Terry co-founded Savvi International, which provides solutions for business performance improvement using Six Sigma, Lean, and Business Process Management techniques. Terry serves as Savvi's chief finance and operations officer.

Since founding Savvi, Terry has been immersed in Six Sigma techniques, helping to design and develop Savvi's training courses in Six Sigma and Lean. In addition, he has extensively taught Six Sigma courses, both in a classroom and as an online instructor.

Dedication

Craig Gygi: To Darren, a true brother.

Bruce Williams: To my mom and dad, Jane and Coe. When it comes to cause and effect, *they* wrote *my* book!

Terry Gustafson: To my incredible wife, Sherrie, for putting up with all my entrepreneurial nonsense without once using the term "dummy."

Publisher's Acknowledgments

We're proud of this book; please send us your comments through our Dummies online registration form located at www.dummies.com/register/.

Some of the people who helped bring this book to market include the following:

Acquisitions, Editorial, and Media Development

Project Editor: Natalie Faye Harris

Acquisitions Editor: Kathy Cox

Copy Editor: Jessica Smith

General Reviewer: Tom Pearson

Editorial Manager: Christine Beck

Editorial Assistants: Erin Calligan, David Lutton, Nadine Bell

Cartoons: Rich Tennant (www.the5thwave.com)

Composition

Project Coordinator: Jennifer Theriot

Layout and Graphics: Carrie A. Foster, Denny Hager, Stephanie D. Jumper, Lynsey Osborn

Proofreaders: Debbye Butler, John Greenough

Indexer: Dakota Indexing

Publishing and Editorial for Consumer Dummies

Diane Graves Steele, Vice President and Publisher, Consumer Dummies

Joyce Pepple, Acquisitions Director, Consumer Dummies

Kristin A. Cocks, Product Development Director, Consumer Dummies

Michael Spring, Vice President and Publisher, Travel

Kelly Regan, Editorial Director, Travel

Publishing for Technology Dummies

Andy Cummings, Vice President and Publisher, Dummies Technology/General User

Composition Services

Gerry Fahey, Vice President of Production Services

Debbie Stailey, Director of Composition Services

Contents at a Glance

Table of Contents

Introduction

● ●

Six Sigma is the single most effective problem-solving methodology for improving business and organizational performance. There's not a business, technical, or process challenge that can't be improved with Six Sigma. The world's top corporations have used it to increase their profits collectively by more than $100 billion over the past ten years. In certain corporations, Six Sigma proficiency on your resume is now a prerequisite to moving into a management position.

If you're part of a Fortune 500 company — particularly a manufacturing company — chances are you've heard about Six Sigma. You may even have been through a training regimen and been part of a corporate initiative or an improvement project. If so, you know the capabilities of Six Sigma; you have witnessed its power and achievements firsthand.

But if, like most people, you're outside of the upper echelons of big business, Six Sigma isn't well known. It has been too expensive and complicated for small- and medium-sized businesses, public institutions, not-for-profit organizations, educational environments, and aspiring individuals. Its potential has remained out of reach for the vast majority of professionals and organizations world-wide.

Fortunately, all this is changing. As the methods and tools of Six Sigma have spread, it has become easier to understand, less expensive to learn, and more straightforward to implement. The mysteries of Six Sigma have been revealed.

Simply stated, Six Sigma is about applying a structured, scientific method to improve any aspect of a business, organization, process, or person. It's about engaging in disciplined data collection and analysis to determine the best possible ways of meeting your customers' needs while satisfying your own, and by minimizing wasted resources and maximizing profit in the process.

About This Book

This workbook is unique. What used to only be available through expensive consultant-led professional training is laid out in simplicity here. This workbook includes step-by-step explanations and examples of the tools, methods, formulas, and tactics of Six Sigma. Exercises and practice problems build your mastery in applying the tools and techniques. And ready-to-use templates and worksheets provide you immediate access to the power of Six Sigma.

Corporate Six Sigma training also uses expensive calculation software like Minitab. Using expensive calculation software is fine if your company can provide you with $1,000 software programs, but everyone else is priced out. Not to worry! In this workbook, we've provided all the formulas and calculations, so that with simple explanations, you can perform these same calculations quickly by hand. The only price is the cost of this workbook (and a box of Number 2 pencils!). Or you can automate them using your favorite spreadsheet software.

Together with the more conceptual *Six Sigma For Dummies*, *Six Sigma Workbook For Dummies* truly forms a 2-volume box set for "Six Sigma in a box." Just add a little practice, and you're ready to join the growing ranks of professionals who list Six Sigma as a critical competency to their success. And be sure to keep a notebook handy for working out problems, as some of them will require a bit more "scrap paper" than even a workbook can provide.

Conventions Used in This Book

Mathematical formulas and variables used in this workbook are written in an *italicized* font. This will help you pick them out from the rest of the text and explanations.

What You're Not to Read

Even after all the hard work we've put into this workbook, we don't expect you to read every word of it! Its purpose is application, so read only what you need to gain mastery of the skill or topic. You don't have to do every practice problem. We've included several problems on each concept just in case you need the practice.

Foolish Assumptions

Six Sigma has a lot of math and statistics in it. We assume you're familiar with basic arithmetic operations — adding, subtracting, multiplying, and dividing. At some points it does get a little more complicated than that, but not much and not very often.

We also assume that you have a context in which to apply the tools and techniques of Six Sigma. It may be a bona fide Six Sigma project you have been assigned to and are working on. Or it may be an improvement effort of your own creation. Or it may even be an aspect of your personal life you want to improve. In any case, as you read through this workbook, try out the tools you're discovering. It's the quickest path to proficiency.

How This Book Is Organized

This workbook is organized along the lines of DMAIC — that's Define, Measure, Analyze, Improve, and Control — the problem-solving methodology of all Six Sigma thinking and working. If you need help with a specific task, you can jump into the workbook at that specific point along the DMAIC roadmap to get the focused practice or guidance you need. Or, if you want to gain a comprehensive mastery of all the skills of Six Sigma, you can follow through from the first page to the last.

Part 1: Getting Started in Six Sigma

In Part I, you find guidance, checklists, and templates for organizing your launch into Six Sigma. This part could be for yourself or it could be for getting an entire organization ready to head down the Six Sigma path. From aligning with key business objectives to forming a management communications plan, there's a lot of preparation when starting a breakthrough improvement journey.

Chapter 1 provides a first-hand, live introduction to the issues of variation and improvement. Chapter 2 gives you tools and worksheets for forming and aligning the improvement work with your organization's key business objectives. Chapter 3 provides checklists, templates, and examples for setting up an organization-wide Six Sigma program.

Part II: Defining a Six Sigma Project

Part II is all about defining the improvement work you do in Six Sigma. If you're starting a Six Sigma project, this is the part for you. You practice generating viable project ideas, find templates for scoping your work, and complete exercises for setting breakthrough objectives and goals.

Chapter 4 contains examples and templates for correctly defining each Six Sigma project. Chapter 5 gives you expertise in all the tools for identifying the potential causes of poor performance. Going through Chapter 6, you discover how to whittle down a host of potential causes to a handful of the "critical few."

Part III: Mastering Measuring

Part III is full of exercises and practice for mastering the skills of measuring. If you don't measure it, you can't know it. If you don't know it, you can't control it. If you can't control it, you're at the mercy of chance. And nobody wants to be in that position!

In Chapter 7, you find exercises for discovering how to collect data and calculate its statistical characteristics. Chapter 8 is a guide to the powerful skills of creating and interpreting charts, graphs, and plots. The practice problems in Chapter 9 show you how to measure the capability of your system or process.

Part IV: Assessing the Right Approach to Your Analysis

Understanding what your measurements mean is the focus of Part IV. In this part, you find exercises that show you how to perform critical analyses of your collected measurements, uncover root causes, and confirm hypotheses.

In Chapter 10, you find calculation templates for analyzing your measurement system. Chapter 11 covers the topic of capability — you find out how to calculate whether your process meets its performance requirements. Throughout Chapter 12 you practice calculating confidence intervals to statistically analyze differences among inputs and outputs.

Part V: Improving and Controlling

The final stages of DMAIC are Improve and Control. Skills for synthesizing improvements to solve problems can be mastered by anyone through the exercises and worksheets provided in this part. And you can't neglect Control — be sure to become proficient in the skills of controlling and maintaining the improvements you make.

Chapter 13 gives you the skills to quantify how one factor affects another. This is done through correlation and curve fitting. Chapter 14 shows you all the aspects of designing, conducting, and analyzing 2^k factorial experiments. In Chapter 15, you practice creating Poka-Yokes, control plans, and statistical process control charts.

Part VI: The Part of Tens

In this part, we provide you with two helpful top ten lists. Chapter 16 debunks the ten most common myths about Six Sigma and Chapter 17 lists the ten most critical things to do to complete a Six Sigma project. And be sure to check out www.dummies. com/go/sixsigmaworkbook for bonus forms that you can print for your own use.

Icons Used in This Book

Throughout the workbook, you'll see symbols in the margins called *icons*. These icons highlight special types of information. When you see any of the following icons, this is what they mean:

Each section of this workbook begins with a brief overview of the topic. After the intro, you see an example problem with a fully worked solution for use as a reference when you work the practice problems. You can quickly locate the example problems by look-ing for this icon.

These are handy points that help you perform and apply some of the trickier parts of Six Sigma more quickly and correctly.

This icon is used in almost every section of the workbook. It lets you know that the associated text summarizes the key application principles, formulas, or procedures needed for that particular skill.

When you see this icon, it alerts you to be aware of a particular risk or pitfall that could cause you trouble.

Where to Go from Here

The beauty of a *For Dummies* book is that you don't have to start at the beginning and work your way through every page. Instead, each chapter is self-contained; you can start with whichever chapter interests you the most and then jump to wherever you want to go next.

Here are some suggestions on where to start:

- ✔ If you already have a Six Sigma project picked out or assigned to you, start in Chapter 4. You'll find practice there on properly defining your problem and its intended solution.

- ✔ If you have a specific Six Sigma task to perform and just need some practice on it, start in the Table of Contents. Find the topic you need and go to it. In no time your skills for that task will be honed and ready to go.

- ✔ If you're forming a Six Sigma initiative for your organization, start in Chapters 2 and 3.

Part I
Getting Started in Six Sigma

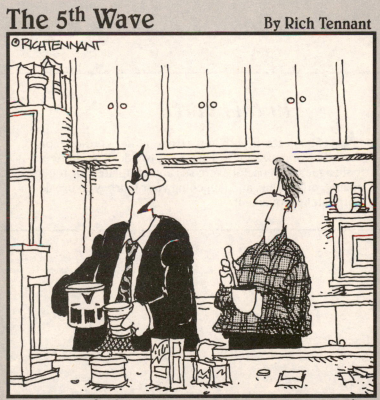

The 5th Wave   By Rich Tennant

"I'm one of the Six Sigma black belts in the company, but several of us still wear suspenders."

In this part . . .

Six Sigma starts with initiative — either your own or your organization's. This part provides you and your colleagues with useful exercises and templates for recognizing, organizing, and launching your journey to breakthrough improvement.

Chapter 1

Getting Ready for Six Sigma: The Effects of Variation

In This Chapter

▶ Realizing that variation is everywhere

▶ Mastering the Six Sigma breakthrough equation

▶ Exploring the effect of variation on business performance

The characterization, measurement, analysis, and control of variation is the central theme of Six Sigma. Every process and every product is affected by variation. Variation — within limits — is okay, and is even desirable. However, you can actually have too much variation. If undesirable variation is out of control, failure is the result!

The key goals of Six Sigma are to fix undesirable variation, ignore variation that doesn't matter, and allow for variation that can't be fixed. Many of the tools and techniques in this workbook help you determine whether your variation is desirable or undesirable. These tools also show you how to fix the variation that can actually be fixed, so that your efforts are concentrated where you can make the most improvement impact.

Before you go any further in this workbook, however, you must accept two undeniable truths about variation: Every output varies and every input varies. Don't you feel better now that you've accepted the fact that variation happens? It's simply a fact of life. You can now focus on finding and correcting as much of that variation as possible — making your processes and products the best they can be. Please also check out www.dummies.com/go/sixsigma workbook for some useful forms you can print out.

Recognizing Variation around You

To get started recognizing the variation around you, use the variation journal in Figure 1-1 to chronicle the variation you encounter in a day of normal activities. Because you have accepted that everything has variation, your daily journal could exceed the size of the Library of Congress if you try to include everything that happens! Instead, try to concentrate on more significant events — events that, if impacted by unacceptable variation, could have a negative effect on your life or job. Figure 1-2 is an example of the entries you might make. Try to record at least 20 key items. As indicated on the worksheet, consider the type of failure that the variation could cause, and whether the variation can be controlled.

Variation Journal

Date:_____

Activity	Undesirable Variation	Effect of Variation	Is Variation Controllable? Yes/No

Figure 1-1:
The Six Sigma variation journal.

Variation Journal

Date:_____

Activity	Undesirable Variation	Effect of Variation	Is Variation Controllable? Yes/No
Arriving at work	Arriving late	Loss of wages, lost business, lost job	Yes
Returning phone calls	Calls returned late	Lost business, irritation of boss	Yes
Accessing server computer	Server slow to respond or not available	Inefficiency, lost data	Maybe

Figure 1-2:
Entry examples for the variation journal.

Evaluating Variation and Business Performance with $Y = f(X) + \varepsilon$

The word "breakthrough" is bandied about all the time, particularly when advertising some product — a breakthrough shaving system, breakthrough hair gel, a breakthrough mousetrap, and on and on. So, you have to be a bit cautious when claiming something is a breakthrough product. But, Six Sigma practitioners don't hesitate to call the basic equation, $Y = f(X) + \varepsilon$, a breakthrough equation. When you apply the concept that all outcomes (Ys) are the result of some number of inputs (Xs) that interact in some way — f, or the function — to produce that outcome, and that there are always some other factors, either known or unknown — ε, or epsilon — that will impact the outcome, then you are well on your way to breakthrough improvements.

The elegance of the $Y = f(X) + \varepsilon$ equation is that it applies to anything and everything — from the simplest process, such as mixing a drink, to the most complex, such as building a space shuttle. After a process is broken down into primary elements, you can then identify the desired outcome, find the inputs that contribute to that outcome, identify those inputs that really matter, recognize where error and variation might occur, and plan improvements that will have a positive impact. This workbook gives you guidance in applying these concepts and conducting improvement activities.

Breaking down $Y = f(X) + \varepsilon$ to a simple process

Following is an example of a simple process with which almost everyone is familiar — cooking eggs. If you apply $Y = f(X) + \varepsilon$ to this process, the results look like this:

- ✔ Outcome (Y) — properly cooked eggs
- ✔ Inputs (Xs) — eggs, oil, heat, pan, timer
- ✔ Function (f) — shells are removed, oil is added to pan, eggs are placed in pan, heat is applied for a specific time, eggs are removed
- ✔ Epsilon (ε) — size of eggs, age of eggs, temperature of eggs, thickness of pan, amount of heat, timer accuracy, type of oil, altitude

Some of these factors can be quantified and controlled, but others can't. The trick is to determine which, if any, of these inputs have a significant impact on the outcome and can be controlled. One of the basic tenets of Six Sigma is focusing efforts only on those inputs that have a substantial impact and that are practical to address. Time and resources would be wasted if you tried to improve the egg-cooking process by changing the altitude!

Applying $Y = f(X) + \varepsilon$: A practice example

As practice, apply the $Y = f(X) + \varepsilon$ equation to a more complicated process, one much like many business processes. Think about the equation as you read the story about a house fire on Elm Street. Then use the worksheet in Figure 1-3 to match elements of the story to the components of the equation. Here's the story problem:

A house catches fire on Elm Street and a neighbor calls 911 to report the fire and give the address. The 911 operator triggers an alarm in the nearest fire station and transmits the address. When the alarm sounds, the firefighters dress, load the truck, and leave the firehouse. Using a current map and an established route plan, they find and take the most direct route to Elm Street. Halfway to Elm Street, they encounter a major traffic jam, which is normal for that time of day, and have to detour. Shortly thereafter, a freak sleet storm forces the truck to slow to a crawl. When the truck finally arrives, the men hook up the hoses, but find that water pressure is low and that water flow to the fire is significantly less than normal. Eventually the flames are extinguished, but only after the house is a total loss. Fortunately, all the residents of the house escaped without injury.

From the perspective of the fire department, identify a primary Y, at least ten important Xs, and the elements of error.

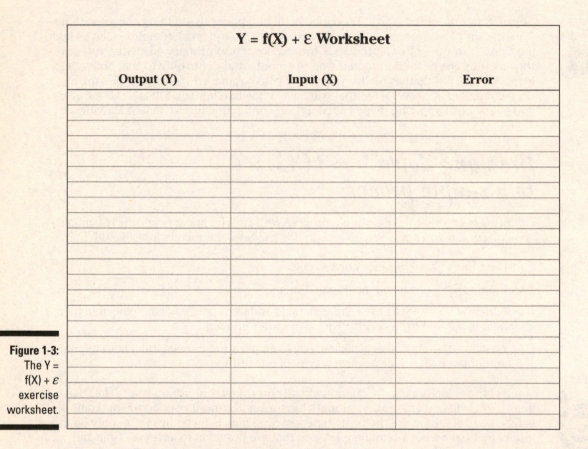

Y = f(X) + ε Worksheet		
Output (Y)	**Input (X)**	**Error**

Figure 1-3:
The Y =
f(X) + ε
exercise
worksheet.

Figure 1-4 is a solution to the practice house fire exercise. Even if your solution includes different items, it's okay. You have at least started thinking how the break-through equation applies to business processes.

Y = f(X)+ ε Worksheet		
Output (Y)	**Input (X)**	**Error**
Put out the fire quickly	911 call	Traffic
	Fire station alarm	Sleet storm
or: Prevent injuries or loss of life	Address of fire	Low water pressure
	Map	
	Route plan	
	Training	
	Firefighter	
	Fire truck	
	Water	
	Hoses	
	Traffic	

Figure 1-4:
The solution to the practice house fire exercise.

Assessing the Impact of Variation on Business Performance

After you realize that variation is prevalent in all processes, you have to determine the effect variation has on your process, and then you have to assess if it's really a problem at all. After all, some variation is inevitable, and you can live with it, right? Well, maybe, or maybe not.

Suppose you're the general manager of Widgets International, the undisputed market leader. You're rightfully proud of your market position, and believe that producing the highest quality widgets has lead you to where you are today. So, you're taken aback when an upstart Six Sigma Yellow Belt dares ask you about the true reliability of your widget production process. "We produce the best darn widgets possible," you retort. "We just can't do much to improve that process. Our rigorous assessments have determined that each and every step in the process is 95 percent reliable. Therefore, the whole process is 95 percent reliable. How can we do better than that?"

The Yellow Belt persists, so you decide to humor her even though you're confident in your figures. "How many steps are there in the production process," she asks. Consulting your most recent production chart, you answer, "We have a total of 20 discrete steps." The Yellow Belt then says, "Let's do some calculations. If each of the first two steps is 95 percent reliable, the chance of a widget making it through both steps without a defect is 0.95 times 0.95, or 90.25 percent." "Uhhh," you respond eloquently, "90 percent is still pretty good, right?" "Well, sure," she says, "but we aren't done yet. The chance of a widget making it through the first three steps without a defect is 0.95 times 0.95 times 0.95, or 85.74 percent." You begin to get a sinking feeling in the pit of your stomach. Sweat begins to run down your face. You begin to see the big picture and stammer, "Are you telling me that this calculation should be made through all 20 steps? What is the bottom line here?" She whips out her calculator and pounds in a few numbers, and then she gives you the bad news: "Well, if each of the 20 steps is 95 percent reliable, the chance of a widget making it all the way through the process without defect is 36 percent."

You feel like you've been whacked with a 2 x 4. "How did you get so smart," you ask Miss Yellow Belt. "This type of analysis is called 'rolled throughput yield, or RTY,' and is part of any basic Six Sigma training," she replies. She again pounds her calculator briefly and says, "And another interesting calculation we can make from this data is Defects Per Unit, or DPU. In this case, the DPU is 1.02." Now you're really stunned. "So what you're telling me is that only about one-third of our widgets make it through the process without a defect, and we can expect, on average, more than one defect per widget? But I know from our latest production report that our final inspection is at 95 percent. Wouldn't that mean we have a tremendous amount of expense, rework, overhead, and excess inventory to make up the difference between the calculated 36 percent rolled throughput yield and our observed 95 percent final inspection?" The Yellow Belt smiled, "Now you know why I'm here."

Finally, you ask the Yellow Belt, "Can you give me a template that I can use to calculate these key ratios for other processes?" Figure 1-5 is a worksheet you can use to calculate the RTY and DPU for your own processes.

Process Step	Description	Yield or Reliability	RTY
1			
2			
3			
4			
5			
6			
7			
8			
9			
10			
11			
12			
13			
14			
15			
16			
17			
18			
19			
20			

Instructions: Start with process step 1, whose RTY is the same as its yield for step 2, and enter the cumulative RTY. Continue for all process steps to calculate the RTY for the entire process.

Figure 1-5: The worksheet for calculating RTY and DPU.

Calculating DPU (From *Six Sigma For Dummies*, p. 138): **DPU**

$$DPU = -\ln(RTY)$$

Remember: 1n is the natural logarithm and can be obtained from any scientific calculator, as well as from math tables.

Chapter 2

Forming a Six Sigma Initiative

*B*elieve it or not, Six Sigma can be applied in several ways — not just at the executive level of a major corporation. At the personal level, you can use the methods and tools of Six Sigma in your everyday life and work to address personal and professional challenges and to solve problems. At the team level, you can conduct formalized improvement projects where a project leader — usually a certified Six Sigma Black Belt — leads a team through a defined improvement process, which can improve a key metric by 70 percent or more. But, at the organizational level, Six Sigma is deployed across your enterprise in such a way that the projects and practices of Six Sigma become part of the organizational culture and functional routine. This chapter helps you understand the activities and tasks needed to successfully complete an organizational-level deployment initiative. You can also print out many forms used in this chapter from www.dummies.com/go/sixsigmaworkbook.

A Six Sigma deployment initiative requires you to align both your business objectives and your organizational framework in support of the management and operational methods of Six Sigma practice. You must determine what you can and can't do yourself and you must augment your resources with the right assistance to go forward. This chapter and Chapter 3 guide you through a deployment initiative. If you aren't performing a deployment initiative and are focused on Six Sigma projects, skip to Chapter 4.

Doing business the Six Sigma way is *easier* after you're familiar with it. Six Sigma is like mastering anything else: Until you figure out how to do it, it's difficult. But after you're comfortable, the task at hand is just so much simpler. For example, consider skiing. Before you actually discover the key to skiing well, it's all a struggle: You fight your way down the hill, you teeter out of balance, and you exhaust yourself as you wrestle the laws of physics. But, if you take a few lessons to really master skiing, what happens? Suddenly you find that doing it right takes much less effort, and your performance and efficiency improve. Business works in the same way: It's difficult, but only until — with Six Sigma — you figure out how to do it right, at which time it becomes much easier.

Planning Your Key Business Objectives (KBOs)

Six Sigma is the most powerful problem-solving tool in business because you won't find a problem or challenge area that can't be improved significantly through the proper application of Six Sigma methods and tools. But, don't forget the risk of turning your team loose with the Six Sigma arsenal: They can charge off and solve the wrong problems. Pursuing paths that aren't important is wasteful for any business. For example, your team would be wrong to invest in improving the production quality of a product that the market doesn't want or to improve the sales efficiency for a product with negative margins.

You can find countless cases of what's known as *functional sub-optimization,* which is improving areas that don't contribute to what's most important. Obviously, improvement is improvement, but in the Six Sigma world, the improvement has to really mean something in the big picture, or it doesn't count.

Your improvements must be tied to *key business objectives* (KBOs), such as growth in market share, improvements in customer satisfaction, or reduction in product defects. As you form your Six Sigma deployment initiative and develop a corps of Black Belts, Green Belts, and other practitioners, you'll be able to identify candidate projects for Six Sigma improvement. But, before these projects are approved, they should be vetted for alignment with your organization's KBOs.

To ensure alignment with your objectives, you need to develop a system and, ultimately, a culture, that looks at the bigger picture. If you do this, the projects themselves generate gains of significant organizational value, the staff becomes aware of what constitutes alignment, and your company culture naturally and consistently focuses on the principle of aligning efforts and performance with KBOs.

Establishing a KBO checklist

Your organization has KBOs, which are identified in places such as annual reports, strategic plans, and operating plans at the organizational level, the business unit level, and the functional level. These KBOs form the basis of your alignment efforts.

Your organizational KBOs may not necessarily be well-defined or even consistent. The effort to define, optimize, and align KBOs across your organization is outside the scope of a Six Sigma deployment initiative — but your alignment effort depends on them. Going forward in your alignment efforts, you'll constantly rely on a set of KBOs. Be sure they're the right ones.

Before performing the alignment exercise, be sure you have all of your company's KBOs in hand. These KBOs are sourced from several areas. Use the following checklist to verify your KBO set:

- ❑ **Find out overall corporate goals.** These goals are identified in annual reports, corporate tag lines, missions, and vision and values statements. They're also articulated in speeches and position papers by key executives. Often, these goals are not identified in measurable, objective terms. You may need to translate amorphous goal statements into quantifiable metrics.

- ❑ **Find out Voice of the Business objectives (VOB).** These objectives are defined in operating plans, budgets, sales or other productivity targets, quotas, and other operating parameters that reflect the goals of the organization. They're in both the core business product and service line areas as well as the support process areas, such as IT, HR, Facilities, and Finance.

- ❑ **Find out Voice of the Customer objectives (VOC).** These objectives, which are critical to the success of your initiative, are typically expressed through the marketing and research efforts that reflect the wishes of the market and of your customers. Certain exercises in *Design for Six Sigma* (DFSS), which is the practice of applying Six Sigma to designing products, services, or business processes, strictly define quantifiable VOC measures.

- ❑ **Make sure objectives are consistent.** Check to verify that your objectives are internally consistent and prioritized and that they tie together logically. Make sure that any inconsistencies have been addressed and rectified.

❑ **Make sure objectives are quantifiable.** Be sure your objectives are in quantified, measurable terms. They should be expressed numerically and in such a way that the results of the projects can be measured and compared to the original values.

❑ **Make sure objectives are current.** KBOs change and in some organizations they change often! Put an update mechanism in place to ensure that you have the current set in front of you.

Verifying your process alignment

With the definition of your key business objectives in hand, you now have the basis for the future evaluation of your project goals and the verification that your process improvement initiative remains aligned with what's most important to the organization. Alignment will be an ongoing cause-and-effect exercise, requiring you to understand the Critical X's that influence the Significant Y's — or in other words, the KBOs.

Use the worksheet in Figure 2-1 to assist you in identifying KBOs. From sources including your organization's mission and vision statements, business unit operating plans, and local functional unit plans, identify the key business objectives. Then, for each objective, identify what quantifiable measure represents these objectives. Upon completing this table, examine the objectives and the metrics for alignment and consistency.

Business Objectives Alignment Worksheet

Date: _____

Process Area	Key Business Objective	Key Metric(s)
Mission/Vision Statement		
Business Unit Operating Plan		
Functional Unit Plans		

Figure 2-1:
The KBO alignment worksheet.

Determining the Proper Training Program

The first step in your deployment initiative is training. You must get your staff up to speed on how to apply the methods and tools of Six Sigma. The training program needs to be precise, and the various training courses need to be delivered in a specific manner and order.

While the initial training period may last from months (for a small organization) to years (for a large corporation or agency), a Six Sigma company never stops training. The initial training for an organization of several hundred people, for example, could be completed in less than six months. For a large corporation like Bank of America, or a huge government agency like the U.S. Air Force, even the initial training can take several years. But, all Six Sigma organizations, regardless of size, continuously follow up with new courses, refresher training, and new-hire training. This section gives you a rundown on how to proceed with your company's own training.

Who will manage the training program?

You must determine who will be responsible for managing your company's training program. Each option in this decision has consequences in terms of the orientation, consistency, and buy-in from your staff. The options include the following:

✔ **The leaders of your profit and loss (P&L) areas and major functional organizations.** Place the ownership of the training program directly within the P&L and functional organizations if you want to orient the overall initiative more directly at bottom-line performance. These organizations directly manage their work, and by managing the Six Sigma training initiative, they focus more directly on results. They can also tailor the training more specifically to their work area. The risks associated with this option include inconsistency in training and some losses in the economy of scale in the training program. But, most companies deploy in this manner and have great success.

✔ **The Six Sigma Deployment Leader, who typically reports directly to the CEO.** Have your Deployment Leader manage the training program if you want to centralize the training and keep it aligned directly to the overall initiative. If you use outside trainers, the Deployment Leader will be in the best position to align the training program with the company KBOs.

✔ **In larger organizations, the training department.** Some companies choose to manage their Six Sigma training program from within their training department.

You may think that an in-house training department is the most logical option, but that's not necessarily the case! True, your training department is in the training business, but it's best to manage the training program through your training department only if you want to generalize your program into a more educational and fundamental skills-based initiative.

Based on the nature of your organization and your goals, determine where you'll base the management of your training program. Communicate this decision to the stakeholders.

Finding the expertise within your organization

Many thousands of people have been involved in Six Sigma initiatives. As a result, capable practitioners are showing up in organizations large and small across all industries and all around the globe. Chances are that someone close to you has knowledge of Six Sigma initiatives.

Before you go any further in your deployment initiative, take the time to assess the level of Six Sigma deployment initiative expertise in your organization. Using Figure 2-2, identify all individuals who have been formally trained in Six Sigma, and specifically document their roles, the number of projects they were involved in, and the results they achieved. Meet individually or in a group with these individuals, and listen to their Six Sigma stories. They will have experienced some form of Six Sigma training, and, more importantly, they may be Green Belts, Black Belts, and perhaps even Master Black Belts. If so, they're capable of defining your program and even conducting some training sessions. Enroll them in the process from this point forward.

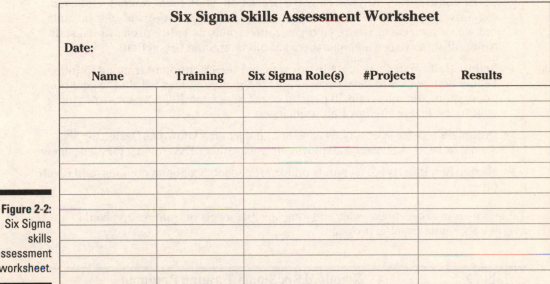

Six Sigma Skills Assessment Worksheet				
Date:				
Name	**Training**	**Six Sigma Role(s)**	**#Projects**	**Results**

Figure 2-2: Six Sigma skills assessment worksheet.

Scoping the training program

Your Six Sigma training program is directly tied to performance. Trainees conduct projects and begin influencing your organization and returning results as part of their initial training regimen, and they continue onward after their training is completed. The number of individuals practicing at the varying levels of Six Sigma capability within your organization is directly a matter of how many are trained and active at any given point in time. You must determine the *scope* of your training program, which means you have to know the number of staff members who will be trained, the level of proficiency they'll be trained to, and in which functions of the organization they'll be trained in.

Because trainees have such a strong influence on behavior and performance, you must scope your training program carefully. Overtraining results in hoards of practitioners undertaking projects faster than they can be properly aligned, or — worse — results in practitioners sitting idly awaiting quality projects. On the other hand, undertraining means insufficient momentum, lost savings, and disenfranchised staff members.

To scope the program properly, note the roles filled in a Six Sigma enterprise:

- ✔ **Executives** participate in a workshop that explains the Six Sigma deployment process, introduces the concepts used by practitioners, and develops the implementation plan.

- ✔ **Senior managers** participate in a workshop that, in addition to an overview of the deployment process and practitioner concepts, sets out the implementation plan and assigns the roles and responsibilities for each of the functional areas of the business.

- ✔ **Black Belts,** as full-time Six Sigma practitioners, are dedicated to working on projects that solve your toughest challenges. Black Belts are necessary only for large and complex issues. Rarely does the Black Belt population exceed 1 to 2 percent of an organization's total staff.

- ✔ **Green Belts** participate in Six Sigma projects on a part-time basis, either as leaders or contributors. Anyone can be a Green Belt: staff, management, and even executives! The Green Belt population is typically 5 to 10 percent of total staff, but we've seen cases where an organization trains its entire professional staff. **Note:** All supervisors and managers should be trained Green Belts.

- ✔ **Yellow Belts** may participate in projects, but the intention of training to the Yellow Belt level is to develop working Six Sigma practices within the general population. You may train 50 percent or more — even 100 percent — of your staff to the level of Yellow Belt proficiency.

- ✔ **Designers** receive specialty training in a subject area known as Design for Six Sigma, or DFSS. A Six Sigma deployment will include DFSS training for all designers.

- ✔ **Master Black Belts** act as hands-on experts, teach Six Sigma courses, and mentor others.

Table 2-1 summarizes these roles and indicates the levels of training involved in an average Six Sigma training program.

Table 2-1	Standard Six Sigma Training Regimen		
Role	**How Many?**	**Standard Training**	**Training Group Size**
Executive	All executives	2- to 3-day workshop	Up to 15
Senior managers	All senior managers	2- to 3-day workshop	Up to 15
Deployment Leader	1	Workshop plus mentoring	1
Champions	1 per organization	5-day intensive instructions	Up to 15
Black Belts	Typically 1 to 2%	4 weeks over 4 months*	15 to 20
Green Belts	Typically 5 to 10%	2 weeks over 2 months	15 to 20
Yellow Belts	Typically 25 to 50%	1 week over 1 month	20
Awareness	Everyone	½-day overview	20 to 100 (or more)
Designers	All designers	Multiple 2- to 3-day courses	12 to 15
Master Black Belts	1 to 2 per organization	Black Belt training plus 2 weeks	5 or fewer

Black Belts are dedicated full time during the four-month training process. They develop and complete a Six Sigma improvement project as part of their training program.

The ranges indicated in Table 2-1 are typical, but not absolute because no set standard exists. Your Six Sigma deployment initiative may vary because every organization is different and each organization has its unique needs and drivers. The drivers that affect your training regimen include:

✔ **Breadth:** How broad must you go in your organization to achieve the results you're looking for? If you're looking for immediate tactical impact in a single work area or line of business, you need only a small team of specialists. Conversely, if you're looking to change the company culture, you'll want a broad initiative.

✔ **Depth:** How serious are your problems and how complex are your challenges? The more complex and problematic, the more Black Belts you'll need. However, many companies operate at a level of complexity below the need for Black Belts. Note that the Six Sigma training industry tends to overtrain.

Many organizations fail to recognize the level and importance of applying Six Sigma to the many areas of design work in an organization. It's not just the design of your products or services, but also the design of your systems, processes, and procedures. Design for Six Sigma addresses all elements of the design process. Don't shortchange your initiative by undertraining designers in DFSS.

Your next exercise is to define the scope of the initiative within your organization. Don't worry about the timing and schedule of training at this point — just focus on the overall scope. Using the worksheet in Figure 2-3, define the number of courses and identify who you expect to undergo training at each level.

Six Sigma Training Program

Date: _____

Six Sigma Role	# Participants	# Courses	Names
Executives			
Senior managers			
Deployment Leader	1	1	
Champions			
Black Belts			
Green Belts			
Yellow Belts			
Awareness			
Designers			
Master Black Belt			

Figure 2-3: Training program worksheet.

Recognizing cultural predisposition

Systems and organizations resist change. And some are more resistant than others. Putting it the other way, some organizations are more ready, willing, and adaptable to change than others. The degree of cultural predisposition toward or against a change initiative like Six Sigma is a key factor in rolling out the training program. If you misjudge the culture and implement the program the wrong way, your initiative may backfire.

Consider the following items when trying to decipher the cultural predisposition of your organization:

✔ **Urgency:** How urgent is the business situation? How much does everyone share that sense of urgency? The more urgent the business drivers, the more aggressively you'll want to implement the training program, celebrate early wins, and stimulate the momentum that moves the key business metrics. Just remember that in this approach, everyone has to be feeling the same degree of pressure.

✔ **Complacency:** How complacent is the environment? The more complacent the environment is, the more tools you'll need to stimulate change. These tools include leadership and support, strong communications, the training of key individuals, strategic program wins, celebrated individual successes, and the use of reward mechanisms.

✔ **Resistance:** How outright will the resistance be? What will be the basis for the resistance? You may have staff members who were involved elsewhere in poorly executed Six Sigma programs or who have otherwise heard negative things about Six Sigma programs. You may have business unit leaders whose empires are at risk once your Six Sigma program begins to shine light in dark places. Often, the most vocal detractors become the most ardent supporters after they've been through training and completed a project. Remember, to move a distribution, you not only move the lead, but also the tail.

✔ **Metrics-averse (a.k.a. "lazy"):** Most pre-Six Sigma organizations prefer to communicate and base decisions on such notable tools as politics, opinion, tradition, and intuition, as opposed to DMAIC (Define, Measure, Analyze, Improve, and Control). Without the intellectual toolset of Six Sigma, it's just easier to work and think in terms of opinion and intuition. Depending on how deep-seated this cultural tumor is in your organization, you'll hear varying degrees of how difficult it is to quantify and measure things.

Defining the training plan

You've determined who will manage the program, identified your organization's internal capabilities, scoped the program, and assessed the cultural predispositions. Now it's time to define the training program plan. Follow these guidelines:

✔ **Determine your training schedule.** First, determine the order of your training classes. Use the worksheet in Figure 2-4 as a guide. We've entered the typical first set of courses and workshops, but the order and timing are up to you.

✔ **Decide what facilities you'll use.** Training courses are usually conducted in groups of about 15. Executive sessions may be smaller while awareness sessions are larger events. In addition, you may be using an e-learning environment (known as a Learning Management System, or LMS) for some of your training.

Often, Six Sigma training is held off-site, using the *alternate venue psychology*, which means you take people out of their ordinary work environments and accompanying mind-sets. The executive sessions may be held in a retreat environment and the regular stand-up courses at a local hotel or training center. Of course, you may also want to use in-house facilities.

Decide whether your Six Sigma training should be held on-site or off-site by considering how important the alternative venue psychology is to your addressing your cultural predisposition factors.

✔ **Choose your resources.** Now it's time to decide who will conduct your company's Six Sigma training. Read on to find out how.

	Six Sigma Training Schedule	
Order	Course / Workshop	Timeframe – Month / Week
1	Executive Workshop	
2	Management Initialization	
3	Leader / Champion	
4	1st Wave Black / Green Belt	
5	Staff Awareness – Basics	
6	2nd Wave Black / Green Belt	
7	1st Wave Yellow Belt	
8	1st Wave Design for Six Sigma	
9		
10		
11		
12		
13		
14		
15		
16		
17		
18		
19		
20		

Figure 2-4:
Six Sigma
training
schedule.

Deciding Who Will Conduct the Training

Until recently, the only viable option for Six Sigma training was to hire an outside training and consulting firm. Because of this, it was simply a matter of selecting the firm that best met your requirements. This is no longer the case. Due to the growth of Six Sigma across industry lines and coupled with the commoditization of material, you now have choices.

That's the good news. The bad news is that one of your choices includes conducting the training yourself, which today is a viable option. Choosing to conduct the training yourself means that you're now facing the "Not Invented Here" syndrome and that you're confronting a classic Make/Buy decision.

You have four general options as to who will conduct the training:

✔ **Contract a Six Sigma systems shop.** These shops are comprehensive providers that contract with you to do it all. They perform the training for all courses, both in stand-up and e-learning mode, and they also provide consulting and mentoring. If they don't have the expertise in-house, they contract it for you. These firms also provide or recommend the software tools — both their own and third-party tools — and conduct applications workshops.

✔ **Contract several boutique Six Sigma trainers.** The Six Sigma industry has numerous specialty trainers that focus on specific niches, such as Belt Training, Design for Six Sigma, Executive Coaching, Project Management, and so on. Some training companies focus on vertical markets, such as health care, financial services, or manufacturing. With this boutique trainer approach, you hire the expertise and buy the software you need, acting as the *systems integrator* to put the pieces together.

✔ **Hire on Six Sigma training expertise and buy materials.** You'll find many qualified Six Sigma Black Belts and Master Black Belts available for hire. In addition, several companies offer training materials for sale. You can hire the instructor talent you need, buy the training materials, and do it all yourself.

✔ **Hire on Six Sigma training expertise and develop materials.** You can do this, if necessary: Hire experts and have them develop a custom set of training materials from a combination of books and other readily available sources of information. You're still likely to buy and not produce some of the software tools — there's no return on investment calculation that justifies developing your own process modeling, portfolio management, or analytical software package — but there may be a role for custom connectivity and reporting software.

In order to make the choices between these options, you apply the same decision process you would apply for any development and staffing challenge: By considering both the value of having this talent reside permanently within your organization as well as the uniqueness of the need. Study Figure 2-5 to understand these tradeoffs. By finding the quadrant that best fits your situation, you'll understand whether to make or buy your training talent.

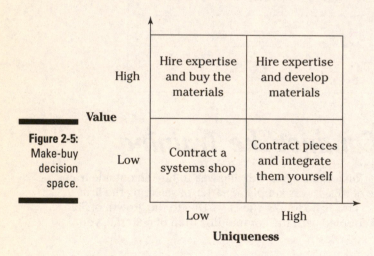

Figure 2-5:
Make-buy decision space.

Follow this checklist to determine which training option is the best fit for your organization:

❑ Is your Six Sigma training regimen relatively typical or will it be uniquely different from standard industry training? Will you need to extensively customize materials before you use them, as opposed to effectively using the industry trainers and materials already available in the marketplace? If you answered yes to either question, you may need to interview some industry trainers and examine curriculum materials to better qualify your company's needs. Note, however, that most organizations are fully satisfied with the industry's standard curriculum.

❑ Can contracted industry trainers effectively teach the material to your staff, or do you want to have in-house staff trainers perform the instruction?

❑ If your needs are so unique that standard training and materials won't work for you, and you want to have in-house trainers perform the instruction, hire (or use your existing) Black Belts and Master Black Belts. They can create custom materials and train your staff.

❑ If you need customized material, but believe that the average marketplace experience is sufficient, contract boutique firms and secure an experienced Deployment Leader to be your systems integrator.

❑ If your needs are standard and you can base your program on existing industry materials, but you want in-house trainers to deliver the instruction, buy the materials and have your instructors deliver the training.

❑ If standard industry materials and trainers will work for you, and you want to outsource your Six Sigma training program, contract with a systems shop.

Even if you've led or been part of a Six Sigma training initiative before, and you've decided to take on the entire training initiative in-house, bring in an experienced mentor — someone to act as a sounding board and who can provide you objective opinions and advice. Whatever you do, don't go down this path alone.

You need to consider the following concepts as you make your decision:

✔ **Uniqueness of material:** Every organization is unique in many ways — the uniqueness is how the organization differentiates itself. But is your organization so different that the fundamental methods and tools of Six Sigma must be extensively modified and tailored before they're applicable in your organization? Probably not.

✔ **Uniqueness of instruction:** You may have unique deployment needs, such that standard materials are applicable, but your instructional approach may need to be different. Perhaps you need a significant e-learning component, multiple-language versions, or industry-specific instruction.

✔ **Empire-building:** The purpose of Six Sigma training is to educate and empower your team with the methods and techniques of Six Sigma so that you can improve the bottom-line performance of your enterprise. Be careful to avoid creating a self-serving Six Sigma training bureaucracy.

✔ **Plethora of expertise:** You can now readily hire industry-specific Six Sigma experts who can effectively train your staff as well as immerse themselves as practitioners in your business.

✔ **Consultant-averse:** Many organizations are culturally (and financially) opposed to using outside consultants. Recognize, however, that not only is the cost of training small compared to the value returned to the business, but also that experience matters in Six Sigma.

✔ **Material and instruction quality:** Every Six Sigma training regimen has common ancestry that traces back to Motorola in the 1980s, but not all material in the marketplace has the same development and production quality. Instructional design is a discipline all its own, but knowing the material doesn't equate to good material and instruction quality.

✔ **Outsourcing:** You can't outsource leadership! Regardless of your approach, your senior-most leaders and managers must be engaged intimately and they must be the driving force behind the program and its progress. These duties can't be contracted, hired-out, or delegated.

After you've chosen your trainer, you're ready to complete the training program make/buy worksheet shown in Figure 2-6. For each category on the worksheet, select either in-house or contract/procure.

Six Sigma Training Program Make/Buy Worksheet			
Category	**Item**	**Develop In-House**	**Contract/Procure**
Training Curricula	Belt Training Curricula		
Training Curricula	Belt Certification Criteria		
Training Curricula	Executive Workshop		
Training Curricula	Management/Initialization Workshop		
Training Curricula	Leader/Champion Curricula		
Training Curricula	All Hands Awareness Curricula		
Training Curricula	Design for Six Sigma Curricula		
e-learning	Curricula		
e-learning	Learning Management System		
Facilities	Classroom Facilities		
Instruction	Belt Instruction		
Instruction	Executive Instruction/Facilitation		
Instruction	Leader/Champion Instruction		
Instruction	Management/Initialization Facilitation		
Instruction	All Hands Awareness Instruction		
Instruction	Design for Six Sigma Instruction		
Software	Analytics		X*
Software	Process Management		X*
Software	Program/Project Tracking		X*
Mentorship	Executive Mentoring		
Mentorship	Deployment Leader/Champion		
Mentorship	Belt Project Mentoring		

Figure 2-6:
Make/buy
worksheet.

* Don't even think about making these software tools. Great tools already exist in the market and are available at reasonable prices.

Teaming for Success: Shopping for Your Implementation Partners

Now that you've decided what you're buying from contractors, you're ready to shop. And lucky for you, like in any other established market, the Six Sigma training marketplace has a healthy selection. You'll find a few great providers, many good ones, many not-so-good ones, and a few really awful ones. It's no trick to find the right partner, but you need to know what to look for.

Six Sigma isn't a regulated industry. You won't find any IEEE or ISO standards or any government, academic, or nonprofit regulatory bodies. It's also not policed or reviewed by a consumer watch group. Instead, it's a cottage industry with a broad and loosely defined set of conventions and practices. The uninformed buyer can waste considerable time and effort and go down paths that lead to frustration and loss. However, on the other hand, the informed buyer can make outstanding choices and reap quick benefits.

The worksheet in Figure 2-7 guides you in selecting and evaluating your implementation partners.

Six Sigma Training Program Source Evaluation Worksheet

Category	Item	Evaluation Criteria	Key Question
Training Firms	Relevance Cultural Alignment Contractual Alignment Comprehensiveness Fulfillment	Industry Expertise Relationship Approach Contract Vehicles Depth and Alignment of Offerings Operations Capabilities	Does the provider understand my business? Are we on the same page? Are we paying according to value received? Does the provider offer what we need? Can they do what they say?
Training Practitioners	Capability Effectiveness Cost	Experience, Resume, References References, Evaluations, Interviews Comparables	Do the trainers know their stuff? Can the trainer effectively train our staff? Am I paying the right price?
Training Materials	Course Catalog Material Quality Material Pedigree Customization Embedded Software Completeness Cost	Depth, Breadth of Offerings Material and Process Inspections Inquiry, Inspection, Comparables Development Process Alignment with Your Selections Bill of Materials Listing Comparables	Does this material cover what we need? Are the materials well designed and developed? Is the material vetted for authenticity? Can the provider make the changes we need? Does the material use the tools we want? Are the materials complete? Am I getting the materials for the best price?
e-Learning	Course Catalog Learning Type (CBT, ALN, and so on.) Material Quality Learning Management System	Depth, Breadth of Offerings Investigation and Review Demonstration, Inspection Functionality, Cost, Performance	Does this cover what we need? Is this the learning modality we want? Are the materials well designed & developed? Is this the right platform for e-learning delivery?
Software Tools	Sourcing (Direct vs. Reseller) Analytics Process Management Program/Project Tracking BPM Software	Technical Support, Integration, Pricing Architecture, Functionality, Pricing, Support Architecture, Functionality, Pricing, Support Architecture, Functionality, Pricing, Support Architecture, Functionality, Pricing, Support	Where should we source our software? Does this properly meet our needs? Does this properly meet our needs? Does this properly meet our needs? Does this properly meet our needs?
Consulting	Membership	Alignment, Experience, References, Interviews	Are we getting the advice and counsel we need?

Figure 2-7: Source evaluation worksheet.

Six Sigma training isn't rocket science. Don't let yourself be bamboozled or slick-talked into anything by being made to feel uninformed, uneducated, or inferior. You're the buyer and you should shop for Six Sigma services just like you would shop for anything else.

Pricing and Contracting Approaches

The Six Sigma training industry has experimented with a number of pricing and contractual approaches — some of which succeeded while others failed. Consider the following options and decide which approach is right for you:

- **Price per wave.** This is the most common pricing approach. With this approach you pay by the course, which is also known in the industry as a *wave* of students. This approach is common enough that you can use it effectively as a basis for comparison in both standup and e-learning environments.

- **Time and materials.** In this consulting-oriented approach, you pay for the time and materials used by the instructor as he teaches the courses.

- **Shared savings.** In this model, which was first pioneered at General Electric in the mid-1990s, the provider receives a percentage of the savings realized by Six Sigma projects. This approach has the benefit of tying the provider's efforts to your bottom-line performance. However, the shared savings approach suffers from potential challenges in accurately assigning value to the projects. This approach may also allow providers to reap a tremendous bonus as a result of your large savings.

- **Volume discounts.** In this approach, you pay less for each additional course or service you use, based on a total volume of goods and services that you use.

- **Expenses.** As a rule, the customer pays all expenses for travel and incidentals incurred by the providers. If you want to do this differently, you'll be running against the grain of the industry.

- **Milestone-based.** Because Six Sigma training programs are lengthy — lasting for months and years — it's commonplace for the program plan to contain review points, or milestones, at which time performance and customer satisfaction are assessed.

Establish your contracts with sufficient measurement points, metrics, and out-clauses. If your first selected partner isn't working out, don't hesitate to make the change.

Chapter 3

Leading and Managing a Six Sigma Initiative

*I*f you're leading or participating in an initiative to deploy the knowledge and apply the methods and tools of Six Sigma across your organization, this chapter, like Chapter 2, helps you through the deployment process. Even if you're not part of a formal deployment initiative, and you instead simply intend to perform Six Sigma projects, don't skip over this chapter. You need to understand how Six Sigma is deployed. In this chapter, you figure out how to form the team that leads and manages your initiative. Chapter 2 shows you how to take aim — aligning the players and determining your implementation partners. Now it's time to fire — it's time to begin the initiative deployment itself.

The word "maybe" doesn't exist in a Six Sigma initiative. You can't simply stick your toe in to test the water (but, we guarantee that the uncharted waters are going to feel at least a little bit uncomfortable!). After you start a Six Sigma initiative, you quickly pass the point of no return. But the good news is that a well-proven and time-tested prescriptive formula for your deployment is available. In this chapter, you apply this formula to your organization and situation, and as a result, you and your organization are well-prepared for the changes and activities to come. Be sure to visit www.dummies.com/go/sixsigmaworkbook for some useful forms you can print out.

Selecting Your Leadership Team

Your Leadership Team should have both the authority and responsibility to ensure that everyone across the organization is properly empowered and supported throughout the life of your Six Sigma initiative. This team is directly accountable for producing the results — the measurable, quantifiable, and significant improvements in key metrics and benchmarks — through facilitation of the initiative process. The makeup of the Leadership Team defines your success. Accordingly, you leave nothing in your initiative to chance — a few things are left to random variation, perhaps, but none are left to chance — and neither should the selection of your Leadership Team.

Approaching the selection process

Part of the selection process is simple: Certain business unit leaders and executives are members of the team automatically. These team members include those who own financial responsibility and key functional processes, such as leaders and executives from the human resources and information technology departments. However, another part of the process is more complicated — particularly in the selection of the Deployment Leader and the Senior Champion or Champions. You also select certain key stakeholders as members of the Leadership Team. Careful selection of these stakeholders is important to the success of your initiative.

Depending on the size of your organization, you may have a large Leadership Team — a dozen or more — which is okay because the Leadership Team isn't a deliberation body that must reach consensus on difficult issues. The entire Team doesn't even always meet as a group. The Leadership Team is more of a SWAT team that fans out across your organization — as well as across your various constituencies — to ensure that your initiative deploys successfully.

Follow these three steps in your selection process:

1. **Identify central organizational roles.**

   To identify these roles, begin by identifying the major direct and supporting processes in the organization and the leaders or owners of those processes and functions. These leaders include:

   • **All leaders accountable for financial performance.** Because financial performance areas are the most important target areas for Six Sigma process improvement, these leaders are by definition part of the Leadership Team.

   • **All leaders of the major enabling process areas.** Examples of these areas include Finance, Accounting, Legal, Procurement, Human Resources, Information Technology, Facilities, and other similar processes that enable your core business processes. Identify these leaders in your organizational structure. Also determine how budgets are assigned and how accountability is measured.

2. **Identify central Six Sigma initiative roles.**

   Here are the three such roles that are part of the Leadership Team:

   • **Communications Leader.** Because communication is so vitally important to a Six Sigma initiative, and because the initiative will have a communications plan, you may consider naming a specific individual to lead the communications activities.

   • **Deployment Leader.** This leader is the individual charged with ensuring that the initiative is deployed across the organization per the deployment plan. Even though this role is traditionally titled as a leadership role, it's more related to management than leadership.

   • **Champion.** This is the true Six Sigma leadership role. The Champion is the senior evangelist who must understand what Six Sigma can and can't do. This person must champion, or support, the initiative's adoption.

3. **Identify other key participants.**

   In addition to the organizational and Six Sigma initiative leaders, you may have other key individuals who belong on your Leadership Team. Identifying these other key individuals is critically important to your success, particularly where change management is concerned. Additional stakeholders may include the following:

   • **An outside board member.** Six Sigma is going to shake things up in your company: Business will be done differently from now on, which results in changes to the way you communicate the status and performance of your company. If you need an advocate who can effectively "carry the water" for you to key shareholders, analysts, sponsors, donors, or other external constituents, you want to include an outside board member on your Leadership Team.

- **An outside advisor.** Your business will be different after Six Sigma. You may modify organization structures, reporting alignments, and other internal institutions. These changes impact the company culture.

  Throughout the Six Sigma process, you may want to have an external advisor — someone who's been through this process before. This outside advisor is someone whom members of the Leadership Team can confide in and seek advice and solace from. You should consider seeking an advisor who isn't part of your training team.

- **Key suppliers.** Your initiative will reach into your supply chain. In fact, you may be implementing Six Sigma now because someone reached into his or her supply chain, and there you were! Suppliers will be directly affected by your initiative, so you may want to include them.

- **Key customers.** Why are you deploying a Six Sigma initiative in the first place? To help serve customers better, of course! The direct beneficiaries of your efforts certainly have a keen interest in how your initiative is accomplished, so keep them informed.

- **Social network leaders.** Remember that all organizations have leaders who don't appear at the top of an organization chart. The cultural changes from the initiative will affect areas of the organization that may be invisible to the official leadership channels — so much so that you would be remiss if you didn't recognize and include individuals who represent the social organization.

- **A training team leader.** If you have selected an outside implementation partner (see Chapter 2 for details), you may want to include a senior member on your Leadership Team.

Many Six Sigma training and consulting firms are rich with statisticians, methodologists, analysts, and engineers, but are short on senior business leadership skills and experience. For this reason, you have to be careful who's chosen for your Leadership Team. For example, your training partner may be an effective facilitator, but he may not belong on your Leadership Team.

Membership on the Leadership Team isn't optional. Everyone chosen must participate because the initiative depends on the performance of every member of the organization. All members must fulfill their roles and responsibilities, and the members of the Leadership Team are no exception. The Team is only as strong as its weakest link.

Because full participation is crucial, many organizations modify the compensation structure of the internal Leadership Team participants and apply incentives to ensure that the job is taken seriously. These incentive changes include the top executives. It's not uncommon for organizations to tie a significant percentage — up to 50 percent — of incentive compensation for their executives directly to Six Sigma performance improvements.

Even if the top management fully supports the initiative as a group, not every individual will be on board. Six Sigma initiatives bring about bold change, which can worry some top management team members. In its relentless pursuit of improvement, Six Sigma shines bright lights into the dark corners of the enterprise where many senior leaders have personal agendas hidden. The successful initiative finds those dark places and exposes the agendas, which often become targets for improvement.

Use the worksheet in Figure 3-1 to make your Leadership Team selections.

Leadership Team Membership Worksheet		
Date:_____		
Area	**Role**	**Individual**
Operations Executive	Business Unit Leader	
P&L Business Unit	Business Unit Leader	
P&L Business Unit	Business Unit Leader	
P&L Business Unit	BusinessUnit Leader	
P&L Business Unit	Business Unit Leader	
Other Business Units	Business Unit Leader	
Finance	Enabling Unit Leader	
Accounting	Enabling Unit Leader	
Procurement	Enabling Unit Leader	
Legal - Contracts	Enabling Unit Leader	
Human Resources	Enabling Unit Leader	
Information Technology	Enabling Unit Leader	
Facilities	Enabling Unit Leader	
Other Support Functions	Enabling Unit Leader	
Communications Leader	Six Sigma Leader	
Deployment Leader	Six Sigma Leader	
Senior Champion	Six Sigma Leader	
Outside Board Member	Stakeholder	
Outside Advisor	Stakeholder	
Key Supplier(s)	Stakeholder	
Key Customer(s)	Stakeholder	
Social Network Leader(s)	Stakeholder	
Training Team Leader	Stakeholder	
Others...		

Figure 3-1:
Leadership
Team
worksheet.

Go, team: Unifying individuals to create a team

After you've selected the individuals for your team, you must forge a team out of them. Unfortunately, individuals don't spontaneously combust to create a team. Creating a team takes work. The dynamics and psychology of teaming are a science and discipline unto itself, and you should keep the following guidelines in mind:

- ✔ Rarely do teams come together simply because a leader calls them together. In other words, simply declaring a group of individuals a team isn't enough. Such an occurrence would be a statistical oddity, for sure.

- ✔ Many times, certain members of the team will perceive a Six Sigma initiative as a great risk to themselves or their constituents. These fears must be carefully addressed or the team won't come together.

- ✔ The team leader — usually the organization's top executive — may not be the right individual to energize and inspire the team. Recognize this fact and figure out how to take the appropriate action, perhaps with the designated Senior Champion.

- ✔ Within teams, cooperation, coalitions, and dissent all change over time. Communications and anticipative action are critical to maintaining team cohesiveness.

Implementing Your Communications Plan

Communications are the tugboats of change. They nudge your supertanker of an organization to a new course and direction. In fact, many organizations have discovered through their Six Sigma communications initiatives how to better communicate in general. Without consistent messages, active listening, and strong reinforcements, no regimen of training or army of consultants can align everyone in the same new way.

Communicating is easy but it's also difficult at the same time. For example, communicating is so easy compared to the vexing details of the business problems that it's often overlooked. The tools of communication are so routine that they're often taken for granted. The need for repetition is so fundamental to changing habits and behaviors, and yet leaders often ignore it for fear of sounding redundant or pedantic. After the initiative feedback says that everyone's tired of hearing about the new program, it's often toned down.

Because a Six Sigma initiative is a retooling of the thinking and behaviors of everyone in the organization, communications are so important that they warrant plans, leadership, and measurements all their own. Don't underestimate the importance of managing communications.

Understanding the two communications plans

You actually have two communications plans to choose from for your Six Sigma initiative. The *Deployment Initiative Communications Plan* identifies and directs how everyone in the organization knows what is occurring during the life cycle of the program. Communications are occurring in all directions: from the top-down and bottom-up, internally and externally, laterally, and informally and formally. With this plan, you ensure that all these channels and forms of communication are enabled and active.

The second type of plan is the *Project Communications Plan.* Because projects are the critical implementation tools of a Six Sigma initiative (see Chapter 4 for more on project tools), they warrant a communications plan all their own. Each project team adheres to the protocol as called for in its Project Communications Plan to ensure that the activities, resources, and focus of the project team are reaching the intended results.

Together, these two communications plans serve as the basis for applying the many tools of Six Sigma management to build momentum and sustain progress. By working with these plans, you can keep everyone aligned, confirm key tenets of the initiative, fight project scope creep, head off rumors, and consistently improve business performance.

Elements of your communications plan

Both the Deployment Initiative Communications Plan and the Project Communications Plan address seven distinct elements. You must be sure that your plans address these. The seven elements are

- **Why:** The purpose for the communication, which is to formally establish and enforce the commitment to communicate certain information.

- **What:** The item of communication. Refer to Figure 3-2 for a summary of the many items of communication in a Six Sigma initiative.

- **By Whom:** The individual responsible for ensuring that the communication occurs (see Figure 3-5).

- **To Whom:** The audience or recipients of the communication.

✔ **When:** The time and frequency at which you deliver the communication.

✔ **How:** The tool or delivery mechanism that you use to communicate. Refer to Figure 3-6 for a list of the many ways you can communicate.

✔ **Where:** The location — physical or virtual — where the recipients find the communicated information.

REMEMBER

The nature of communication varies over the life cycle of the initiative, including the content of what's communicated, to whom and by whom it's communicated, when it takes place, and what tool of choice is most applicable. How differently would you communicate during the initialization phase as opposed to the deployment phase? How would you change the nature of your communications during the expansion phase? And, finally, what would your communications be like during the sustaining phase? Keep these questions in mind as you read — you put them to use in an exercise at the end of the chapter.

The following sections cover these elements in more detail. In the section, "Writing your communications plan," you build your own communications plan so you can see how the process includes these seven elements.

What's to communicate?

Six Sigma initiatives communicate considerable amounts of information across the organization. Figure 3-2 is a list of the major items communicated. So that you better understand the contents and purpose of each item in your plan, complete the figure by writing a brief explanation of each.

Items of Six Sigma Communication		
Item	**Where Used**	**Explanation**
Purpose	Initiatives, Projects, Controls	
Plans	Infrastructure, Projects, Experiments, Controls	
Methods	Measurements, Experiments Analyses	
Lexicon	Both Formal and Informal Language	
Metrics	Within Projects and Across the Business	
Analyses	Projects, Controls	
Experiments	Projects, Studies	
Reports	Initiatives, Projects, Controls	
Budgets	Projects	
Action Items	Projects	
Schedules	Projects	
Success Stories	Initiatives, Projects, Controls	
War Stories	Initiatives, Projects, Controls	
FAQs	Initiative	
Elevator Pitch	Initiative	
Indicators	Processes and Management	
Attitude	Across the Business	

Figure 3-2:
Items of communication.

Before the initiative can proceed beyond the Leadership Team, one critical item of communication must be prepared — *the elevator pitch*. The Six Sigma elevator pitch, which is a common way of defining and describing your initiative in a smooth, brief, passionate, and consistent manner, is a cornerstone of the initiative's communications plan. Brevity is important here — the elevator pitch got its name because you should be able to give the entire spiel during a short elevator ride. If you create anything longer, you risk losing your audience.

In Figure 3-3, you craft your own Six Sigma elevator pitch. Take your time on this task — it's not easy to boil down your entire initiative to a crisp and clever definition. You only have to address four topics to complete the elevator pitch. They're laid out for you in the figure.

Here's a purposefully generic example of an elevator pitch. It covers each of the topics from Figure 3-3 in a handful of sentences that can be spoken in about a minute:

> *We're embarking on a long-term, continuous improvement effort called Six Sigma. It's not a fad; it's a well-proven approach to reducing inefficiencies and increasing effectiveness across all aspects of our business. Our industry is faced with increasing global competition against both the quality and price of our products and services. Our Six Sigma program will give us the tools to constantly eliminate the things that are holding us back. This will require all of us to learn new tools and ways of doing things, but as a result we'll be a stronger company, and each of us will be more agile and valuable.*

Now try creating your own elevator pitch. Even though ours is generic, make yours passionate and specific to your situation.

The Six Sigma Elevator Pitch

Floor	Item	Statement
Ground Floor	Identify the initiative and what itís about.	
Mezzanine	Explain why it's so important to be doing it.	
Balcony	Articulate the benefits for the organization.	
Penthouse	Show what the initiative means to the individual.	

Figure 3-3: The elevator pitch.

Great work — you've completed one of the most difficult communications! The next communication, the frequently asked questions (FAQ) list, is much easier. In Figure 3-4, you see a set of commonly asked questions about Six Sigma. Complete the worksheet by answering the questions. Feel free to add new questions that you think may be asked in your organization.

Who does the communicating?

Everyone communicates in Six Sigma. Communications happen from the top-down — from the highest levels of leadership down to the last hourly worker or volunteer. They also occur from the bottom-up, from anyone in the organization who sees a problem that needs fixing or a way to do something better, up to those who can actually do something about it. Communications are also *lateral* — which means that methods and tools are shared and results are verified across and between projects and departments. And they're both outside-in, with inputs from customers, suppliers, and stakeholders, and inside-out, with inputs going from the organization to these constituents. Finally, communications are also very much bidirectional, with everyone listening as much as he or she is being listened to.

Six Sigma FAQs		
Subject	**Question**	**Answer**
Basic Information	What is Six Sigma all about? Isn't Six Sigma just for manufacturing? We've seen all these various "quality" intiatives come and go. What makes this one different? What's with all the goofy belts? Isn't this really just a job-reduction initiative? Does this mean more consultants?	
How It Affects Me	How will this affect my job? How will this affect my department or team? How does this affect my career opportunities? We're so busy now; how can we possibly take on a new initiative? Do we all have to become math geeks?	
How It Affects the Company	How does this make us a better company? Does this mean another reorganization? Will the managers understand and support this? How's it going to roll out? Where do we start? How does this affect our customers? How does this affect our suppliers?	
How It Works	Where did the term – and the movement – come from? What has this meant for other businesses like ours? Is there a great book that describes it? Do we really have to achieve Six Sigma? How will this affect our company culture?	

Figure 3-4: Six Sigma frequently asked questions.

Figure 3-5 shows a matrix of each general class of participant. Because communications are bidirectional, each class is listed on both axes. You may identify others that you can include for your organization. Take the time to consider what type of communication goes in each square. Ask the following questions:

- Which communications are most important to the effectiveness of the initiative?

- Are there any communications that are unlikely to ever occur? Why? Should they?

- Which communication channels are likely to be exercised the most?

- Which communications are the most unusual — but critical to the initiative nonetheless?

- Do any communications pose a risk to the success of the initiative? What should be done about it?

- Which communications are most vulnerable to being disrupted? What would you do to protect them?

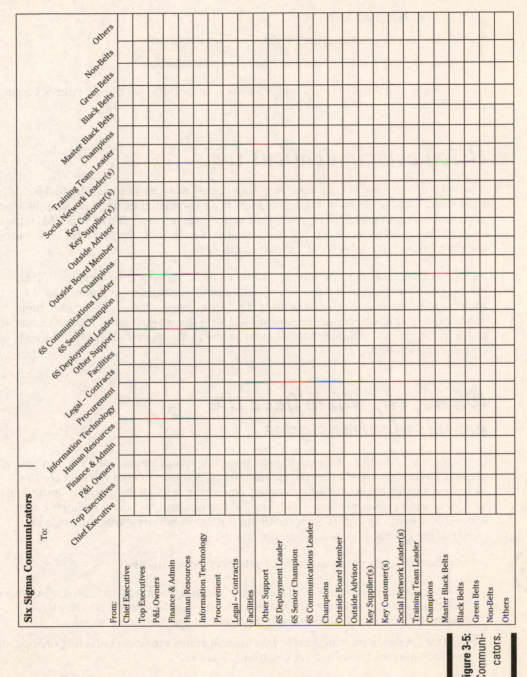

Figure 3-5: Communicators.

Timing is everything

You should communicate at four different times:

- ✔ At a milestone event or point of achievement
- ✔ At a periodic time interval
- ✔ At an impromptu time that's right for communication
- ✔ At an impromptu time that's wrong for communication

Like with any major initiative, all four cases will come into play during your Six Sigma deployment.

Using communications tools

You can communicate in countless ways with countless types of tools. Figure 3-6 categorizes many standard tools of communication into a list, including the typical applications of each tool. Study this table to discover how many tools are available to you. This table also shows you the different powers and applicability of each tool. You can't use all the tools all the time. Instead, it's a matter of the right combination.

As an exercise, consider and identify when it's most appropriate to use each tool. Which tools are most useful to each of your communicators from Figure 3-5? When in the process of your initiative or project would you use each tool? Which are most powerful and efficient in your organization? Using the worksheet in Figure 3-6, make notes in the "When" column that help you identify and organize the uses of these communication tools.

Where, oh, where have the communications gone?

Environment dramatically affects the nature of communications, which is why formal presentations are staged in formal environments, and why off-site retreats are the backdrop for new, out-of-the-box thinking. One of the original Six Sigma training firms took corporate executives to a ranch in rural Arizona and had them riding the range and herding cattle as part of their reorientation. Don't underestimate the role and power of environment in your communications.

Follow these guidelines as you prepare your Six Sigma initiative:

- ✔ To command everyone's attention, senior management should use the podium of its most revered settings to announce and present information at key times. Anything less will denigrate the importance of the program.

- ✔ Off-site retreats have proven to be effective venues for concentrating change efforts with managers and other organizational leaders.

- ✔ Senior managers and process owners should regularly venture into the organization and conduct formal communications events as well as informal encounters within the environment of the Six Sigma projects and work processes that are in the midst of change.

- ✔ One-on-one sessions in non-threatening environments enable key communications.

- ✔ Because online "environments" are vital in today's technological world, tools such as an internal Web site and a newsletter, which include all key communications and a link to repositories, should be developed and maintained throughout the initiative.

The Communications Toolkit

Tool	Application	When
Formal Documents	Project Definition, Status, Reports; White Papers; Plans; Procedures	
Dashboards (BPM Applications)	Near Real-time Business and Systems Status; Scorecarding	
Formal Presentations	Awareness; Briefings; Reviews; Training; Approvals	
Repositories	Reference Information; Templates and Tools	
Six Sigma Newsletters	Achievements; Success Stories; Initiative Status	
Column in Other Newsletters	Achievements; Success Stories; Initiative Status	
Memos and Letters	Directives; Questions & Concerns; Answers	
Surveys	Employee Morale, Program Momentum, Customer Opinion, Supplier Information	
Videotapes	Personalized Records; Team-Building; Levity	
Face-To-Face	Questions & Answers; Understanding & Empathy; Reinforcement	
Impromptu Presentations	Knowledge Transfer	
Informal Discussions	Knowledge Transfer	
Meetings	Consensus Building; Group Decision-Making	
Telephone Calls	Private Discussions At-A-Distance	
Stories	Team Development; Consensus-Building	
Advertisements	Sales; Momentum; Alignment	
Trinkets and Mementos	Momentum-Building; Rewards; Recognition; Team-Building	
Congratulations	Public Recognition; Support; Momentum	
E-mail*	Private Discussions At-A-Distance; Directives; Group Communications	
Town Halls	Consensus-Building; Catharsis; Diversity; Group Communications	
CEO Memo to Employees	Awareness; Consensus-Building	
Posters and Banners	Advertising; Momentum; Alignment	
FAQs	Create a Common Language; Address Issues and Concerns	
Pamphlets	Mini-Tutorials - Reminders; Refreshers	
Brown Bag Lunches	Knowledge-Sharing; Consensus-Building	
Intranet Posting Updates	Status; Knowledge-Sharing	
Phone Hotline	Questions & Answers; Understanding & Empathy; Reinforcement	
Milestone Recognition Events	Recognition of Achievement	
Suggestion and Question Box	Anonymous Input; Catharsys; Diversity	
Quality Quiz or Crossword Puzzle	Skills Development; Levity	
The Bullhorn	Sometimes you just have to shout it from the mountain-top!	

* e-mails are never completely private.

Figure 3-6: Communications tools.

Writing your communications plans

After completing your communications planning, you're ready to assemble each of the elements into the two communications plans. Figure 3-7 contains a template for organizing your Deployment Initiative Communications Plan. Using the materials and results from the exercises you performed throughout the chapter, write your plan.

Six Sigma Deployment Initiative Communications Plan

I. **Cover**
    Title, Date, Release Version, Author, Approval(s)

II. **Role and Purpose**
    State the role this plan will play within the organization.

III. **Values**
    Identify the way your organization values and uses communications.
    Indicate the communications responsibilities for executives, managers, practitioners, and staff.

IV. **Items of Communication**
    Identify the scope of the communications plan.
    Indicate key items to be communicated.

V. **Key Personnel**
    List the principal author and responsible parties for this plan.
    Confirm participation and approval from the top organization executive(s).
    Indicate who will be responsible for issuing and responding to the communications items.

VI. **Timing**
    Indicate communications items by milestone.
    Indicate communications items by fixed frequency.

VII. **Tools**
    List the different tools to be used and by whom.
    Indicate where certain tools are inappropriate as well.

VIII. **Environment**
    Identify where published reports, presentations, letters, and other pertinent communications will be archived and accessible for reference.
    Indicate other facilities, environments, information technologies, and channels to be used.

IX. **Measurement & Analysis**
    Identify key measures of successful communications and how the analyses of these measures will lead to improvements.

Figure 3-7:
Building the Six Sigma communications plan.

Figure 3-8 contains a template for organizing your Project Communications Plan. Using the materials and results from the exercises you performed throughout the chapter, write your plan.

Six Sigma Project Communications Plan					
What	**By Whom**	**To Whom**	**When**	**How**	**Where**
Project Charter	Black Belt/Project Lead	Project Team, Process Owner, Six Sigma Champion	Prior to Project Approval	Document and Presentation	Program Archives
Project Team Meeting Notices and Agendas	Black Belt/Project Lead	Project Team, Other Invitees	<Date/Day/Time/Duration>	Notices, Calendars, Documents	<Meeting Location>
Meeting Minutes	Black Belt/Team Scribe	Distribution List	Day After Meeting	e-mail	Program Archives
Team Work/Action Items	Black Belt/Project Lead	Project Team, Six Sigma Champion	TBD	e-mail, Phone Call	Program Archives
Status Reports and Progress Reports	Black Belt/Project Lead	Project Team, Process Owner, Process Owner, Process Owner,	<per Milestone Events>	e-mail	Program Archives
Project Budget	Black Belt or Project Financial Analyst	Six Sigma Champion, Project Analyst	<per Project Budget>	e-mail	Program Archives
Project Reviews	Black Belt/Project Lead	Six Sigma Champion Six Sigma Champion, Project Analyst	<per Milestone Events>	Notices, Calendars, Documents	<Meeting Location>

Figure 3-8: Project Communications Plan.

Selecting Software Products and Integrating Information Technology Architectures

The software tools for Six Sigma sort into two major categories: practitioner tools and management tools. In this section, you identify your needs and determine which of these tools is right for you.

Yours, mine, or ours: Platform questions

REMEMBER

The first issue to address is the extent to which you need your data and software applications to be designed and implemented for enterprise use, which depends primarily on the size and scope of your organization and your initiative. If you're deploying Six Sigma across a large organization, you need enterprise-class tools. If your implementation is in a small organization or single department, desktop tools should be sufficient. To decide whether you need to use enterprise-class tools, answer the questions in Figure 3-9.

Six Sigma Enteprise vs. Desktop Worksheet	Yes	No
Is your Six Sigma intiative being deployed across your entire organization?		
Is your organization presently enabled with "enterprise" type applications?		
Do you intend to use outsourced Web applications as your program software?		
Is your Six Sigma program going to affect more than 1,000 staff memebers?		
Do you have customers who require integrated data systems?		
Do you anticipate having more than 20 Black Belts?		

Figure 3-9: Enterprise computing worksheet.

Did you answer "Yes" to all the questions in Figure 3-9? If any of your answers were "No," chances are great that you won't be using enterprise tools.

Practitioner tools

Six Sigma practitioners use a variety of tools when performing the measurements, analysis, and improvements of business processes. These tools are summarized in Figure 3-10. Use this checklist to verify that you have selected tools that fulfill each of these needs.

Figure 3-10: Practitioner software tools.

Practitioner Software Tools		
Tool	**Applications**	**Software**
Process Modeling	Process Definitions, Material Flow, Value Stream Identification, Resources Cycle Times, Functional Alignments (Swimlanes)	☐
Simulation	Process Timing, Resource Consumption, Patterns, Bottlenecks	☐
Analytics	Measurement Systems Analysis, Graphical Analysis, C&E Matrix, Time-Series, Descriptive Statistics, ANOVA, Advanced Statistics, Process Capability and Capability-Complexity Analysis, Tolerance Analysis, Regression, Exploratory Analysis, Mutivariate Analysis	☐
Design of Experiments	Robust Experiments, Multi-Factorial Designs, Response Surface Designs, Taguchi Designs	☐
Design	Axiomatic Design, QFD, Kano Modeling, Robust Design, TRIZ, Pugh Concept Selection	☐

Management tools

Management tools enable and assist project management, facilitate communications, aid learning and retention, and provide a repository for future reference. Figure 3-11 is a checklist of the management tools required. Verify that you have capabilities in place for performing these functions.

Figure 3-11: Management software tools.

Management Software Tools		
Tool	**Applications**	**Software**
Communications	Leadership, Motivation, Statusing, Informing, Explaining, Listening, Direction, Correction, Rewarding, Celebration	☐
Program and Portfolio Management	Initiative-level tracking and management of program performance; Ideation; Project Selection; Alignment; Prioritization	☐
Project Management	Project-level budgeting, schedules, resources, milestones, methodology, benefits, risks, controls	☐
Reporting	Statusing, Actions, Results, Recommendations, Achievements, Failures, Challenges, Lessons-Learned, Best Practices, Dashboards, Balanced Scorecard	☐
Knowledge Management	Methods and Tools repositories, Best Practices Reference Databases, Collaboration, Plans, History and Archives	☐
Learning Tools	Lectures; e-Learning; Handbooks; Guides	☐

Enterprise Integration, SOA, and BPM

In addition to the practitioner and management software tools specific to Six Sigma program execution, there are other information technology contributions to a Six Sigma initiative. These contributions are based on leveraging the existing technology infrastructure and application programs already in use across your organization. These programs may include such critical systems as financial and accounting applications, customer management software, supply chain and delivery management, procurement software, design tools, and more. Many existing business processes are encoded formally within these systems or informally in the way people use them, and, as a result, your Six Sigma initiative will eventually address these systems.

Make sure your IT department uses the following technologies:

- **Enterprise Application Integration and Service-Oriented Architectures:** Your Six Sigma reporting tools, dashboards, and other measures of business performance will require you to extract information from these systems. Use connectivity tools, middleware, and other forms of *Enterprise Application Integration* (EAI) to extract the data. Increasingly, *Service-Oriented Architectures* (SOAs) are used as an abstraction layer to make data extraction simpler.

- **Business Process Management:** *Business Process Management* (BPM) systems extend the functionality of process management and process analysis tools into proactive simulation and control of key components of the business.

Defining and Implementing Your Management Plan

Your Six Sigma initiative is a long-term commitment to a new way of performing everyday business. Six Sigma involves both a shift in thinking to a measurable basis for setting objectives and performance, as well as the development of a project orientation to approaching and solving problems. Your organization will undergo an extended programmatic effort to deploy the knowledge, methods, and tools of Six Sigma and will develop the infrastructure, communications, incentives, and control systems.

Your Six Sigma initiative has a life cycle with four distinct phases:

- **Initialization:** This is the phase you're in right now — the process of preparing and developing the infrastructure and support systems needed to begin the initiative.

- **Deployment:** In this phase, the many elements of the infrastructure are deployed. Training and project work begin, and the first results come in.

- **Expansion:** After the initial deployment phase is completed, you expand the program to encompass the entire organization, including key suppliers and customers.

- **Sustaining:** This is the most challenging phase of all because you have to sustain the gains — and these aren't the gains in bottom-line performance. They're the gains in cultural agility. This is the phase of transitioning from "the new initiative" to "the way we work."

Unfortunately, Six Sigma doesn't happen magically. To accomplish a successful Six Sigma initiative, you need to create and work with an Initiative Management Plan.

The Six Sigma *Initiative Management Plan* is similar to other initiative plans because it requires a complete and thorough consideration of all aspects of the initiative and a fully documented and traceable set of measures and controls.

Figure 3-12 is a checklist for your plan. As you prepare your plan, be certain that each of the elements in the checklist is included.

Initiative Management Plan Checklist

Phase	Management Task	Complete
Initialization	Business Objectives	☐
	Scope of Initiative	☐
	Leadership Team Selection / Assignments	☐
	Communications Plan Definition	☐
	Human Resources	☐
	Definition of Training Regimen	☐
	Critical Success Factors	☐
	Timeline of Major Milestones	☐
	Risk Factors and Contingency Plans	☐
	Revision and Update Management	☐
	Policies	☐
Deployment	Leadership Team Initiation Workshop	☐
	Infrastructure Readiness	☐
	Communications Elements	☐
	Information Technology	☐
	Human Resources Alignment	☐
	Initial Training Waves	☐
	First Projects / Process Improvement Areas	☐
	Results, Reports, Communications	☐
Expansion	Lessons Learned – System / Plan Updates	☐
	Scope Adjustments	☐
	Training Waves	☐
	Additional Projects / Process Improvements	☐
	Results, Reports, Communications	☐
	<repeat>	☐
Sustaining	Lessons Learned – System / Plan Updates	☐
	Infrastructure Adjustments	☐
	Cultural Incentive Realignments	☐
	Institutionalization Elements	☐
	Additional Projects / Process Improvements	☐

Figure 3-12:
The Initiative Management Plan checklist.

Part II
Defining a Six Sigma Project

The 5th Wave   By Rich Tennant

"Okay, maybe a decent Six Sigma initiative will improve our business performance, but I still think these sulphur pools and twines of barbed wire in the hallways are slowing us up in some ways."

In this part . . .

From the topmost to the lowest level applications, Six Sigma uses the Define-Measure-Analyze-Improve-Control (DMAIC) project methodology to achieve break-through improvement results. In this part, you go through exercises and worksheets that build your mastery of defining the problem to be solved and the project effort that will solve it. Consistent improvement requires your careful study and precise scoping of what the problem actually is.

Chapter 4

Putting the Right Foot Forward: Defining a Six Sigma Project

Prior chapters show you how to form an overall Six Sigma initiative in your organization, how to gather the necessary resources, and how to make sure your initiative meets the goals of your organization. Through these chapters, you discover how to lead and manage your initiative and how to make sure your team, lines of communication, and technologies are all in place. So, now you think you're ready to leap in with both feet, frantically attacking every problem in sight and slashing and burning your way through all that variation, error, and waste, right? Not so fast!

Correctly defining your project is a critical tipping point in your Six Sigma initiative — a misstep here can totally derail the whole shebang. Selecting and scoping projects, particularly in the early stages of an initiative, must be done in a rational, orderly process because nothing causes a loss of confidence in an initiative more than a failure at the outset. Your first projects must have extremely high chances for clear success. These first wins build confidence and momentum in your improvement efforts. Anything less is the kiss of death.

This chapter provides you with the tools and techniques to ensure that your project selection process gets your initiative off on the right foot.

Getting Project Ideas by Using the Business Case Writing Tool

After you've reined in your sense of urgency to get started, you're ready to kick-off an orderly project selection process. The first step is to look around for projects, right? Not exactly; that's still a bit premature. The first step is to identify the *problem areas* of the business. By using a tool called a *business case*, you can identify where in the business problems are occurring, provide a summary description of the situation, and estimate the potential value of improvement efforts. The intent here isn't to define a Six Sigma project, but to clearly illuminate where projects are needed the most.

The description of the business problem doesn't need excessive detail at this point — the detail comes with the definition of the associated projects.

In order to stimulate you to find problem areas in your business, following is a checklist of red flag items, any one of which could indicate a business problem area to address:

❏ Product returns   ❏ Low quality   ❏ Capacity restraints

❏ Receivable collection issues   ❏ Low yield   ❏ Long cycle times

❏ Stressful work   ❏ Rework   ❏ Excessive inventory

❏ Chaotic or complicated workflow   ❏ Waste   ❏ Customer complaints

Q. After you've identified a potential problem area, it's time to prepare the business case. An effective business case must include the following elements:

- The specific system or process being scrutinized

- The area of the business affected

- The base goal or objective not being met

- The resulting problems or issues

- The estimated impact, in dollars or another metric

Underline each of these business case elements in the following statement:

Our accounts receivable performance for the finance invoicing area isn't meeting the goal of 47 days sales outstanding. Overall this poor performance is causing cash flow and budget problems that are costing us as much as $4 million per year.

A. Here's what the statement looks like with the business case elements underlined:

Our <u>accounts receivable</u> performance for the <u>finance invoicing</u> area isn't meeting the goal of <u>47 days sales outstanding</u>. Overall this poor performance is causing <u>cash flow and budget problems</u> that are costing us as much as <u>$4 million per year</u>.

1. Here's a business case example. Find and underline each of the five required business case elements:

Procedures call for all shipments to be turned over to the carrier within four hours of receipt at the dock. Shipping dock A has an average time of more than 12 hours, resulting in storage issues and customer complaints. We had to add 100 square feet of storage to the dock, and have lost three customers this month due to late shipments.

Solve It

Use the following template to create business cases and to start the process of selecting appropriate Six Sigma projects:

The performance of _____ isn't meeting the goal of _____ in the area of _____. This results in _____ causing these negative effects: _____.

Prioritizing and Aligning Projects with Business-Customer-Process Scorecards

Hopefully by now you've identified a number of problem areas in your business and have prepared business cases for each (if you haven't, check out the previous section,

"Getting Project Ideas by Using the Business Case Writing Tool," for tips). So now the question is "What criteria should I use for selecting appropriate Six Sigma projects?" Here are just a few options: Alphabetical, random, highest dollar, and even by throwing darts. But be careful! Even though you've identified legitimate problem areas that will yield good candidates for projects, haphazard project selection can still hamper or derail your initiative.

Always keep in mind that to obtain the maximum benefit from your initiative, you must link your Six Sigma project selection with the strategic needs of the business.

Take a look at Figure 4-1, which illustrates the overall concept of aligning Six Sigma with business goals and objectives.

Objective	Phase	Output
Link Six Sigma to business priorities	Recognize → Define	Project identification and launch
Achieve breakthrough improvement	Measure → Analyze → Improve → Control	Solution to the problem and a final report
Integrate into day-to-day business	Realize	Implementation and financial benefit

Figure 4-1: Project alignment to business needs.

At this critical point in the selection process, you probably have a number of "Voices" shouting at you and demanding attention: the *Voice of the Customer* (VOC), *Voice of the Process* (VOP), and *Voice of the Business* (VOB). Often you find these Voices competing with each other for your attention. For example, the VOC wants lower prices, better pizza, and faster delivery, the VOP wants the best possible ingredients regardless of the cost, and the VOB wants to make more money.

Take the Three Sigma Pizza Emporium for example. This business has a number of problems, and the Six Sigma team didn't know where to start on improvement efforts. So, the team completed a *business-customer-process scorecard,* which is shown in Figure 4-2.

Name of Ark Process	Impact on Customer Needs - Internal or External (VOC)	Improvement Need or Amount (VOP)	Importance to Meeting Business Goals and Objectives (VOB)	Overall Ranking
Processes that need some amount of improvement (from Business Cases)	The effect this process has on meeting the needs and expectations of the customer	A rating based on existing performance levels that are required to meet the needs of the business	The effect improving this process will have on existing goals and objectives of the business	The score resulting from multiplying the ratings in the three columns
Inventory management	2	1	4	8
Staffing and training	3	3	2	18
Phone-in ordering	4	2	3	24
Preparing pizza	**5**	**4**	**3**	**60**
Delivering pizza	5	2	5	50

Impact ratings: 1=Little 2=Somewhat 3=Moderate 4=High 5=Extreme

Figure 4-2: Business-customer-process scorecard.

After multiplying the three column rankings for each process, the Six Sigma team at the Three Sigma Pizza Emporium decided that making pizza was the place to start improvement efforts. The team identified several key projects in that area.

Figure 4-3 is a blank scorecard template you can use to prioritize the problem areas for your potential Six Sigma projects by considering all the important Voices in your process. You can print this form from www.dummies.com/go/sixsigmaworkbook.

Name of Ark Process	Impact on Customer Needs - Internal or External (VOC)	Improvement Need or Amount (VOP)	Importance to Meeting Business Goals and Objectives (VOB)	Overall Ranking
Processes that need some amount of improvement (from Business Cases)	The effect this process has on meeting the needs and expectations of the customer	A rating based on existing performance levels that are required to meet the needs of the business	The effect improving this process will have on existing goals and objectives of the business	The score resulting from multiplying the ratings in the three columns

Figure 4-3: Business-customer-process scorecard template.

Impact ratings: 1=Little 2=Somewhat 3=Moderate 4=High 5=Extreme

Project Definition 1: Writing a Problem Statement

Before mounting your white horse and leaping right into solving your business problems, you need to define and describe the problem by using a *problem statement*. This tool clarifies the issue by specifically identifying what has to improve to meet your goal, the magnitude of the problem, where the problem occurs, and the financial impact. The problem statement can then be used to communicate the problem to the people whose support you need.

Following is a checklist that shows all the critical elements of a successful problem statement:

❑ A description of the problem and the metric used to describe it.

❑ The process name and location of the problem.

❑ The time frame over which the problem has been occurring.

❑ The size or magnitude of the problem.

Q. The Six Sigma team at the Three Sigma Pizza Emporium created a problem statement to pinpoint the business's problems with pizza production. The first draft of the problem statement read as follows:

"There is a problem with the number of undercooked pizzas."

A. When the team presented this problem statement to the General Manager, his response was, "So what? I knew that!" The team leader told the team to try again, using the checklist above. The next draft read as follows:

"In the last six months, 5 percent of pizzas had to be scrapped prior to

boxing due to undercooking. The boxers had no procedures for sending pizzas back for additional cooking time. In addition, 2 percent of the pizzas delivered to customers were undercooked, resulting in 125 customer complaints. Pizza scrapping cost the company $23,550 during the last six months, in addition to a loss of customers."

If you compare the new statement with the previous critical elements checklist, you see that all critical elements have been included. The General Manager now has a clear picture of the problem, and he will no doubt support the Six Sigma projects conducted by the team in this area.

2. Now it's your turn to help the Three Sigma Pizza Emporium team write another problem statement. If you recall from the scorecard created in the section "Prioritizing and Aligning Projects with Business-Customer-Process Scorecards," pizza delivery was the second-ranked problem area. Take the following incomplete statement, and rewrite it as an effective problem statement, making sure to include all items from the checklist:

"Customers are complaining about delivery times."

_____
_____
_____
_____
_____
_____

An example solution to this practice problem is located at the end of this chapter. Of course, there is no single right answer. The only requirement is that your solution contains all the necessary elements.

Solve It

_____

Following is a blank problem statement template to help you organize your thoughts as you prepare for your next project:

A description of the problem _____

_____

The metric used _____

_____

Specifically where the problem is occurring_____

_____

How long the problem has been occurring _____

_____

The size or magnitude of the problem _____

_____

Project Definition 11: Writing an Objective Statement

One more tool is important for you to make sure that your improvement project launches properly. This tool is called an *objective statement*, which directly addresses the problem statement. In order to be effective, the objective statement must contain all of the following elements: It must improve some *metric* from some *baseline* to some *goal,* in some amount of *time* with some *positive impact* on some corporate *goal or objective.* Simply put, the objective statement must indicate the level of improvement expected from improvement efforts, including specific, quantifiable amounts and the time required to complete.

Six Sigma practitioners often use a memory jogger, called SMART, to help write effective objective statements. Each letter reminds you of a goal to achieve in your statement:

- ✔ *Specific:* Make sure that the specific deliverables and outcomes are stated and that you answer the question, "What's the specific purpose of this project?"

- ✔ *Measurable:* Be sure that your objective is both quantifiable and verifiable and that it includes such things as quality, quantity, cost, and timeliness.

- ✔ *Aggressive, but Attainable:* A challenging objective makes the project interesting and fulfilling, while also providing worthwhile returns. However, don't try to solve world hunger.

- ✔ *Relevant:* The objective must be relevant to business goals.

- ✔ *Time bound:* You must state a definitive time frame for reaching your objective.

Q. The Three Sigma Pizza Emporium team created an objective statement. The first draft of the statement for pizza production looked like this:

"Retrain employees to reduce the number of undercooked pizzas."

A. The team leader sent the team back to the drawing board with instructions to include all the critical elements required for a proper objective statement. The team's next effort read as follows:

"Our goal is to reduce the number of pizzas scrapped from undercooking from 5 percent to less than .05 percent by June 30. In addition, we also want to reduce the number of undercooked pizzas that reach customers from 2 percent to zero by the same date. Doing so will help restore our image as a quality pizza parlor and will save the company $50,000 annually."

If you compare the new draft to the required elements mentioned at the beginning of this section, you'll find that all are included.

---

3. Returning again to the Three Sigma Pizza Emporium situation, see if you can help the team prepare an effective objective statement for the pizza delivery problem. Take the following incomplete statement and rewrite it as an effective objective statement, making sure to include all required items:

"Improve pizza delivery times."

_____

_____

_____

_____

_____

_____

An example solution to this practice problem is at the end of this chapter. Of course, there is no single right answer. The only requirement is that your solution contains all of the necessary elements.

Following is a blank objective statement template to help you organize your thoughts as you prepare for your next project:

The metric to be improved _____

_____

The current baseline _____

_____

The goal _____

_____

The time frame for improvement _____

_____

The corporate goal or objective _____

_____

The impact on the goal or objective _____

_____

Launching a Project

You're probably chomping at the bit to launch your project. You've written the business case, you've made sure your identified problem area is important to the company, and you've written a problem statement and an objective statement. So, you say, let's go! However, don't get ahead of yourself — there are still a few things to remember and manage as the project starts.

To make sure the launch process is orderly, follow this checklist:

- ❑ Identify everyone who has to approve the project.
- ❑ Obtain written approval.
- ❑ Identify the people impacted by your project.
- ❑ Notify the impacted people of what's to come.
- ❑ Get final approval from the project team leader.
- ❑ Identify Six Sigma skill levels (Belts) that are needed.
- ❑ Identify the process members who will participate.
- ❑ Identify the entire project team by name.
- ❑ Fire!

Solutions to Defining a Six Sigma Project

1 Here's a solution to the business case example:

Procedures call for all <u>shipments</u> (*the specific process*) to be turned over to the carrier <u>within 4 hours of receipt</u> (*the base goal not being met*) at the dock. Shipping dock A (*area of the business affected*) has an average time of more than 12 hours, <u>resulting in storage issues and customer complaints</u> (*the resulting problem*). We had to <u>add 100 square feet of storage to the dock, and have lost three customers this month</u> (*the impact*) due to late shipments.

2 Now it's your turn to help the Three Sigma Pizza Emporium team write another problem statement. If you recall from the scorecard created in the section "Prioritizing and Aligning Projects with Business-Customer-Process Scorecards," pizza delivery was the second-ranked problem area. Take the following incomplete statement, and rewrite it as an effective problem statement, making sure to include all items from the checklist:

"Customers are complaining about delivery times."

An effective problem statement for this case reads as follows:

"Since June 30, the average time to deliver a pizza within our market area, a 15-mile radius, is 35 minutes. During this time we had a low of 22 minutes and a high of 66 minutes, and we exceeded our advertised guarantee of 30 minutes 55 percent of the time. The result of these slow delivery times is customer complaints, free pizzas to the customer, and a loss of business. Free and scrapped pizzas resulted in a revenue loss of $23,800 during the period. Driver costs for redelivery cost the company an additional $6,600. Lost customers are estimated to represent $45,000 in annual business."

3 Returning again to the Three Sigma Pizza Emporium situation, see if you can help the team prepare an effective objective statement for the pizza delivery problem. Take the following incomplete statement and rewrite it as an effective objective statement, making sure to include all required items:

"Improve pizza delivery times."

An effective objective statement for this case reads as follows:

"Our objective is to reduce the number of pizzas delivered in more than 30 minutes from 55 percent to less than 5 percent by June 30 of next year. Doing so will further enhance our image of excellence and will save the company over $60,000 annually."

Chapter 5

Brainstorming the Inputs to Your Process

. . . .

In This Chapter

▶ Creating diagrams to identify inputs

▶ Developing process flow maps

▶ Sorting inputs with CT trees

. . . .

*E*very process, every product, every event — what do these all have in common? Each is comprised of, or caused by, some number of *inputs,* known in Six Sigma parlance as Xs, which take their place in the equation, $Y = f(X)$. Before you can start improving your outcome, or Y, you have to first identify all of the inputs that created this outcome. Without tools and a rigorous process, identifying inputs is a daunting task.

Even something as simple as a #2 lead pencil has an astounding number of inputs — wood, paint, metal, rubber, graphite, and all the people, machines, and processes to mine, refine, produce, mold, bend, shape, spindle, ship, receive, and assemble the parts. Now, consider something as complex as an automobile — you have steel, plastic, rubber, paint, aluminum, glass . . . well, you get the picture.

Six Sigma practitioners have developed tools and techniques to act as catalysts to facilitate the identification of the inputs into a process or product. Because the rest of this workbook deals with categorizing, measuring, improving, and controlling inputs, it's important that you're proficient in identifying these inputs. So, in this chapter, you find out how to prepare a series of diagrams, each one of which digs you deeper and deeper into the world of inputs.

All Together Now: Brainstorming with Your Team to Create Affinity Diagrams

An *affinity diagram* is a diagram that's the result of an exercise where members of a group write their ideas on small paper notes and sort the ideas into logical categories. Brainstorming has always been an effective tool for generating a large number of ideas — and the first step in creating an affinity diagram is a brainstorming session. Brainstorming works because the ideas and knowledge generated by two or more people acting as a group are always greater than those of the sum of the people acting individually.

Here's the traditional cycle of a brainstorming session:

1. **Agree on a subject.** The group must first agree on the category or condition to be the subject of the session.

2. **Encourage participation.** Each team member should be encouraged to participate.

3. **Discourage criticism.** Ensure that everyone understands that debates and criticism aren't allowed.

4. **Decide on a contribution method.** Members can contribute in rotation or in free flow. Just make sure everyone is heard.

5. **Promote equality.** Ensure that every member has an equal opportunity to be heard.

6. **Listen.** Hear and respect the ideas of others — there are no stupid ideas.

7. **Record ideas.** Make sure all ideas are written down.

8. **Continue as long as necessary.** Stop only after no more new ideas are offered.

9. **Edit.** Review the list for clarity and duplicates.

10. **Repeat.** Repeat the process for all identified categories.

After you've generated a whole truckload of ideas, you can start your affinity diagram. The process of creating an affinity diagram stimulates an effective gathering and organization of the ideas into natural groupings — groupings that start to pinpoint the essence of a problem and provide the raw material for a breakthrough solution.

Likely more than one person in the brainstorming group already knows what's causing the problem — these people just don't know that they know. After the ideas are generated and organized, the light will come on and the entire group will say, "Ahhh, so that's the problem!"

Q. Here's a checklist for generating an affinity diagram:

1. Write down the problem or issue.

Be sure that the topic is clear and concise enough to address in one session. "How do we boil the ocean?" is too broad. However, "Why is our server computer crashing?" is a more suitable topic to delve into.

2. Conduct a brainstorming session for the problem.

Follow the brainstorming steps that we outlined earlier in this section. Spend a minimum of 15 minutes, and as long as necessary, discussing this issue.

3. During the discussion, have the participants write each of their ideas on a separate sticky note, with only one idea per note.

Avoid using ideas that are single words. Instead, use phrases or sentences. For instance, unacceptable ideas for the topic "Why is our server computer crashing?" would be: "stupidity," "junk," "evil spirits," or "who knows?" Acceptable ideas would be: "Users are poorly trained," "Computer hardware is obsolete," and "Software is incompatible."

Continue as long as necessary. It's not unusual to generate more than 100 notes.

4. **Post all of the sticky notes on a smooth surface, such as a wall or whiteboard.**

   Without discussion, have the participants sort the notes into a few logical categories — usually around five, but in no case more than ten. Encourage participants to move notes from category to category to where they fit best.

   Sorting in silence helps participants focus on meaning and not on the emotion or baggage that arises in most discussions.

5. **After all the sorting is done, instruct the participants to create titles for the categories.**

   A category title should fit the notes bundled under it. Don't force titles or notes into places they don't fit. When the sorting process is done, create an affinity diagram.

A. The affinity diagram should look something like the following:

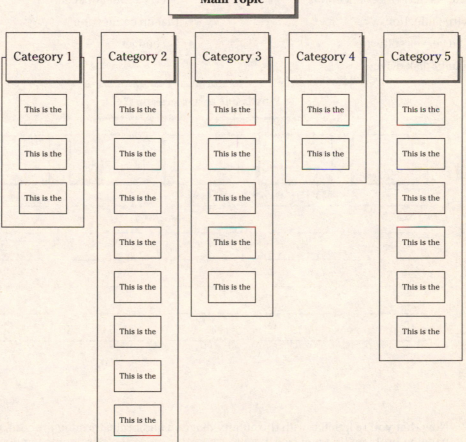

1. Following is a short list of ideas that may have been generated in a brainstorming session on the topic, "Why is our server computer crashing?" Review the ideas, and then enter each in one of the category columns in the included figure. After entering all the ideas, add suitable category titles. Here are the brainstorming ideas:

- Obsolete hardware
- Poor training
- Large applications
- Incompatible software
- Power surges
- Weak firewall
- Server room too warm
- Excess network connections
- Virus infection
- Old server software
- Faulty disk drive

- Old virus software
- Spyware
- Power brownouts
- No new-hire training
- Macintosh computers
- Linux software
- Microsoft software
- Server room not secure
- Dial-up connection
- No budget

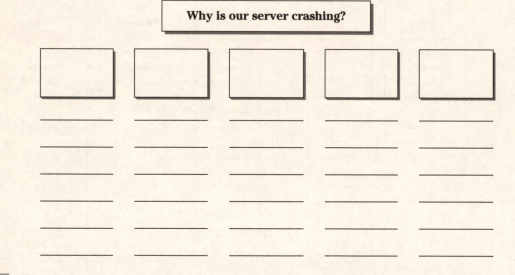

Why is our server crashing?

Solve It

Now that you're familiar with the affinity diagram and brainstorming process, pick a nagging problem that you face in your job, gather several other people familiar with the issue, and conduct an affinity exercise using the blank template in Figure 5-1. You can print it from www.dummies.com/go/sixsigmaworkbook.

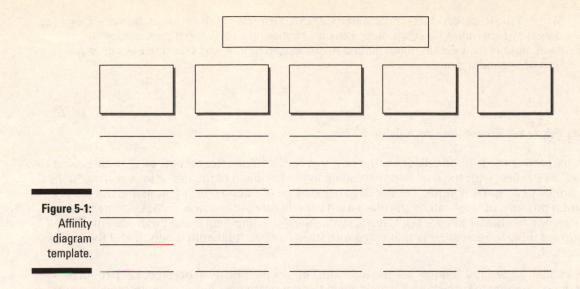

Figure 5-1:
Affinity
diagram
template.

Dem Bones: Creating Fishbone Diagrams

After you create an affinity diagram, take it a step further and drill down a bit into the inputs to find the causes of variation by using a very useful tool called the cause-and-effect diagram, which is also called the Ishikawa diagram or, because of its appearance, the fishbone diagram (see Figure 5-2).

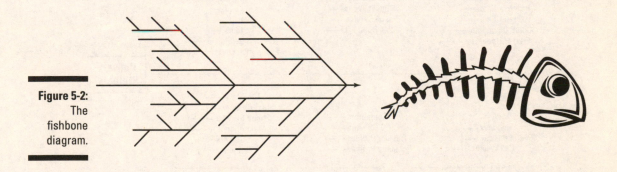

Figure 5-2:
The
fishbone
diagram.

The fishbone diagram, which was created by Kaoru Ishikawa, a quality management pioneer in Japan, is used to explore all the potential causes (inputs) that result in a single output. Even though an affinity diagram helps you group inputs into general categories, the fishbone diagram goes a step further and links inputs together to help you dig for the true root causes of variation.

Many of the ideas produced in an affinity diagram exercise may not be causes at all, or they may turn out to be symptoms of the root cause. In a fishbone diagram exercise, each input is explored in depth, linked to associated inputs, and classified as either a root or secondary cause.

Q. Using Figure 5-2, create your own fishbone diagram.

A. In constructing the fishbone diagram, the problem or condition (the output, or Y) is entered at the "head" of the fish, with the backbone extending to the left. Each of the major intersecting "bones" is a primary category of input. These categories may be the same ones identified in the affinity diagram process, or they can be the often-used generic categories, such as Measurement, Man (or People), Method (or Process), Materials, Machine (or Equipment), and Environment. The important thing to remember is that categories need to fit your identified output and the inputs generated.

The smaller, horizontal "bones" are the individual inputs previously generated. Each input is examined carefully to make sure it's not only in the right category, but also to determine whether it's a direct input at all. If an input turns out to be only indirectly contributing to the outcome, and primarily affects another input, these indirect inputs are placed as "sub-bones" connected to another input. Of course, if, upon examination, a generated idea has no impact at all on the outcome, this idea is discarded and not entered on the fishbone diagram.

The following is an example of a completed fishbone diagram.

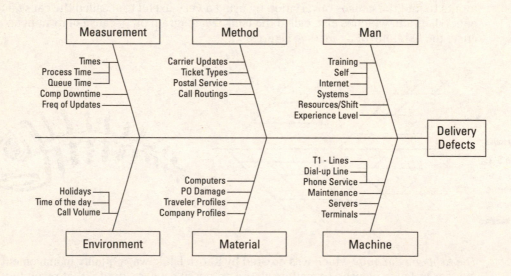

2. Following are some of the inputs from the affinity diagram exercise from earlier in the chapter. Find an appropriate spot for each input on the fishbone diagram template in the included figure. Look long and hard at each one — if you come to the conclusion that an item simply doesn't have an impact on the outcome, don't enter it. If an item appears to be an indirect input, enter it as a diagonal under another input. If you find that an item does impact the outcome, but doesn't fit any of the five categories, create a new category of your own. Remember, like in the affinity diagram exercise, your output is continuous server crashes. Here's a hint to help you: The server itself has a functioning uninterruptible power supply, but the computer room doesn't. Here are the inputs for this fishbone diagram exercise:

- Power surges
- Weak firewall
- Macintosh computers
- Server room too warm

- Virus infection
- Power brownouts
- Old virus software
- Spyware

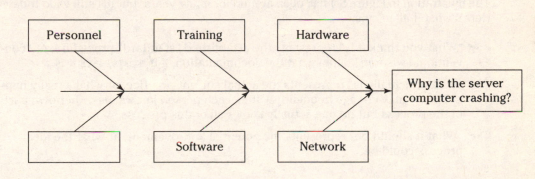

Solve It

Now, using the problem from your own company that you chose in the previous section, along with the affinity exercise results you brainstormed, create a fishbone diagram using the blank template in Figure 5-3. You can also print it from www.dummies. com/go/sixsigmaworkbook.

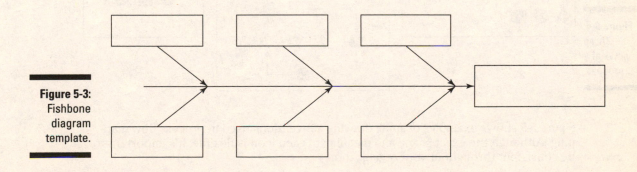

Figure 5-3:
Fishbone
diagram
template.

Examining Your Processes with Process Flow Maps

After you've generated a number of potential inputs into your selected outcome and have begun to categorize and analyze these inputs, it's time for you to take the next step. Even though you've been looking at the possible causes of your outcome, you haven't yet taken a look at the whole system, or process, of which your outcome is the end result. Before you can make improvements to your process, which will give you the outcome that you want, you have to know what the process really is. One way to examine a process is to use a graphical representation of a process called a *process flow map*. But beware of a process flow map if you haven't verified that it represents what's really occurring.

The illustration in Figure 5-4 has been around for many years, but it's still valid today. Here's what it all means:

✔ "What you think it is" represents the established "standard" procedure, or "conventional wisdom"; often what the documentation, if it exists, says it is.

✔ "What it actually is" represents the actual current practice, or what's really happening. It may change frequently. Often, each person knows his or her own part of the process but no one actually knows all of this process.

✔ "What it should be" represents the potential improvement, or what the ideal process could be.

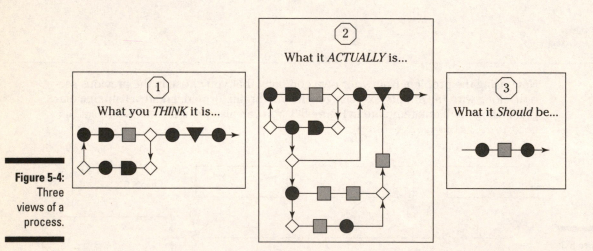

Figure 5-4: Three views of a process.

Figure 5-5 shows examples of some drawing conventions used in process flow mapping. Although the exact shape and meaning of each icon is flexible, it's important to be consistent throughout your organization.

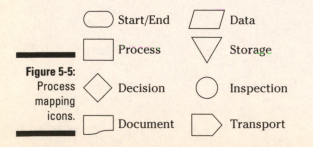

Start/End   Data

Process   Storage

Figure 5-5: Process mapping icons.

Decision   Inspection

Document   Transport

Q. Create an example of a simple process map for a process that starts with a customer feeling hungry and finishes with the customer eating pizza.

A. The following figure represents the example process flow map.

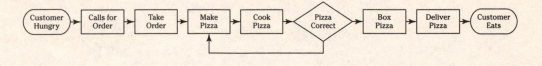

3. Create a process flow map for the following manufacturing process: This process starts with metal parts entering a machine and coating shop and ends with the finished parts moving to inventory. Below are all the steps in this process, but they're not in any particular order. After reviewing these steps, create a process flow map using the symbols shown in Figure 5-5. Be sure to use every step once. Here are the steps:

- Scrap
- Drill holes
- Initial inspection
- Move to coating
- Clean part
- Inspect holes
- Mark for drilling
- Scrap
- Light sanding
- Dip in plastic coat

- Store
- Final inspection
- Scrap
- Install in drill jig
- Prepare inventory report
- Install in dip jig
- Move to store room
- Smooth holes
- Chemical bath

For even more practice, create a process flow map for a process you use every day in your job.

Finding Critical Fruit in the CT Tree

A CT tree is another diagrammatic way of sorting and displaying inputs, but with a different wrinkle. Affinity and fishbone diagrams sort inputs by type, but a *CT tree* sorts inputs by what is *Critical To* (Six Sigma crowds are pretty original, aren't they?) the major contributors to the success of your desired outcome. What makes the CT tree particularly useful is that it relates inputs to specific outputs that you're interested in. This is the only such tool that starts with the outcome of interest and backs into the causes.

Q. Try your hand at creating your own CT tree.

A. Review the example CT tree in the following figure:

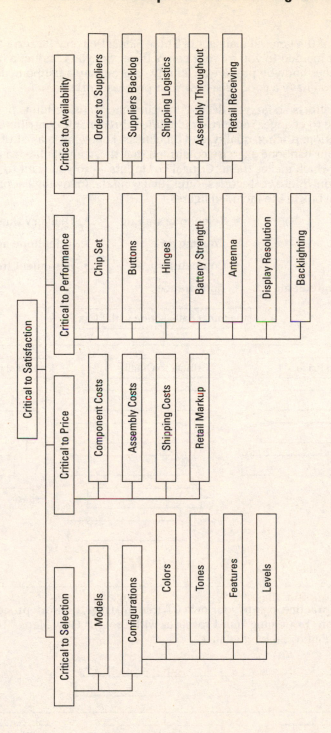

4. Assume that you're the general manager of Three Sigma Delivery Pizzeria and that you've been getting your crust handed to you by your competition. So, you conduct a brainstorming session with your employees and you prepare an affinity diagram and a fishbone diagram. You then map your process so you have a good idea how your process works.

As a result of the efforts so far, you decide that customer satisfaction is poor, and that this is the outcome you have to change. You further identified three major contributors that are critical to customer satisfaction: pricing, quality, and timeliness. Following is a list of inputs identified in brainstorming. Your fishbone exercise confirmed that these inputs have a potential impact on your outcome — which makes them "Critical To" inputs — so you want to further classify them by the three major contributor categories. After reviewing the following list of inputs, write each one in the appropriate box in the included figure:

- Available lines
- Taste
- Packaging
- Cost of extra ingredients
- Telephone staffing
- Cooking time
- Competition
- Appearance
- Delivery time
- Telephone answering
- Ingredient freshness

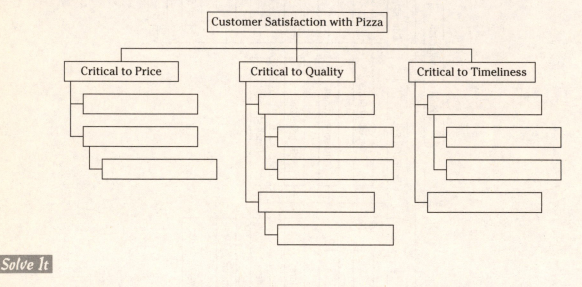

Solve It

For further practice, create your own CT tree by using the work process you selected in the section "Examining Your Processes with Process Flow Maps." Use the CT tree template in Figure 5-6 for guidance.

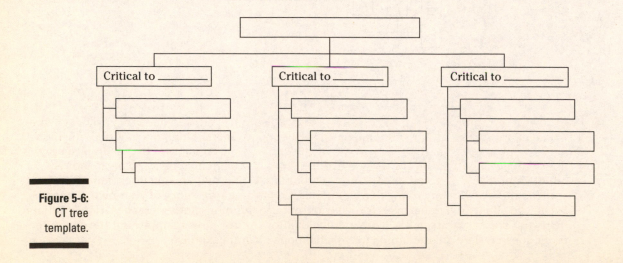

Figure 5-6:
CT tree
template.

Solutions to Brainstorming the Inputs Problems

1 Following is a short list of ideas that may have been generated in a brainstorming session on the topic, "Why is our server computer crashing?" Review the ideas, and then enter each in one of the category columns in the problem figure. After entering all the ideas, add suitable category titles. Here are the brainstorming ideas:

- Obsolete hardware
- Poor training
- Large applications
- Incompatible software
- Power surges
- Weak firewall
- Server room too warm
- Excess network connections
- Virus infection
- Old server software
- Faulty disk drive

- Old virus software
- Spyware
- Power brownouts
- No new-hire training
- Macintosh computers
- Linux software
- Microsoft software
- Server room not secure
- Dial-up connection
- No budget

The following figure shows an example solution. Keep in mind that the relationships between possible inputs are not hard and fast, and that they depend on the perspective of the participants. One of the strengths of this type of exercise is the diverse views, which create out-of-the-box solutions.

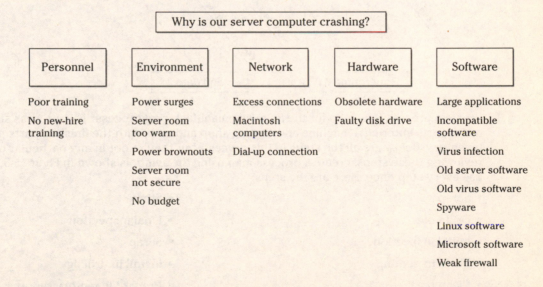

2 Following are some of the inputs from the affinity diagram exercise from earlier in the chapter. Find an appropriate spot for each input on the fishbone diagram template in the problem figure. Look long and hard at each one — if you come to the conclusion that an item simply doesn't have an impact on the outcome, don't enter it. If an item appears to be an indirect input, enter it as a diagonal under another input. If you find that an item does impact the outcome, but doesn't fit any of the five categories, create a new category of your own. Remember, like in the affinity diagrams exercise, your output is continuous server crashes. Here's a hint to help you: The server itself has a functioning uninterruptible power supply, but the computer room doesn't. Here are the inputs for this fishbone diagram exercise:

- Power surges
- Weak firewall
- Macintosh computers
- Server room too warm
- Virus infection
- Power brownouts
- Old virus software
- Spyware

See the following figure for the solution. Upon closer examination, you should have found that the power surges, brownouts, and the room temperature were all related. You probably created a new category called Environment (or something similar) for these items. Though the server itself has an uninterruptible power supply, the air conditioning in the server room was often shutting down, causing temperature increases. So, you probably decided that the power fluctuations didn't affect the server directly, but could be a root cause and should be further investigated.

You also may have realized that the combination of the weak firewall and the old virus software leaves the server vulnerable to infection. Even though the weak firewall itself doesn't impact the server, it could be a contributing root cause, which means that it should be flagged for further study and measurement.

Spyware, while annoying, doesn't cause the server to crash. And, Macintosh computers, which we're using to write this workbook, obviously have nothing to do with the issue at hand and shouldn't be persecuted by jealous PC users.

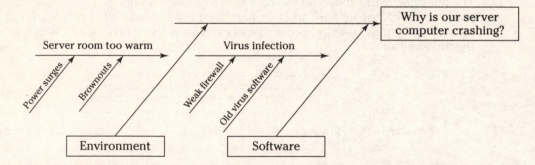

3 Create a process flow map for the following manufacturing process: This process starts with metal parts entering a machine and coating shop and ends with the finished parts moving to inventory. Below are all the steps in this process, but they're not in any particular order. After reviewing these steps, create a process map using the symbols shown in Figure 5-5. Be sure to use every step once. Here are the steps:

- Scrap
- Drill holes
- Initial inspection
- Move to coating
- Clean part
- Inspect holes
- Mark for drilling
- Scrap
- Light sanding
- Dip in plastic coat

- Store
- Final inspection
- Scrap
- Install in drill jig
- Prepare inventory report
- Install in dip jig
- Move to store room
- Smooth holes
- Chemical bath

The following figure is an example solution. Even though your process map may not be exactly the same, if the steps are in a sequence that doesn't create sequential gaps, the process map is useful.

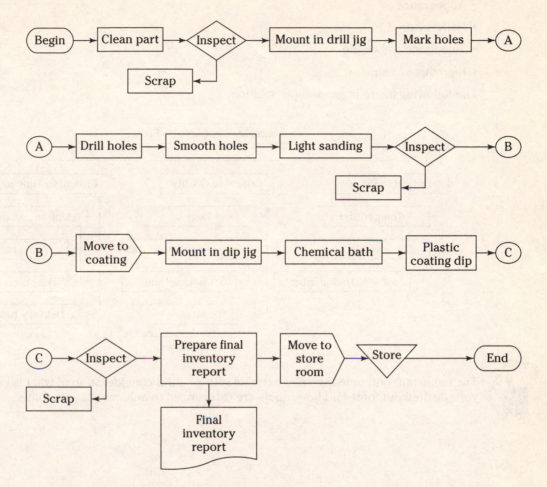

4   Assume that you're the general manager of Three Sigma Delivery Pizzeria and that you've been getting your crust handed to you by your competition. So, you conduct a brainstorming session with your employees, and prepare an affinity diagram and a fishbone diagram. You then map your process so you have a good idea how your process works.

As a result of the efforts so far, you decide that customer satisfaction is poor, and that this is the outcome you have to change. You further identified three major contributors that are critical to customer satisfaction: pricing, quality, and timeliness. Following is a list of inputs identified in brainstorming. Your fishbone exercise confirmed that these inputs have a potential impact on your outcome — which makes them "Critical To" inputs — so you want to further classify them by the three major contributor categories. After reviewing the following list of inputs, write each one in the appropriate box in the problem figure:

- Available lines
- Taste
- Packaging
- Cost of extra ingredients
- Telephone staffing

- Cooking time
- Competition
- Appearance
- Delivery time
- Telephone answering
- Ingredient freshness

The following figure is an example solution.

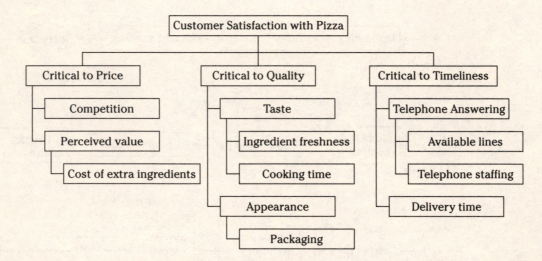

The important outcome from this exercise is the careful consideration of what is critical to your desired outcome and how inputs are categorized to achieve that outcome.

Chapter 6

Prioritizing Which Inputs to Address

Chapter 5 shows you how to identify, classify, and start to prioritize the inputs into a product or process, how to conduct a rousing group get-together, how to create diagrams that look like dead fish, and how to determine whether your system or process really works like you thought it did. You also discover that some inputs are critical to one thing or another, while others aren't. If you've already perused that chapter, no doubt you're now chomping at the bit, ready to charge in on your white horse and fix everything in sight. (If you haven't already perused Chapter 5, you should probably do so now.)

In order to concentrate improvement efforts on only those inputs that have a significant impact, you need to prioritize your inputs so that limited resources can be applied to what will produce the greatest improvement. This chapter shows you how. You can also print some of the forms used in this chapter from www.dummies.com/go/sixsigmaworkbook.

Weeding and Pruning the Input Garden: Using Pareto Diagrams

The *Pareto Principle,* or the 80-20 rule as it's sometimes called, is as true today as it was 100 years ago when Vilfredo Pareto observed that 80 percent of all grain in Italy came from 20 percent of the farmers. Applying the Pareto concept to inputs is a powerful way to sort out "the vital few" from "the trivial many." If you remember that 20 percent of inputs produce 80 percent of the results, you can narrow your focus down significantly.

Q. Create your own Pareto diagram.

A. The most common way to apply Pareto analysis in Six Sigma is to relatively rank inputs based on the amount of impact each has on the outcome. You then create a

visual representation, a *Pareto diagram,* of the input ranking, such as a bar chart, that quickly identifies which critical inputs are ranked the highest, as in the following figure.

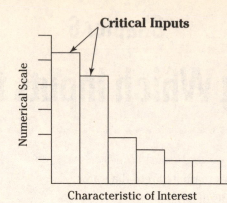

Critical Inputs

Numerical Scale

Characteristic of Interest

Don't try to apply this concept too early in your improvement process. You first need to identify all the inputs before you can start sorting out the vital few (see Chapter 5 for how-to info on input gathering).

1. Your BelchFire 5000 coupe is a bit of a gas hog, so you decide to apply the Six Sigma principles to improve your gas mileage. In an affinity diagram exercise with your bowling buddies, you brainstormed the following list of inputs that impact your gas mileage:

✔ Gas brand/type	✔ Passenger weight
✔ Idle time	✔ Accessories used
✔ Driving speed	✔ Weather
✔ Vehicle maintenance	✔ Engine size
✔ Tire pressure	✔ Transmission type
✔ Tire brand	✔ Aerodynamics

Follow these steps to finish this practice problem:

   1. Place the inputs into a fishbone diagram.

   Use the following figure and the generic categories shown on the template.

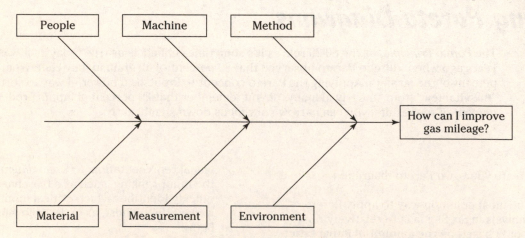

   2. After you've placed the inputs in the diagram, relatively rank them to clearly differentiate the impact of each on your outcome.

   Even though the degree of impact for some inputs may be intuitively obvious, the impact of others may not be. Use the discussion and analysis from the Affinity and Fishbone exercises in Chapter 5 to help establish rankings. You may also want to explore any data that's readily available to help confirm or refine your rankings.

You can use any ranking method you want, as long as the differences in impact are clear. For this practice exercise, use a ranking of 0 to 10, with 10 being the greatest impact and 0 being no impact at all. Place your ranking score next to each input on the fishbone diagram.

You may be tempted at this point to start taking measurements to help you rank your inputs. You could measure the change you get in gas mileage for different brands of gas or you could evaluate gas mileage for different passenger weights and for different driving speeds. This type of measurement is a powerful way to identify the critical inputs, but unfortunately it takes a huge effort. Remember, the whole point is to avoid expending effort to measure an input that doesn't have a significant impact on the problem.

3. **Put the ranked inputs into a Pareto diagram to get a clear, visual indication of which inputs are critical inputs.**

Using Microsoft Excel or any other chart-making application, enter your ranked inputs into an appropriate chart format, such as a bar chart. Make the vertical axis the ranking scale and the horizontal axis the inputs. After the chart is finished, indicate which inputs are critical by putting a mark, such as an "X," on the 2 to 3 highest bars. Also indicate which inputs are candidates for further measurement and analysis.

Solve It

Cementing the Foundation: Creating SIPOC Diagrams

SIPOC (pronounced sy-pok) when spoken with a guttural inflection sounds like a Klingon curse on Star Trek. In reality, however, it's an acronym for one of the most fundamental steps in the Six Sigma process.

SIPOC — which stands for Suppliers-Inputs-Process-Outputs-Controls — is a tool for building high-level process maps that consider the impact of suppliers and the requirements of customers. In this context, both suppliers and customers may be external or they may be people, systems, or processes within the same organization.

A SIPOC diagram is based on simple process flow maps, but it delves much further — providing immediate feedback as to which inputs are critical to the process output. A SIPOC diagram focuses on inputs, outputs, customers, and suppliers, and provides the foundation for significant DMAIC (Define-Measure-Analyze-Improve-Control, the basic Six Sigma process) improvement.

Following are the steps you take to complete a SIPOC diagram:

1. **Identify the process you want to map and then define the scope and boundary points.**

   Be sure to use action verbs to describe what the process is supposed to do. A key to creating a SIPOC diagram is to correctly identify the current process before moving on to the other parts of the diagram.

2. **Identify the outputs. Describe the products or services produced by the process.**

3. **Define the customer or customers.**

   Name the people, processes, or organizations that receive the outputs. As part of this step, define the customer requirements by listing what they demand and what they're entitled to.

4. **List all of the inputs to the process — identify the people, information, materials, and other resources necessary for the process to produce the identified outputs.**

5. **Identify the sources, or suppliers, of the inputs.**

_0._ Create a SIPOC diagram for the order-taking portion of a pizza order process for the Three Sigma Pizza Delivery company, which is struggling with poor customer satisfaction and is examining all interactions with customers to find areas for improvement.

_A._ The following figure is an example of the completed SIPOC diagram.

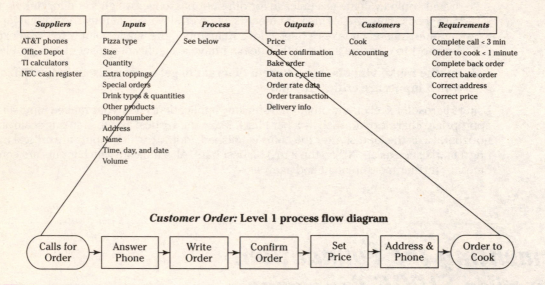

Suppliers	Inputs	Process	Outputs	Customers	Requirements
AT&T phones	Pizza type	See below	Price	Cook	Complete call < 3 min
Office Depot	Size		Order confirmation	Accounting	Order to cook < 1 minute
TI calculators	Quantity		Bake order		Complete back order
NEC cash register	Extra toppings		Data on cycle time		Correct bake order
	Special orders		Order rate data		Correct address
	Drink types & quantities		Order transaction		Correct price
	Other products		Delivery info		
	Phone number				
	Address				
	Name				
	Time, day, and date				
	Volume				

Customer Order: Level 1 process flow diagram

Calls for Order → Answer Phone → Write Order → Confirm Order → Set Price → Address & Phone → Order to Cook

_2._ Practice creating a SIPOC diagram for the process of building a #2 lead pencil. Penrod Pencils, Inc., buys all the pencil components, builds the pencils, and sells them to a pencil wholesaler. Following is all the information you need to complete a SIPOC diagram for the pencil process. The data is in random order, so you have to carefully consider where each item fits in the included figure, which is a SIPOC template. Here's a hint: The template includes the exact number of boxes in each category.

- 6-inch graphite rods
- Finished pencil
- Pencil packages
- Grant's Graphite
- Form wood barrel
- Erasers
- Woody's Wood
- Glue wood barrel
- Wood sheets
- Finished pencil assembly
- Paint pencil
- Stan's Steel Parts
- Cut graphite rods
- Eraser assembly
- Wood glue
- Finished barrel assembly
- Insert eraser in clasp
- Reasonable price

- Rubber rods
- Oswald Office Product Distributors
- Yellow paint
- Cut rubber rods
- Finished wood barrel
- Polly Paint
- Timely delivery
- Package pencils
- Attach eraser assembly
- Eraser clasp
- Consistent quality
- 6-foot graphite rods
- George Glue Emporium
- Packaged pencils
- Ralph's Rubber Products
- Packard Packaging Products
- Insert graphite rod in wood barrel

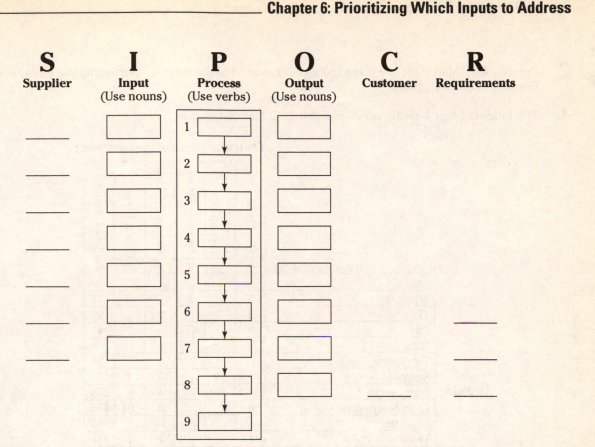

S Supplier	**I** Input (Use nouns)	**P** Process (Use verbs)	**O** Output (Use nouns)	**C** Customer	**R** Requirements
____	☐	1 ☐	☐		
____	☐	2 ☐	☐		
____	☐	3 ☐	☐		
____	☐	4 ☐	☐		
____	☐	5 ☐	☐		
____	☐	6 ☐	☐		____
____	☐	7 ☐	☐		____
		8 ☐	☐	____	____
		9 ☐			

Solve It

Untangling Webs: Creating a Cause-and-Effect Matrix

In Six Sigma, Y = f(X). In other words, all outcomes (Ys) are the result of certain inputs (Xs) and the forces that act on them. In simplest terms, this formula is based on cause and effect.

REMEMBER

The Cause and Effect Matrix, or *C&E Matrix,* helps Six Sigma practitioners make a link between multiple inputs and the resulting outcomes. By identifying and prioritizing these relationships, you can explore and graphically display the possible causes of a problem or condition, which allows you to then search for the root cause.

In many applications, the C&E Matrix relates process inputs and outputs to customer requirements — don't forget the Voice of the Customer! In other instances, the C&E Matrix relates inputs to outputs in order to focus your improvement efforts and resources.

Q. Create a C&E Matrix for the pizza order process used in the section "Cementing the Foundation: Creating SIPOC Diagrams."

A. The following figure represents a possible C&E Matrix example:

		Outputs (Voice of the Customer)					
		Hot Pizza	Correct Ingredients	Delivery Time	Proper Cooking	Burnt Pizza	Rank order sum
	Customer ranking	9	7	9	8	10	
Inputs	Name						0
	Address	5		8			117
	Time	5		5			90
	Day	4		5			81
	Date						0
	Telephone number			4			36
	Recipe		10		4	7	172
	Ingredients	4	10		4	8	218
	Oven temperature	8			8	10	236
	Cook time	5		7	10	8	268
	Volume	7		8	7	1	231
	Preparation time			9			81
	Ingredient availability		10	10			160
	Delivery	7		10			150

3. Complete a C&E Matrix for a service with which almost everyone is familiar — Internet access. In this exercise, you're going to be the customer who's using the C&E Matrix to decide on an Internet service provider (ISP). Here's the scenario: After brainstorming and preparing an affinity diagram with the members of your family, you identified seven outcomes, or customer requirements, for Internet service that are important to your family. In addition, you identified seven inputs from an ISP that impacts these requirements. Following are 14 items — seven inputs and seven outputs — in random order:

✔ Ease of use

✔ Short setup

✔ Access on the road

✔ Web filter

✔ Quick log-on

✔ Setup time

✔ Remote coverage

✔ Fast downloads

✔ Transfer rate

✔ Log-on time

✔ Kids can use it

✔ ISP stability

✔ Ability to block sites

✔ Reliability

Following are the steps to complete the C&E matrix that will help you make an ISP selection decision:

1. **Sort these items into inputs and outputs. Use the worksheet at the end of these steps as a template.**

2. **Place each output (customer requirement) in a column heading.**

3. **Rank each customer requirement using a scale from 1 to 5, with 5 being a must-have down to a 1, which is a nice feature, but isn't critical.**

   In this exercise, assume the following rankings: Ability to block: 1; Access on road: 2; Quick log-on: 3; Short setup: 3; Fast downloads: 4; Reliability: 4; Kids can use it: 5.

4. **List each input in a row heading.**

   These important inputs are often called *critical-to-customer characteristics,* or CTCs for short.

5. **Rank the relationships between the inputs and outputs by placing a value of 1, 3, or 9 at the intersections.**

   Nine indicates a strong relationship, 3 a medium relationship, and 1 a weak relationship. Leave a blank if no relationship exists. This ranking scale is somewhat arbitrary, but be sure that you clearly distinguish between strong and weak relationships.

6. **Calculate the rank order sum for each input to determine its relative priority.**

   To do so, multiply each input's individual relationship value by its corresponding customer requirement ranking value, and then add the multiplied values across the row.

   For example, if an input has a medium, or 3, relationship with a particular output that has a customer ranking of 5, enter 3 times 5, or 15, in the intersecting square.

7. **To complete the C&E Matrix, enter the rank order sums from highest to lowest in a Pareto diagram, such as a bar chart. The most important inputs are now obvious.**

Outputs (Voice of the Customer)

Rank order sum

Customer ranking

Inputs

Performing a Failure Modes Effects Analysis (FMEA)

Failures in products or processes are inevitable. However, remember that the key premise of Six Sigma says that variation is everywhere and is in everything. Six Sigma also says that even though you can't eliminate all variation, you can detect and eliminate the most harmful variation and allow for the variation that can't be totally eliminated.

The fact is that every input has the potential to fail and cause problems with the outcome. Remember the words of the great philosopher, Kenny Rogers: "Every hand's a winner and every hand's a loser." It's the same with inputs. Each one can be successful in contributing to the desired outcome, but any one of them also can cause a catastrophic failure. Huge companies have been destroyed by the simplest of process errors — errors that could have been prevented if a *Failure Modes Effects Analysis* (FMEA) had been performed.

Q. Define and explain *Failure Modes Effects Analysis* (FMEA).

A. An FMEA is a structured approach to identifying the potential ways a product or process can fail and to identifying how you can detect the failure and its effects so you can reduce the risk of either occurrence or impact, or both. Keep these points in mind for the next problem.

4. As the general manager of Three Sigma Pizza, you want to continue your efforts in making customers happier. After preparing an affinity diagram and a C&E Matrix for your pizza preparation process, you have chosen one input — pizza cooking time — as a candidate for a Six Sigma improvement project. Before kicking off the project, you want to prepare an FMEA to focus the project where it will have the most impact. Using the following template, follow these steps to complete your FMEA:

| Process name: | FMEA Template | | | | | | | |
| Date: | | | | | | | | |
Process step	Potential failure mode	Potential failure effects	Severity	Potential causes	Occurence	Current Controls	Detection	RPN

1. **Select and enter your input variables.**

   In this exercise, use "Pizza cooking time" as the input. Proper consideration at this step can eliminate trivial factors from further consideration. Only list variables that have been identified from your previous work — such as a C&E Matrix, an affinity diagram, a Pareto diagram, or a SIPOC diagram — instead of listing every possible factor.

2. **Enter potential failure modes (the consequences if the input variable isn't properly controlled) associated with each individual input variable you list. Each variable may have more than one failure mode.**

   As a hint to get you going in this exercise, use "Cooking time too short" and "Cooking time too long" as the input.

3. **Enter the potential failure effect the failure mode would have on your product or process.**

   A failure mode may have more than one effect, so be sure you identify all of them as separate line items.

4. **Quantify the severity of the failure modes by assigning each a severity score, from 1 to 10.**

   The more severe the effect, the higher its score. Even though all identified failure modes may have some impact on your customer, that impact won't be the same for each.

   In the following figure are some guidelines for ranking the severity of each failure mode's impact on your customer. The 1-to-10 scale is most common in industrial applications because it allows for wider variation among the results. Narrower score ranges, such as 1 to 5, make it easier for teams to agree. The key is to be consistent.

RATING	DEGREE OF SEVERITY
1	Customer will not notice the adverse effect, or it is insignificant
2	Customer will probably experience slight annoyance
3	Customer will experience annoyance as a result of poor performance
4	Customer dissatisfaction as a result of poor performance
5	Customer is made uncomfortable or their productivity is reduced by the continued poor performance
6	Customer complains as a result of performance issue
7	High degree of customer dissatisfaction due to being unable to use a portion of the product
8	Very high degree of dissatisfaction due to loss of performance
9	Customer has lost total use of product
10	Customer has lost total use of product and will never return

5. **Enter the potential causes of each listed failure mode and then assign occurrence scores, which rank the likelihood of a failure occurring, for each of the potential causes.**

   At this point, you can generate your identified causes in a brainstorming session with those directly involved in the system, product, or process.

   The following figure shows guidelines for ranking the likelihood that a failure mode will occur. A score of one means that there is very little chance that the failure will occur. The scoring scale goes up to ten, which says that a failure is certain. Your organization may modify or adopt these scoring guidelines to fit your specific market and situation, but remember that consistency in rating factors is the key.

RATING	LIKELIHOOD OF OCCURRENCE
1	Likelihood of occurrence is remote
2	Low failure rate with supporting documentation
3	Low failure rate without supporting documentation
4	Occasional failures
5	Relatively moderate failure rate with supporting documentation
6	Moderate failure rate without supporting documentation
7	Relatively high failure rate with supporting documentation
8	High failure rate without supporting documentation
9	Failure is almost certain based on data
10	Assured of failure based on data

6. **Identify and list the controls that are currently in place to prevent each failure mode's cause.**

7. **Score each control to determine its ability to detect the failure mode before harm or damage is done or to prevent the failure mode from ever occurring.**

   The following figure shows guidelines to help you rate detectability. Obviously it's more beneficial to your customer, and your process, if you prevent the failure rather than detect it after it has already occurred. However, when failures do occur, the best case scenario is that it's detected before reaching the customer.

RATING	ABILITY TO DETECT
1	Sure that the potential failure will be found or prevented before reaching the next customer
2	Almost certain that the potential failure will be found or prevented before reaching the next customer
3	Low likelihood that the potential failure will reach the next customer undetected
4	Controls may detect or prevent the potential failure from reaching the next customer
5	Moderate likelihood that the potential failure will reach the next customer
6	Controls are unlikely to detect or prevent the potential failure from reaching the next customer
7	Poor likelihood that the potential failure will be detected or prevented before reaching the next customer
8	Very poor likelihood that the potential failure will be detected or prevented before reaching the next customer
9	Current controls probably will not even detect the potential failure
10	Absolute certainty that the current controls will not detect the potential failure

8. **Compile and analyze your FMEA work.**

   Calculate a Risk Priority Number, or RPN, for each failure mode cause by multiplying the severity, occurrence, and detectability scores together for that mode. The highest RPN numbers indicate the highest risk and show you where your initial efforts should be concentrated.

Now that you've identified the highest priority items, you can set proposed actions, assign responsibility, and agree on a due date. This use of the FMEA turns the analysis into a proactive and actionable document.

You should always attempt to reduce the RPN by preventing the failure mode rather than detecting it. The idea is to make it impossible for the failure to occur.

After the improvement actions have been accomplished and documented, enter new scores for severity, occurrence, and detectability. A new RPN gives you a clear indication of whether your efforts have been successful. You can then decide to take further actions on this failure mode, or move on to the next highest priority item.

Solutions to Prioritizing Inputs Problems

1 Following is an example solution to the Pareto Diagram exercise, including a fishbone diagram that identifies and ranks the inputs (see following figure).

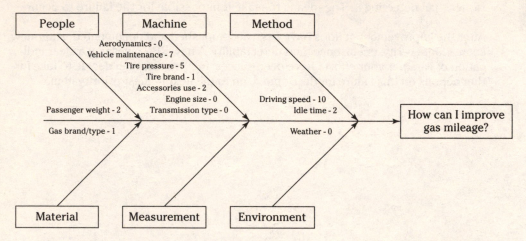

A Pareto diagram helps visualize the critical inputs. (See the following figure).

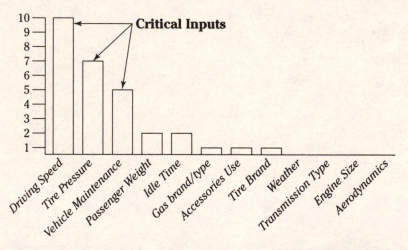

In this case, driving speed, tire pressure, and vehicle maintenance are singled out for further measurement and analysis. Even though you may be tempted to immediately start improvement efforts in all three areas, you still have no data confirming that any of these inputs is the culprit. Measurements will narrow the choices even further, so you may not have to lighten up that lead foot quite yet.

Engine size, transmission type, and aerodynamics shouldn't be ranked. Even though you have no doubt that these inputs have a very definite impact on gas mileage, they aren't controllable, which means they aren't points of improvement leverage. For the same reason, weather should not be ranked. However, in some circumstances, you may have the flexibility to not drive in bad weather. In that case, weather would be ranked, possibly as a critical input.

2 Using the entire list of SIPOC elements, the following figure shows an orderly and detailed representation of the pencil production process.

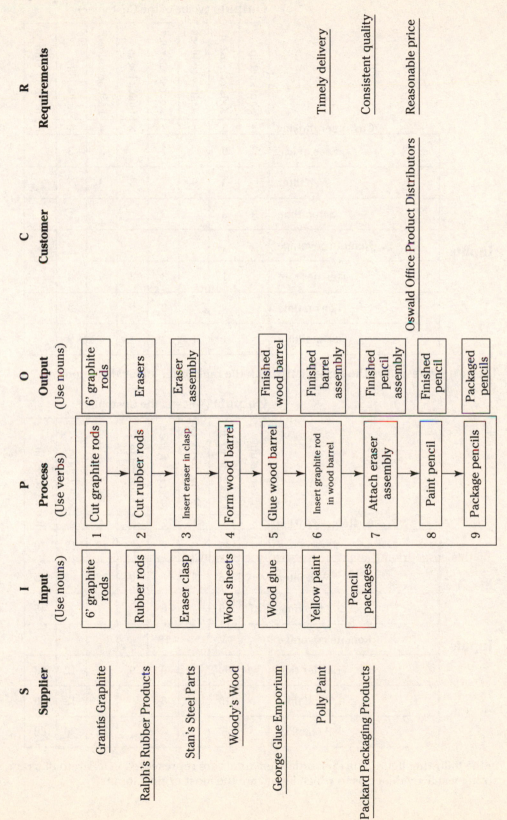

3 The following figure shows the C&E Matrix with the raw relationship scores.

Outputs (Voice of the Customer)

	Short setup	Kids can use it	Ability to block	Access on road	Quick log-in	Fast downloads	Reliability	Rank order sum
Customer ranking	3	5	1	2	3	4	4	
Ease of use	3	9		1		3	3	
Web filter		3	9		3	3		
Setup time	9	3		3				
Remote coverage		1		9				
Transfer rate		1		3	3	9	3	
Log-on time		3		3	9		3	
ISP stability		1	1	3		3	9	

Inputs (label for rows)

The next figure shows the same Matrix with the rank order sum calculations.

Outputs (Voice of the Customer)

	Short setup	Kids can use it	Ability to block	Access on road	Quick log-in	Fast downloads	Reliability	Rank order sum
Customer ranking	3	5	1	2	3	4	4	
Ease of use	9	45		2		12	12	70
Web filter		15	9		9	12		45
Setup time	27	15		6				48
Remote coverage		5		18				23
Transfer rate		5		6	9	36	12	68
Log-on time		15		6	27		12	60
ISP stability		5	1	6		12	36	60

Inputs (label for rows)

In the following figure, the rank order sum totals are represented in a Pareto diagram, giving strong visual evidence as to which inputs are the most critical inputs.

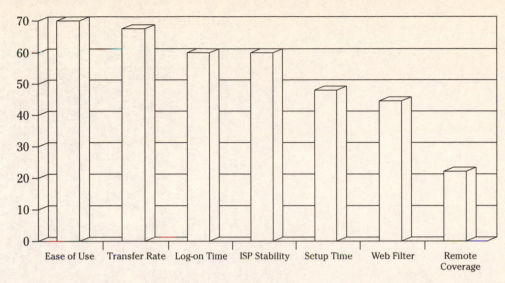

4 The following figure is a solution to the FMEA exercise. Though your FMEA solution may not look much like this one, you need to be sure that you made logical assumptions and conclusions as you entered the data.

Process name:									
Date:			**FMEA Template**						
Process step	Potential failure mode	Potential failure effects	Severity	Potential causes	Occurence	Current Controls	Detection	RPN
Pizza cooking time	Time too short	Doughy crust	8	Inaccurate timer	1		10	80
		Unmelted cheese	8	Pizza removed too early	6		4	192
		Raw ingredients	8	Timer not set	7		4	224
		Cold pizza delivered	8	Placed in oven after timer started	4		4	128
				Staff inattention	9		4	288
	Burnt crust	9	Inaccurate timer	1		10	90
	Burnt cheese	9	Pizza removed too late	6		4	216
	Burnt ingredients	9	Timer not set	7		4	288
			Placed in oven before timer started	4		4	144
			Staff inattention	9		4	324

Be sure that your improvement efforts are focused on the highest RPN, because this is where you can have the most impact.

Part III
Mastering Measuring

The 5th Wave   By Rich Tennant

"Eliminating conflicts along the production line is a big part of our Six Sigma initiative."

In this part . . .

What you don't measure, you can't know. What you don't know, you can't control. And if you can't control, you're left to the whims of chance. Measurement is the first step in improvement. This part provides you with exercises to build your expertise in measuring and knowing the critical outputs and inputs of the product or system you're improving.

Chapter 7

Categorizing Data and Calculating Measures of Variation

. . . .

In This Chapter

▶ Determining what kind of data you have

▶ Calculating means, modes, and medians

▶ Calculating how much variation is in a set of data

▶ Separating variation into its short-term and long-term components

. . . .

You're reading this book with one goal in mind: Improving your process. However, you have to remember that improving your processes requires that you understand variation. And, to understand variation, you need to figure out how to categorize data by type and how to summarize it with some simple tools. After you understand what type of data you have, where it's located, and how it varies, you're much closer to understanding and improving your processes. Read on — this chapter guides you through the process of understanding and categorizing your data.

Differentiating Data Types

Data comes in different shapes and sizes. If you know what kind of data you have, you can then figure out what type of analysis and what tools or methods you need to use in your Six Sigma work. Your data values will either be able to be placed into named categories (this data is called *attribute* or *categorical data*) or will follow a continuous scale (this data is called *continuous* or *variable data*).

Attribute or categorical data is used to describe a named attribute of the characteristic or process. This type of data is *discrete,* which means that the data can be counted, ranked, or sorted, but not added, subtracted, or averaged. For example, if you had one red ball and one blue one, it makes no sense to try to average the color.

You can ask yourself a simple question about your data that tells you whether it's continuous: "Can I meaningfully add or subtract values of this data?" If the answer is "yes," you have continuous data.

Q. You have a set of data for an ice cream store that tells you what flavors are on the menu:

Chocolate	Chocolate chip cookie dough
Strawberry	Raspberry cheesecake
Butter pecan	Rocky road
Vanilla	Pistachio
Neapolitan	Orange sherbet
Mint chocolate	Bubble gum

What type of data is this?

A. The ice cream flavors in this list are clearly named categories, which makes it attribute data.

Q. Now consider having more detail for the ice cream, such as how many cartons of each flavor were sold last week. Using the following table, determine what kind of data you have:

Flavor	Cartons Sold
Chocolate	22
Strawberry	14
Butter pecan	3
Vanilla	19
Neapolitan	7
Mint chocolate	8
Choc. chip cookie dough	9
Raspberry cheesecake	11
Rocky road	3
Pistachio	1
Orange sherbet	2
Bubble gum	6

A. The additional information shown in the table for the flavor categories is important. Ask yourself: "Can I meaningfully add or subtract values of this data?" For example, can you add all the carton numbers together to get a meaningful total? Yes! Or, can you subtract the number of chocolate cartons from the number of vanilla cartons to find out how many more cartons of chocolate ice cream were sold than vanilla? Yes again! These answers tell you that this additional data is continuous.

1. Packages entering a sorting facility are labeled as having either "urgent" or "normal" priority. What kind of data is this characteristic of the packages?

Solve It

2. You're collecting weight measurements of a plated contact switch. The measurements are in grams. What type of data is this?

Solve It

3. Each final inspection record for manufactured disk drives is stamped with a date code. What type of data are these date code stamps?

4. Student grades are given as A, A–, B+, and so on. Is this attribute or categorical data? What about grades given on a numerical grade point scale: A = 4.00, A– = 3.67, B+ = 3.33, and so on? Is this attribute or categorical data? What is the advantage of a numerical grade point scale?

Solve It

Calculating Measures of Variation Location

To begin to understand variation in your data, you have to be able to describe it with numbers. The most basic numerical measures are those that quantify the location of the central tendency of your variation — or, in other words, the values that are most likely to occur.

When you have continuous data, you can calculate three different measures of variation location:

- **Mode:** The *mode* of a set of data is the single value that is most frequently observed and is associated with the highest peak of a distribution.

- **Median:** The *median* of a set of data is the single value where half the data is below and half is above. The median is the preferred measure of variation location when your collected data contains *outliers,* or extreme data points well outside the range of other data.

  You determine the median by ordering your collected data from least to greatest and counting the total number of points. If you find an odd number of data points, the median is the middle value, or the one exactly halfway through the list. If you find an even number of data points, the median is the average of the two points in the middle of the list.

- **Mean:** The *mean* — or average — of a set of data, is represented mathematically by the symbol $\bar{x}$:

$$\bar{x} = \frac{\sum x_i}{n}$$

where

- $\bar{x}$ (pronounced "ex bar") is the symbol representing the calculated mean.

- x_i represents each of the individual measurement values.

- Σ, the Greek capital letter sigma, tells you to sum up (add) all the individual measurements.

- n is the number of individual measurements in your data set.

Q. For the following collection of pressure measurements (kPa), calculate the mode, median, and mean.

247	228	232	251
237	248	240	246
252	261	242	247
263	239	229	246
262	243	244	263
267	233	246	249

A. Sorting the data from least to greatest helps you find the mode and the median:

Value	Order	Value	Order
228	1	246	13
229	2	247	14
232	3	247	15
233	4	248	16
237	5	249	17
239	6	251	18
240	7	252	19
242	8	261	20
243	9	262	21
244	10	263	22
246	11	263	23
246	12	267	24

When going through the calculations for all the measures of central location, remember the following:

- The mode is the data value that is observed most frequently. For this pressure data, you can see that the value of 246 kPa occurs three times — more than any other — making it the mode.

- The median is the exact middle value of the rank-ordered data. For the 24 points of this data set, the middle value lands between ordered points 12 and 13. That makes 246 kPa the median.

- Determining the mean is more calculator intensive. But the calculation is still straightforward: You add up all the individual data values and divide by the number of individual data points, 24, which gives you 246.6 kPa as the mean.

- The following figure is a *dot plot* (see Chapter 8 for practice on creating dot plots) of the collection pressure measurements. You can see how symmetrical the variation is. When variation is symmetrical, the mode, median, and mean are often nearly identical.

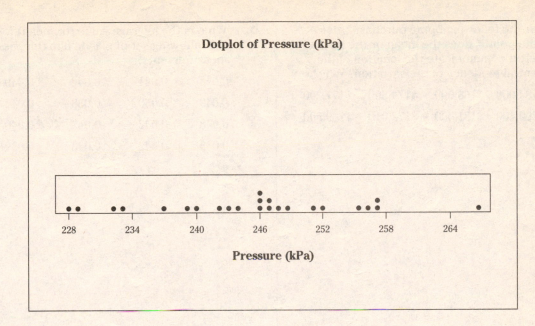

When a set of data with variation is not symmetrical, the mode, median, and mean are often different. Don't be surprised when this happens.

5. Find the mode, median, and mean of the following collection of process cycle time measurements:

8	19	9	10
21	8	10	8
11	11	13	21

Solve It

6. What is the average grade point of the following class of students? What is the median?

3.33	3.00	3.67	3.00
3.67	3.00	3.33	3.00
0.33	3.67	3.33	3.33
3.33	3.33	3.67	3.67
3.00	3.33	3.00	4.00

Solve It

7. For the following home purchase price data points, does the mean or the median better communicate the location of the central tendency of the variation? Why?

| $184,000 | $168,000 | $174,500 | $177,200 |
| $292,400 | $181,000 | $172,010 | $169,900 |

Solve It

8. What is the average value (or mean) for the following set of plastic film thickness measurements:

0.044	0.041	0.046	0.049
0.049	0.050	0.038	0.044
0.048	0.042	0.043	0.040
0.039	0.042	0.043	0.039

Solve It

Variety Is the Spice of Life: Measuring Variation Spread

The central location of the variation in your data is only the first of two critical parameters you need to quantify. The second parameter is the measure of how much *variation spread* you find in your data around its central location. Table 7-1 summarizes three different measures of variation spread.

Table 7-1	Summary of Statistical Measures of Variation Spread	
Measure of Variation Spread	**Definition**	**Comments**
Range	$R = x_{MAX} - x_{MIN}$	Simple. Preferred metric for sets of data with only a few (2 to 9) members. Drawback: Greatly influenced by outliers.
Variance	$\sigma^2 = \dfrac{\sum (x_i - \overline{x})^2}{n - 1}$	Useful for more advanced experimentation and analyses.
Standard deviation	$\sigma = \sqrt{\dfrac{\sum (x_i - \overline{x})^2}{n - 1}}$	Most commonly used for data sets with 10 or more members. More accurate than the range metric for larger data sets.

EXAMPLE

Q. What is the range, variance, and standard deviation in the dollar values for the following set of invoices?

$5,242.18	$5,194.04	$5,263.70	$5,188.45
$5,217.21	$5,200.50	$5,073.54	$5,167.45

A. The range (R) in the dollar value in this collection of invoices is the difference between the greatest (x_{MAX}) and the least (x_{MIN}). By identifying these extreme values in the data, it's easy to plug them into the formula and arrive at the answer:

$$R = x_{MAX} - x_{MIN} = \$5,263.70 - \$5,073.54 = \$190.16$$

To calculate the variance (σ^2), you must first calculate the mean, $\bar{x}$, which ends up being $5,193.38. At this point, laying out a calculation table is helpful:

x_i	$x_i - \bar{x}$	$(x_i - \bar{x})^2$	x_i	$x_i - \bar{x}$	$(x_i - \bar{x})^2$
$5,252.18	$48.80	$\$^2$ 2,381.34	$5,217.21	$23.83	$\$^2$ 567.65
$5,194.04	$0.65	$\$^2$ 0.43	$5,200.50	$7.11	$\$^2$ 50.60
$5,263.70	$70.32	$\$^2$ 4,944.24	$5,073.54	−$119.84	$\$^2$ 14,362.15
$5,188.45	−$4.94	$\$^2$ 24.36	$5,167.45	−$25.93	$\$^2$ 672.35

Notice how all the squared $x_i - \bar{x}$ terms are positive. And notice how when you square them, you end up with the weird units of $\$^2$, or *squared dollars*. As strange as that may seem, it's ok! There's no such thing in the real world, but there is in the ethereal math universe. It all works out in the end.

Next, you add up all the squared dollar terms and divide the sum by one less than the number of points in your data set ($n - 1$):

$$\frac{\sum(x_i - \bar{x})^2}{n - 1} = \frac{\$^2 23,003.11}{8 - 1} = \$^2 3,286.16$$

For now, this calculated variance number is just a first step to obtaining the standard deviation (σ). Later, the variance will help you determine which factors contribute to overall variation when designing experiments to improve your processes. As you mature in statistics, variance measures become very useful tools.

The final calculation is for the standard deviation (σ). After you've found the variance, it's extremely easy to find the standard deviation — you just take the square root:

$$\sigma = \sqrt{\sigma^2} = \sqrt{\$^2 3,286.16} = \$57.33$$

As you can see, with the standard deviation, you've come back down to Earth and are again using the real-world units of dollars, instead of squared dollars. And now you have a quantitative measure of how much variation spread you have in your data.

Many computer programs and calculators automatically perform the tedious intermediate steps to calculate the variance and standard deviation. All you have to do is enter the raw data. A great example is Microsoft Excel or any other spreadsheet application. Master these tools to make your Six Sigma life much, much easier!

9. Calculate the range, variance, and standard deviation for the set of process cycle time measurements given in Problem 5 of this chapter.

Solve It

10. Calculate the range, variance, and standard deviation for the class grade point data in Problem 6.

Solve It

11. Calculate the range and standard deviation for the set of home purchase prices in Problem 7 in two ways: first, with all eight data points and second, by excluding the $292,400 point. With the elimination of just one data point, how are the range and standard deviation measurements affected?

Solve It

12. Calculate the standard deviation for the set of plastic film thickness measurements in Problem 8.

Solve It

Time Warp: Separating Short-Term and Long-Term Variation

Quantifying variation spread can be tricky because it changes over time. Over a short period of time, the variation you observe is smaller than it will be over a longer period of time. One of the first tasks of the Six Sigma practitioner is to separate observed variation into these two buckets — short-term and long-term.

The basic formula for standard deviation captures *all* the variation occurring within a set of data. So, when your data set covers enough time to include the influence of all the special-cause variables and factors, it's a measure of the long-term variation.

$$\sigma_{LT} = \sqrt{\frac{\sum (x_i - \overline{x})^2}{n - 1}}$$

To extract the short-term variation from a set of data, you have to find the average range between the sequential data points:

$\sigma_{ST} = \overline{R}\left(\frac{1}{1.128}\right)$ where $\overline{R} = \frac{\sum R_i}{n - 1}$. So combining together you get $\sigma_{ST} = \frac{\sum R_i}{1.128(n - 1)}$.

Never try to calculate the short-term standard deviation on anything other than a sequential set of measurements. That is, only perform this calculation on a set of measurements that's in the order that the measurements were taken. You have to use the correct order because the calculation of the short-term standard deviation is based on the natural ranges that occur between the characteristics' measurements. If the order of the measurements is altered at all, your answer will be smaller than it should be.

Q. Water level measurements of a well have been recorded for the last 40 months (recorded in order from oldest measurement to newest, from left to right and top to bottom):

5.7	4.4	4.6	1.3
5.7	5.6	4.2	5.3
9.5	10.0	9.3	11.7
9.5	8.3	7.9	9.3
4.7	4.3	6.4	5.0
6.0	3.9	5.5	5.5
4.5	5.5	5.7	7.6
7.5	7.4	8.0	9.1
9.1	8.9	8.9	10.1
12.1	11.2	9.5	10.0

Chart this variation over time and calculate both the long-term and the short-term standard deviations.

A. First, create a chart of this variation over the course of the 40 months of measurements, starting with the oldest recording (month 1) and continuing to the most recent (month 40). The following figure shows one chart example:

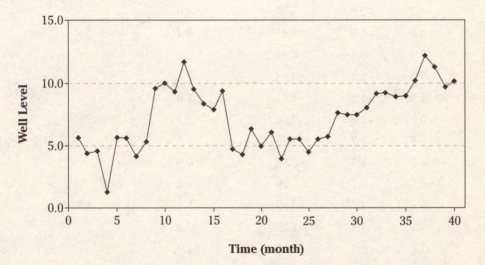

You can see how the variation changes over time, displaying a smaller amount of variation over any given short subset of months as compared to the large variation that occurs over the full-time scale.

An immediate calculation table helps in calculating both the long-term and the short-term standard deviations if you're doing these by hand. Start by calculating the mean ($\bar{x} = 7.2$) for the values. Notice how the intermediate calculations in the columns of the following table are laid out to enable the final results:

Month	x_i	$x_i - \overline{x}$	$(x_i - \overline{x})^2$	$R_i = \lvert x_i - x_{i-1} \rvert$
1	5.7	–1.5	2.25	NA
2	4.4	–2.8	7.84	1.3
3	4.6	–2.6	6.76	0.2
4	1.3	–5.9	34.81	3.3
5	5.7	–1.5	2.25	4.4
6	5.6	–1.6	2.56	0.1
7	4.2	–3.0	9.00	1.4
8	5.3	–1.9	3.61	1.1
9	9.5	2.3	5.29	4.2
10	10.0	2.8	7.84	0.5
11	9.3	2.1	4.41	0.7
12	11.7	4.5	20.25	2.4
13	9.5	2.3	5.29	2.2
14	8.3	1.1	1.21	1.2
15	7.9	0.7	0.49	0.4
16	9.3	2.1	4.41	1.4
17	4.7	–2.5	6.25	4.6
18	4.3	–2.9	8.41	0.4
19	6.4	–0.8	0.64	2.1
20	5.0	–2.2	4.84	1.4
21	6.0	–1.2	1.44	1.0
22	3.9	–3.3	10.89	2.1
23	5.5	–1.7	2.89	1.6
24	5.5	–1.7	2.89	0.0
25	4.5	–2.7	7.29	1.0
26	5.5	–1.7	2.89	1.0
27	5.7	–1.5	2.25	0.2
28	7.6	0.4	0.16	1.9
29	7.5	0.3	0.09	0.1
30	7.4	0.2	0.04	0.1
31	8.0	0.8	0.64	0.6
32	9.1	1.9	3.61	1.1
33	9.1	1.9	3.61	0.0
34	8.9	1.7	2.89	0.2
35	8.9	1.7	2.89	0.0

Month	x_i	$x_i - \bar{x}$	$(x_i - \bar{x})^2$	$R_i = \|x_i - x_{i-1}\|$
36	10.1	2.9	8.41	1.2
37	12.1	4.9	24.01	2.0
38	11.2	4.0	16.00	0.9
39	9.5	2.3	5.29	1.7
40	10.0	2.8	7.84	0.5

With the intermediate calculation table in hand, you're now in position to calculate the short-term and long-term standard deviations:

$$\sigma_{LT} = \sqrt{\frac{\sum (x_i - \bar{x})^2}{n-1}} = \sqrt{\frac{244.43}{40-1}} = 2.50$$

$$\sigma_{ST} = \frac{\bar{R}}{1.128} = \frac{1.29}{1.128} = 1.15$$

As it always should be, the short-term variation is less than the long-term variation. This makes sense because over the long-term, factors and influences enter in, shifting the entire variation or causing it to drift or fluctuate more than it does over any given short period.

---

13. For a sequential set of 70 bolt torque measurements, the sum of the squared error, $\sum (x_i - \bar{x})^2$ is 3,750 and the sum of the interpoint ranges is 178. What are the short-term and long-term standard deviations for this set of data?

Solve It

14. Complete the following calculation table to determine the short- and long-term standard deviations for a 35-point set of plate density measurements:

No.	x_i	$x_i - \overline{x}$	$(x_i - \overline{x})^2$	$R_i = \lvert x_i - x_{i-1} \rvert$
1	103			
2	95			
3	113			
4	92			
5	112			
6	97			
7	90			
8	81			
9	89			
10	77			
11	98			
12	86			
13	86			
14	83			
15	90			
16	84			
17	84			
18	87			
19	53			
20	62			
21	63			
22	77			
23	85			
24	86			
25	75			
26	86			
27	85			
28	89			
29	94			
30	103			
31	93			
32	109			
33	91			
34	96			
35	90			
	$\overline{x} = \dfrac{\sum x_i}{n} =$		$\sigma_{LT} = \sqrt{\dfrac{\sum (x_i - \overline{x})^2}{n-1}} =$	$\sigma_{ST} = \dfrac{\sum R_i}{1.128(n-1)}$

Solve It

15. Complete the following calculation table to determine the short- and long-term standard deviations for a 30-point set of cycle time measurements:

No.	x_i	$x_i - \bar{x}$	$(x_i - \bar{x})^2$	$R_i = \|x_i - x_{i-1}\|$
1	42			
2	42			
3	44			
4	39			
5	40			
6	48			
7	47			
8	61			
9	49			
10	57			
11	57			
12	47			
13	46			
14	55			
15	55			
16	56			
17	60			
18	47			
19	40			
20	41			
21	47			
22	36			
23	45			
24	39			
25	46			
26	28			
27	54			
28	52			
29	50			
30	53			
	$\bar{x} = \dfrac{\sum x_i}{n} =$		$\sigma_{LT} = \sqrt{\dfrac{\sum(x_i - \bar{x})^2}{n-1}} =$	$\sigma_{ST} = \dfrac{\sum R_i}{1.128(n-1)} =$

Solve It

Solutions to Categorizing Data and Calculating Measures of Variation Problems

1 Packages entering a sorting facility are labeled as having either "urgent" or "normal" priority. What kind of data is this characteristic of the packages?

"Urgent" and "normal" are named attributes of the packages. These values can't be meaningfully added or subtracted. Clearly, what you have here is attribute or category data.

2 You're collecting weight measurements of a plated contact switch. The measurements are in grams. What type of data is this?

Weight measurements in grams would look something like: 2.45, 3.78, 1.23, and so on. There's no limit to the possible weight measurements — they could be anything within a range of numbers. Also, this data can be meaningfully added or subtracted. For example, the combined weight of a 1.23 gram switch and a 3.78 gram switch would be 4.01 grams. Clearly, what you have here is continuous or variable data.

3 Each final inspection record for manufactured disk drives is stamped with a date code. What type of data are these date code stamps?

Even though they may appear to be numerical, these date stamps are instead categorical. For example, have you ever tried to calculate Tuesday and a half? Or, can you find an answer to Thursday plus Friday? These situations don't make sense, which tells you that these data stamps are attribute or category data.

However, you can organize this data through the sequence of the days of the week: Sunday, Monday, Tuesday, and so on. When you can categorize attribute data in this way, it's called *ordinal data*.

4 Student grades are given as A, A–, B+, and so on. Is this attribute or categorical data? What about grades given on a numerical grade point scale: A = 4.00, A– = 3.67, B+ = 3.33, and so on? Is this attribute or categorical data? What is the advantage of a numerical grade point scale?

When you have letter grades, you have attribute data. You can't add an A to a B! And you can't mathematically find an average of an A and a C grade. But, if you cleverly assign a numerical value to each letter grade, such as A = 4.00, A– = 3.67, and so on, voila, you immediately transform your data from attribute to continuous data. Now, you can find an average or a numerical difference between students' grade point averages. Imagine the nerdy teacher who came up with this idea!

5 Find the mode, median, and mean of the following collection of process cycle time measurements:

8	19	9	10
21	8	10	8
11	11	13	21

The first thing to do is to rank the data from least to greatest, like this:

Order	Value	Order	Value
1	8	7	11
2	8	8	11
3	8	9	13
4	9	10	19
5	10	11	21
6	10	12	21

The mode is the value in the data that occurs most frequently. In this case, the most frequent value is 8, which occurs three times.

The median is the value at the midpoint of the ranked list of data. For a set of 12 measurements, the sixth and seventh ordered numbers separate the bottom half from the top half. For the set of data in this problem, the sixth ranked point is 10 and the seventh is 11. So, the median is the point midway between these two values, which is 10.5.

The mean of the data set is found by taking the sum of all the measurements and then dividing by the number of measurements in the set:

$$\bar{x} = \frac{\sum x_i}{n} = \frac{150}{12} = 12.5$$

6 What is the average grade point of the following class of students? What is the median?

3.33	3.00	3.67	3.00
3.67	3.00	3.33	3.00
0.33	3.67	3.33	3.33
3.33	3.33	3.67	3.67
3.00	3.33	3.00	4.00

Using the formula for the average, you can find the mean of these student grades:

$$\bar{x} = \frac{\sum x_i}{n} = \frac{63.99}{20} = 3.20$$

You find the median by ranking the grade data from least to greatest:

Order	Value		Order	Value
1	0.33		11	3.33
2	3.00		12	3.33
3	3.00		13	3.33
4	3.00		14	3.33
5	3.00		15	3.67
6	3.00		16	3.67
7	3.00		17	3.67
8	3.33		18	3.67
9	3.33		19	3.67
10	3.33		20	4.00

For this 20-student data set, the median falls between the 10th and 11th ordered points. So, the median is 3.33.

7 For the following home purchase price data points, does the mean or the median better communicate the location of the central tendency of the variation? Why?

$184,000	$168,000	$174,500	$177,200
$292,400	$181,000	$172,010	$169,900

The mean for this home price data is $189,876 and the median is $175,850. One way to see the difference between the mean and the median is to plot them graphically along with a dot plot of the raw data, like in the following figure.

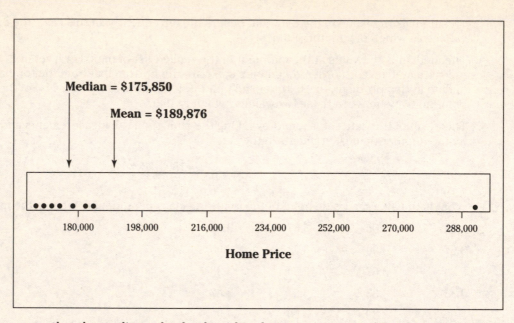

You can see that the median value lands within the main grouping of the data. The mean, however, is pulled outside the main cluster of the data by the one outlier point at $292,400.

8 What is the average value (or mean) for the following set of plastic film thickness measurements:

0.044	0.041	0.046	0.049
0.049	0.050	0.038	0.044
0.048	0.042	0.043	0.040
0.039	0.042	0.043	0.039

To calculate the mean or average, you take the sum of all the data values and divide by the number of points in your data set:

$$\bar{x} = \frac{\sum x_i}{n} = \frac{0.697}{16} = 0.044$$

9 Calculate the range, variance, and standard deviation for the set of process cycle time measurements given in Problem 5.

The range is the maximum minus the minimum values:

$$R = x_{MAX} - x_{MIN} = 21 - 8 = 13$$

After first calculating that $\bar{x}$ equals 12.4, the calculation table shown here contains the intermediate calculations required to calculate the variance:

x_i	$x_i - \bar{x}$	$(x_i - \bar{x})^2$	x_i	$x_i - \bar{x}$	$(x_i - \bar{x})^2$
8	−4	16	10	−3	9
19	7	49	8	−4	16
9	−3	9	11	−1	1
10	−2	4	11	−1	1
21	9	81	13	0	0
8	−5	25	21	8	64

With this table in hand, you calculate the variance with the following formula:

$$\sigma^2 = \frac{\sum (x_i - \bar{x})^2}{n-1} = \frac{263}{16-1} = 23.9$$

With the variance calculated, you can now simply take the square root to get the standard deviation:

$$\sigma = \sqrt{\sigma^2} = \sqrt{23.9} = 4.9$$

10 Calculate the range, variance, and standard deviation for the class grade point data in Problem 6.

The range is the maximum minus the minimum values in your set of data:

$$R = x_{MAX} - x_{MIN} = 4.00 - 0.33 = 3.67$$

Calculating the variance is easier if you use a calculation table, like the one shown here:

x_i	$x_i - \overline{x}$	$(x_i - \overline{x})^2$		x_i	$x_i - \overline{x}$	$(x_i - \overline{x})^2$
3.33	0.13	0.017		3.33	0.13	0.017
3.00	−0.20	0.040		3.33	0.13	0.017
3.67	0.47	0.221		3.33	0.13	0.017
3.00	−0.20	0.040		3.33	0.13	0.017
3.67	0.47	0.221		3.67	0.47	0.221
3.00	−0.20	0.040		3.67	0.47	0.221
3.33	0.13	0.017		3.00	−0.20	0.040
3.00	−0.20	0.040		3.33	0.13	0.017
0.33	−2.87	8.824		3.00	−0.20	0.040
3.67	0.47	0.221		4.00	0.80	0.641

After creating a calculation table, use the intermediate values in the table to calculate the variance and standard deviation:

$$\sigma^2 = \frac{\sum \left(x_i - \overline{x}\right)^2}{n-1} = \frac{10.34}{20-1} = 0.54, \text{ and}$$

$$\sigma = \sqrt{\sigma^2} = \sqrt{0.54} = 0.74$$

11 Calculate the range and standard deviation for the set of home purchase prices in Problem 7 in two ways: first with all eight data points and second by excluding the $292,400 point. With the elimination of just this one data point, how are the range and standard deviation measurements affected?

With all the data points, the range for the home price data is

$$R = x_{MAX} - x_{MIN} = \$292,400 - \$168,000 = \$124,400$$

However, if you remove the $292,400 outlying point, the range becomes

$$R = x_{MAX} - x_{MIN} = \$184,000 - \$168,000 = \$16,000$$

With all the data points, the calculation table for the home price data looks like this:

x_i	$x_i - \overline{x}$	$(x_i - \overline{x})^2$
$184,000	−$5,876	$² 34,530,314
$168,000	−$21,876	$² 478,570,314
$174,500	−$15,376	$² 236,429,064
$177,200	−$12,676	$² 160,687,314
$292,400	$102,524	$² 10,511,119,314
$181,000	−$8,876	$² 78,787,814
$172,010	−$17,866	$² 319,202,889
$169,900	−$19,976	$² 399,050,564

Using this intermediate calculation table, the standard deviation for eight data points can be calculated as

$$\sigma = \sqrt{\frac{\sum(x_i - \overline{x})^2}{n-1}} = \sqrt{\frac{\$^2 12,218,377,588}{8-1}} = \$41,779$$

By simply eliminating the $292,400 row from the intermediate calculation table, the calculation for the standard deviation changes to

$$\sigma = \sqrt{\frac{\sum(x_i - \overline{x})^2}{n-1}} = \sqrt{\frac{\$^2 1,707,258,273}{7-1}} = \$5,855$$

You can see from the two different range and standard deviation calculations that both measures of variation spread are sensitive to outliers.

12 Calculate the standard deviation for the set of plastic film thickness measurements in Problem 8.

After calculating the mean ($\overline{x} = 0.044$), an intermediate calculation table is always a good next step for calculating the standard deviation:

x_i	$x_i - \overline{x}$	$(x_i - \overline{x})^2$	x_i	$x_i - \overline{x}$	$(x_i - \overline{x})^2$
0.044	0.001	0.0000003	0.048	0.005	0.0000222
0.041	−0.002	0.0000058	0.042	−0.002	0.0000033
0.046	0.002	0.0000047	0.043	−0.001	0.0000004
0.049	0.005	0.0000277	0.040	−0.004	0.0000133
0.049	0.005	0.0000253	0.039	−0.004	0.0000169
0.050	0.007	0.0000440	0.042	−0.002	0.0000023
0.038	−0.005	0.0000262	0.043	−0.001	0.0000008
0.044	0.001	0.0000005	0.039	−0.005	0.0000242

You can then use these intermediate values to calculate the standard deviation of the data set:

$$\sigma = \sqrt{\frac{\sum(x_i - \overline{x})^2}{n-1}} = \sqrt{\frac{0.0002178}{16-1}} = 0.0038$$

13 For a sequential set of 70 bolt torque measurements, the sum of the squared error, $\sum(x_i - \overline{x})^2$ is 3,750 and the sum of the interpoint ranges is 178. What are the short-term and long-term standard deviations for this set of data?

The short-term standard deviation is calculated from the following equation:

$$\sigma_{ST} = \frac{\sum R_i}{1.128(n-1)}$$

REMEMBER

By knowing the sum of the interpoint ranges and the number measurements, you can plug directly into this equation to solve for the short-term standard deviation:

$$\sigma_{ST} = \frac{178}{1.128(70-1)} = 2.3$$

The long-term standard deviation is calculated from the equation

$$\sigma_{LT} = \sqrt{\frac{\sum(x_i - \overline{x})}{n-1}}$$

REMEMBER

By knowing the sum of the squared error and the number of measurements, you can plug directly into this equation to solve for the long-term standard deviation:

$$\sigma_{LT} = \sqrt{\frac{3,750}{70-1}} = 7.4$$

14 Complete the following calculation table to determine the short- and long-term standard deviations for a 35-point set of plate density measurements:

No.	x_i	$x_i - \bar{x}$	$(x_i - \bar{x})^2$	$R_i = \left\| x_i - x_{i-1} \right\|$
1	103	14.9	222.4	NA
2	95	6.9	47.8	8
3	113	24.9	620.7	18
4	92	2.9	8.5	22
5	112	23.9	571.9	21
6	97	8.9	79.5	15
7	90	1.9	3.7	7
8	81	−7.1	50.2	9
9	89	0.9	0.8	8
10	77	−11.1	122.9	12
11	98	9.9	98.3	21
12	86	−2.1	4.4	12
13	86	−2.1	4.4	0
14	83	−5.1	25.9	3
15	90	1.9	3.7	7
16	84	−4.1	16.7	6
17	84	−4.1	16.7	0
18	87	−1.1	1.2	3
19	53	−35.1	1231.0	34
20	62	−26.1	680.5	9
21	63	−25.1	629.3	1
22	77	−11.1	122.9	14
23	85	−3.1	9.5	8
24	86	−2.1	4.4	1
25	75	−13.1	171.2	11
26	86	−2.1	4.4	11
27	85	−3.1	9.5	1
28	89	0.9	0.8	4
29	94	5.9	35.0	5
30	103	14.9	222.4	9
31	93	4.9	24.2	10
32	109	20.9	437.4	16
33	91	2.9	8.5	18
34	96	7.9	62.6	5
35	90	1.9	3.7	6

$$\bar{x} = \frac{\sum x_i}{n} = 88.1 \qquad \sigma_{LT} = \sqrt{\frac{\sum (x_i - \bar{x})^2}{n-1}} = 12.8 \qquad \sigma_{ST} = \frac{\sum R_i}{1.128(n-1)} = 8.7$$

$$88 \qquad\qquad\qquad 12.8 \qquad\qquad\qquad 8.7$$

15 Complete the following calculation table to determine the short- and long-term standard deviations for a 30-point set of cycle time measurements:

No.	x_i	$x_i - \bar{x}$	$(x_i - \bar{x})^2$	$R_i = \lvert x_i - x_{i-1} \rvert$
1	42	–5.4	29.5	NA
2	42	–5.4	29.5	0
3	44	–3.4	11.8	2
4	39	–8.4	71.1	5
5	40	–7.4	55.3	1
6	48	0.6	0.3	8
7	47	–0.4	0.2	1
8	61	13.6	184.1	14
9	49	1.6	2.5	12
10	57	9.6	91.5	8
11	57	9.6	91.5	0
12	47	–0.4	0.2	10
13	46	–1.4	2.1	1
14	55	7.6	57.3	9
15	55	7.6	57.3	0
16	56	8.6	73.4	1
17	60	12.6	157.9	4
18	47	–0.4	0.2	13
19	40	–7.4	55.3	7
20	41	–6.4	41.4	1
21	47	–0.4	0.2	6
22	36	–11.4	130.7	11
23	45	–2.4	5.9	9
24	39	–8.4	71.1	6
25	46	–1.4	2.1	7
26	28	–19.4	377.7	18
27	54	6.6	43.1	26
28	52	4.6	20.9	2
29	50	2.6	6.6	2
30	53	5.6	31.0	3

$$\bar{x} = \frac{\sum x_i}{n} = 47.4 \qquad \sigma_{LT} = \sqrt{\frac{\sum (x_i - \bar{x})^2}{n-1}} = 7.7 \qquad \sigma_{ST} = \frac{\sum R_i}{1.128\,(n-1)} = 5.7$$

Chapter 8

A Picture's Worth 1,000 Words: Measuring with Charts and Graphs

. . . .

In This Chapter

▶ Determining the shape of variation with dot plots and histograms

▶ Comparing variation distributions with box and whisker plots

▶ Setting up scatter plots to explore relationships between characteristics

▶ Creating process behavior and time series charts to see how a characteristic changes over time

. . . .

Nothing communicates an idea better than a clear picture. And besides just looking impressive, a good chart quickly reveals the important story within your data and helps your team see previously hidden relationships between key inputs and outputs. You and your team will be able to compare and contrast what you think is happening with what you actually see in the charts and graphs. You should master creating the basic charts in this chapter and should religiously use them as the very first battery of tests you perform on all your data. You'll be amazed at the rapid insight you gain.

Putting Dot Plots or Histograms to Use

The purpose of dot plots and histograms is to graphically show you where variation occurs within a critical characteristic — whether it's all lumped together within a narrow interval or evenly spread out over a wide range of values. A *dot plot* or *histogram* will immediately tell you how frequently various values occur in your data and will provide clues to the sources of the variation.

You create a dot plot or histogram by following the same simple process for both. Follow these steps:

1. **Create a horizontal line representing the scale of measure for the characteristic you're charting.**

2. **Divide the length of the horizontal scale into ten to twenty equal "buckets" between the smallest and largest observed values.**

3. **For each measurement in your data set, place a dot in the corresponding bucket along the horizontal axis.**

   Stack up successive dots that occur within the same bucket. To create a histogram, simply replace the stacked dots with a bar of the same height.

4. **Repeat Step 3 until you've placed a dot on the chart for each measurement.**

Interpret your dot plot or histogram by looking for the following basic patterns:

- ✔ What shape does the data form? Do the dots (or bars) on the graph form a single bell-shaped curve or hump? Or is there a uniform distribution across a range of values? Are the dots clumped together with one side trailing out more than the other?

- ✔ Where is the *mode,* or tallest peak of the distribution, located? Is there one peak or are there multiple peaks?

- ✔ At what point along the horizontal axis of your dot plot or histogram do the stacked dots or bars seem to balance out like a teeter-totter? This point is the approximate location of the variation *mean,* or average.

- ✔ What is the *range*? The distance along the horizontal axis between the largest dot (x_{MAX}) and the smallest dot (x_{MIN}) is the range ($R = x_{MAX} - x_{MIN}$).

- ✔ Are there *outliers* (specific points that don't seem to fit the grouping of the rest) in your data? Are they either too far to the right or too far to the left of the rest of the data to be concluded as coming from the same set of circumstances that created all the other points?

Q. Create a dot plot chart for the following set of cycle time measurements and describe the nature of the variation:

8.4	6.4	9.5	11.6
11.4	12.5	4.6	8.5
11.2	6.8	7.6	5.6
5.3	7.0	7.5	4.8
7.9	8.2	9.3	8.3
8.3	8.3	11.7	8.8

A. Start by creating a horizontal line representing the cycle time scale of measure. On the left end, place a tick mark for the smallest value in the data set. On the right end, place a tick mark for the largest value. Your line should look like this:

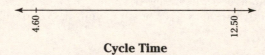

Cycle Time

Now, divide the horizontal scale between the max and min into equal-sized buckets. For this example, try ten divisions. So, take the distance between the max and the min and divide it by ten to find the *bucket width*:

$$\text{bucket width} = \frac{x_{MAX} - x_{MIN}}{\text{number buckets}} = \frac{12.5 - 4.6}{10} = 0.79$$

Using this bucket width value, calculate and draw in the remaining tick marks along the horizontal axis to create the ten dot plot buckets:

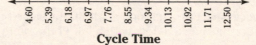

Cycle Time

Now for the fun part! Place a dot for each data point in the corresponding bucket. For example, the 11.4 cycle time measurement lands between 10.92 and 11.71. So, place a dot for this data point in the 10.92 – 11.71 bucket, like this:

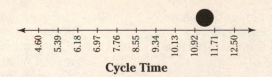

If a datapoint falls right on a bucket division, place it in either one of the buckets. As long as you don't put it in both, you're okay! The min and max data points will always fall into the lowest and highest buckets, respectively. Here's what the completed dot plot for this example looks like:

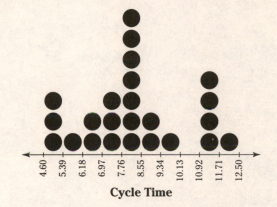

What does this dot plot tell you about the nature of the variation? Well, it actually reveals quite a lot. Note the following:

- The shape of the variation distribution appears somewhat bell-shaped. Most cycle time measurements are clustered around the middle of the distribution, with the frequency of occurrence trailing off as you move farther out from the middle (but, as you can see, there are some extra points near the min and max).

- The mode (the tallest peak in the dot plot) and the mean (the pivot point on the horizontal axis where all the dots balance) both seem to be at about the same spot — in the 7.76 – 8.55 bucket, maybe at a value of about 8.2. Check this rough visual estimate with an actual calculation of the mean (see Chapter 7 to find out how to calculate the mean). How close is the visual estimate?

- The spread of the variation is easily seen in the dot plot. The cycle time measurements range from 12.5 to 4.6.

- There aren't any outlying data points that are far out on either side of the rest of the variation.

---

1. Create a 10-bucket dot plot or histogram with the following purchase order data:

$1,115.43	$ 872.09	$1,300.96	$1,562.73
$1,550.19	$1,614.07	$ 797.54	$1,137.42
$1,531.71	$ 904.88	$ 996.95	$ 824.33
$ 813.01	$ 926.97	$ 974.96	$ 799.78
$1,031.56	$1,081.77	$1,263.90	$1,094.13
$1,106.64	$1,092.60	$1,572.41	$1,188.11

Solve It

2. Use your dot plot or histogram from Problem 1 of this chapter to describe the variation of the purchase order data. What's the shape of the variation distribution? Where's the variation centered? How spread out is the variation? Are there any outliers in the data?

Solve It

3. Draw a 12-bucket dot plot or histogram for the following processing time measurements. Keep some scrap paper handy!

7.1	5.6	7.7	5.9
6.3	6.4	6.0	7.8
7.7	7.5	6.8	5.6
5.7	7.8	7.0	5.3
6.2	7.7	9.2	11.3
6.6	6.3	7.9	6.1
5.2	6.2	6.3	6.6

Solve It

4. Use your dot plot or histogram from Problem 3 of this chapter to describe the variation of the process time measurements. What's the shape of the variation distribution? Where's the variation centered? How spread out is the variation? Are there any outliers in the data?

Solve It

Setting Up Box and Whisker Plots

Sometimes you need to quickly compare two or more variation distributions of the same characteristic. It's like standing two people back-to-back to see who's taller. But, in this case, you're asking questions such as "Which distribution is more spread out?" and "Which has the higher central location?" This is when *box and whisker plots* come in handy.

These plots, which are usually called box plots, can be created by following these steps:

1. **Rank order each of the sets of data, from smallest value to largest value, that you'll be including in your box plot.**

2. **Separately for each set of data, divide your rank-ordered data into fourths, or *quartiles*, as statisticians like to say:**

   • From x_{MIN}, the smallest observed point, to a point called Q_1 is the lower quartile of the points in your data set.

   • From Q_1 to the *median* of your data set is the second quartile of the points (see Chapter 7 to find out how to calculate the median of a data set).

   • From the *median* to a point called Q_3 is the third quartile.

   • From Q_3 to x_{MAX}, the largest point in your data set, is the fourth quartile.

3. **Draw a horizontal or vertical axis to place the box plot on.**

   Create a numerical scale along this axis that spans from just below the smallest value of all the data sets to just above the largest value.

4. **For the first data set, locate along the axis the points for x_{MIN}, Q_1, the median, Q_3, and x_{MAX}.**

5. **Draw a box between the Q_1 and Q_3 points.**

6. **Place a heavy line through the box at the point of the median.**

7. **Draw whisker-like lines extending from the Q_1 and Q_3 points to x_{MIN} and x_{MAX}, respectively.**

8. **Repeat these same steps for each successive subgroup distribution you're including for comparison with your box plot.**

   On the same axis, draw each successive distribution next to the previous one. You now have a graphical picture for comparing the variation distributions to each other.

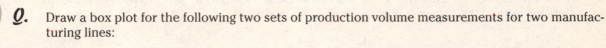

Q. Draw a box plot for the following two sets of production volume measurements for two manufacturing lines:

Line A				Line B			
116,788	105,804	105,355	110,463	107,819	86,065	100,173	78,915
118,669	96,947	112,454	114,794	84,479	84,400	89,366	96,238
103,414	110,412	114,032	109,262	93,802	96,099	83,925	121,554
100,161	94,586	114,142	92,078	79,970	91,956	107,792	104,966
107,654	118,804	107,049	100,351	118,956	129,140	82,318	87,221
99,974	99,949	122,249	108,432				

After you draw the plot, describe the similarities and differences between each line's performance.

A. The first step in creating a box plot is to rank order each set of data. Here are the ordered results for each production line:

Order	Line A	Line B		Order	Line A	Line B
1	92,078	78,915		13	108,432	96,238
2	94,586	79,970		14	109,262	100,173
3	96,947	82,318		15	110,412	104,966
4	99,949	83,925		16	110,463	107,792
5	99,974	84,400		17	112,454	107,819
6	100,161	84,479		18	114,032	118,956
7	100,351	86,065		19	114,142	121,554
8	103,414	87,221		20	114,794	129,140
9	105,355	89,366		21	116,788	
10	105,804	91,956		22	118,669	
11	107,049	93,802		23	118,804	
12	107,654	96,099		24	122,249	

With the data rank ordered, you can easily pick off the x_{MIN} and x_{MAX} points for each set of measurements. For Line A, x_{MIN} = 92,078 and x_{MAX} =122,249. For Line B, x_{MIN} = 78,915 and x_{MAX} = 129,140.

Finding the median for each data set is also easy. (Refer back to Chapter 7 if you need a quick refresher!) The Line A median is 108,043 and the Line B median is 92,879.

To find Q_1 and Q_3, just look for the data points that correspond to the first and third quarters of the data. For Line A, with 24 data points, you divide by four so each quarter consists of 6 points. That means that Q_1 will be the average of the sixth and seventh points in the rank ordered data (100,256), and Q_3 will be the average of the 18th and 19th points (114,087). For Line A, that leads to Q_1 being 100,256 and Q_3 being 114,087. For Line B, with 20 data points, Q_1 is at the fifth rank-ordered point (84,400) and Q_3 is at the 15th (104,966).

With the calculation of all these points prepared, your next step is to create an axis to put your box plots on. You can make your axis either up and down (vertical) or left to right (horizontal). It really doesn't matter. This axis represents the scale of measure of your data. So, if your scale of measure *feels* natural to be seen left to right rather than up and down, make your axis horizontal. Time is a good example of a variable that is usually plotted left to right. Temperature is one that is normally vertical. For the production volume data of this example, a vertical axis will work fine. Draw a vertical line for the axis, create tick marks along its length to indicate the scale, and plot points for each of the values — x_{MIN}, Q_1, median, Q_3, and x_{MAX}:

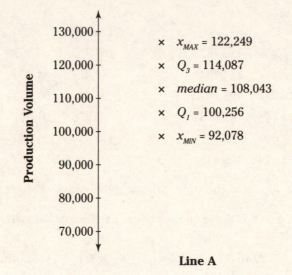

Line A

For the box plot for Line A, all you need to do now is draw the box between the Q_1 and Q_3 points. Then draw thin whiskers from the box edges out to x_{MIN} and x_{MAX}. You complete the box plot for Line A by putting the line through the box at the point of its median, like this:

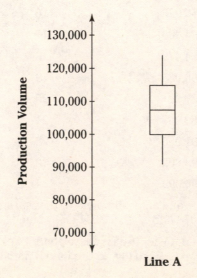

Line A

Now, follow the same steps to add a box plot for the Line B data to the same plot. It ends up looking like this:

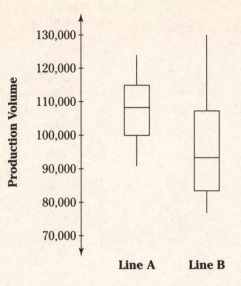

From the completed side-by-side box plots, you can easily see the similarities and differences between the performances of the two manufacturing lines. The variation for Line B is much more spread out than Line A. Line B also has its central location lower than Line A, and Line B's data isn't symmetrical — it's skewed to the lower production volume values. If you wanted to select the production line that consistently produces higher volumes, you'd definitely pick Line A, even though Line B had the highest single measurement.

5. Create a box plot for the following set of monthly sales figures. Make sure you have scrap paper handy.

$13,245	$38,267	$21,576	$16,151
$60,231	$15,705	$32,689	$13,168
$30,221	$24,036	$22,154	$22,409

Solve It

6. Describe the variation of the monthly sales data from Problem 5 of this chapter. Now suppose the monthly sales data is from the previous twelve months. What amount of sales would you expect for the next month following?

Solve It

7. Three products — A, B, and C — are being compared for warranty returns. Using the data below, which shows the monthly number of warranty returns, create box plots for all three products.

Product A

20	17	18	18
27	22	22	20

Product B

32	31	31	24
27	32	34	32
32	33	30	30
28	39	31	32

Product C

20	29	16	16
14	24	20	22
16	20	29	24

8. Using the box plots from Problem 7 of this chapter, describe the differences and similarities between the warranty performance of the three products. Keep scrap paper on hand!

Seeing Spots: Using Scatter Plots

Scatter plots help you explore the relationship between two characteristics. As the values for Characteristic A increase, for example, what happens to values for Characteristic B? Do they also increase? Or do they decrease? Or neither?

To create a scatter plot, you must have pairs of measurements for each observation — measurements for each characteristic taken at the same point in time, under the same conditions. Otherwise, there's no basis for exploring the relationship between the two characteristics or variables.

You can create a scatter plot by going through the following steps:

1. **Form data pairs that represent *x-y* points from the collected data.**

   For each observation, pair the simultaneously measured values for the two characteristics together to form an *x-y* point that can be plotted on a two-axis *x-y* graph.

2. **Create a two-axis plotting framework.**

   To create your framework, draw two axes, one horizontal and the other vertical. Draw one axis for each of the two characteristics you're exploring.

   The scale for each axis should be in the units that correspond to its assigned characteristic — millimeters for length, pounds for weight, minutes for time, number of defects found on an inspected part, or whatever the units may be that quantify the characteristics you're exploring.

3. **Plot each *x-y* pair as a point on the two-axis framework.**

Scatter plots can be created when one of the two characteristics is not measured on a continuous scale, but instead consists of attribute data (see Chapter 7). For example, the characteristic of "production volume" (measured on a continuous units-per-hour scale) can be plotted against the characteristic of "production line ID" (perhaps named Line A and Line B).

You interpret your scatter plot by looking for relationships or patterns between the two plotted characteristics. Look for:

- **Graphical correlation between the two plotted characteristics or variables.** If there's no pattern in the plotted points — just a random scattering of points — then there's no correlation or relationship between the characteristics. Clustering of the plotted points or patterns that follow the shape of a line or a curve reveal correlation between the two variables.

- **Direction of correlation between the variables.** When there are patterns, does an increase in one variable lead to an increase in the other? Or a decrease in one lead to a decrease in the other? If so, there is a *positive* relationship between the variables. But if a change in one variable leads to a change in the opposite direction for the other, there is a *negative* relationship between the variables.

- **Strength of effect between the variables.** How drastic or steep is the linear relationship between the variables? If a small change in one variable leads to a large change in the other, you're observing a strong effect between them.

Q. The company you're working for has had problems with its compressed air supply — sometimes the compressor equipment can't supply the demanded production flowrate. You've found some historical data that includes measurements of the compressed air flowrate and another variable, the speed setting of the production line, that you think may factor into the compressed air performance. The measurements for each of these variables were taken at the same time, once each week. Here's a listing of the data you've found. Is there any relationship between production speed setting and compressed air pressure?

Week	Production Speed Setting	Compressed Air Pressure (psi)	Week	Production Speed Setting	Compressed Air Pressure (psi)
1	22.6	85	15	22.1	107
2	21.5	111	16	20.5	119
3	23.3	79	17	22.3	103
4	24.5	73	18	22.5	91
5	24.4	79	19	23.2	90
6	25.1	68	20	22.6	86
7	20.4	113	21	22.6	98
8	22.7	90	22	22.6	104
9	24.3	85	23	24.6	81
10	21.7	95	24	22.9	94
11	22.2	110	25	22.8	96
12	21.0	110	26	22.4	91
13	20.8	106	27	25.4	62
14	21.8	96			

A. What do you think? Is it clear from the listed data whether a relationship exists between the two variables? Creating a scatter plot will help you answer this question.

The first step is to recognize that each week's measurements form an *x-y* data pair. That's because each measurement is linked in time. For this example, assign the production speed settings to the horizontal axis and the compressed air pressure to the vertical axis.

Begin your scatter plot by creating the horizontal and vertical axis framework and by plotting each week's data pair, like this, for Week 1:

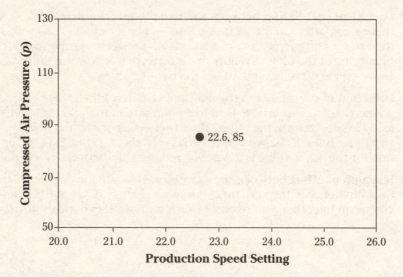

Notice how the plotted point lines up with the 22.6 value on the horizontal axis and the 85 psi value on the vertical axis. Finish creating the scatter plot by repeating this process for all the weeks' data pairs:

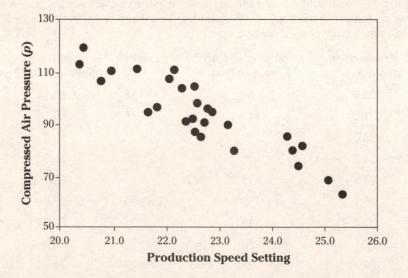

Is there a pattern here? Yes. The plotted points follow a trend that slopes downward as you move from left to right. This means you've discovered a relationship between the production speed setting and the compressed air pressure variable. As the production speed setting increases, the compressed air pressure goes down. And, as you decrease production speed, air pressure goes up. This is a negative relationship.

The strength of the relationship is determined by the slope of the general line formed by the plotted data. The figure below draws in a line that roughly fits the pattern in the plotted points.

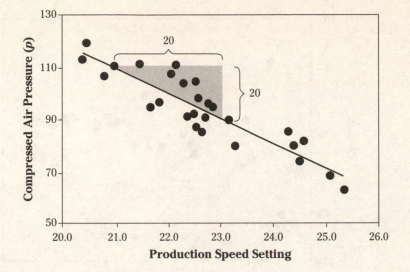

For every 2 units of increase in production speed setting is a 20 psi decrease in the air pressure. Another way of saying this is that there is a 10 psi change in air pressure for every 1.0 change in the production speed setting. Knowing this fact about the relationship helps you forecast what the pressure will be for any setting of production speed, and vice versa.

---

9. A company performed an experiment where glue samples were allowed to cure for different lengths of time. They then measured the force required to peel away the glue bond. Create a scatter plot by using the following data. Make sure you have plenty of scrap paper!

Sample	Cure Time (Days)	Peel Force (Lbs)	Sample	Cure Time (Days)	Peel Force (Lbs)
1	5.24	8.0	6	5.16	7.4
2	4.93	7.2	7	5.42	8.3
3	4.91	7.0	8	5.32	7.7
4	4.52	6.7	9	5.39	7.8
5	4.63	6.6	10	4.79	7.0

Solve It

---

10. Describe the relationship, if any, between the cure time and the peel force variables from the scatter plot of Problem 9 of this chapter.

Solve It

11. Describe the relationship, if any, between the Input X3 variable and the Output variable shown in the following scatter plot:

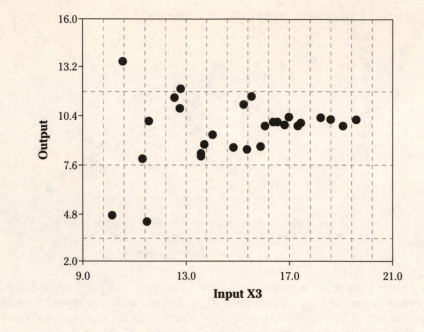

12. Describe the relationship, if any, between Variable D and Variable C shown in the following scatter plot:

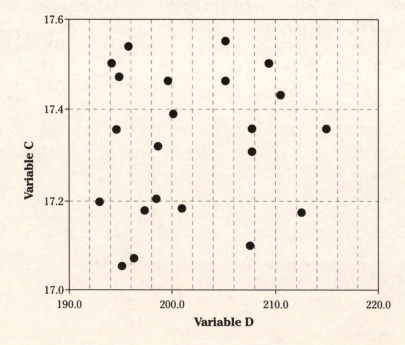

Solve It

Hindsight Is 20/20: Using Process Behavior or Time Series Charts

Dot plots, histograms, box plots, and scatter plots all neglect an important variable — time. To see how a characteristic changes over time, you have to plot its measurements in the sequence or series in which they occurred. When variation behavior is linked to time, you're then able to link process behavior and changes back to historical events or conditions — such as the changing of a work shift, the gradual dulling of a cutting tool, or the steady jitter of the status quo.

A *time series or process behavior chart* is made by simply plotting measured performance on a vertical scale against a horizontal scale representing the progress of time. When a process is free of special causes or outside influences, its behavior, or measured performance, bounces randomly around a central, flat level on the behavior chart. Most of the observed variation will be clustered close to this central level. And, every now and then, some measurements will land farther away from the central level. This variation will be completely random over time, without patterns or trends.

You interpret your behavior chart or time series plot by looking for signs of variation that are out of the ordinary. After you've identified non-normal behavior, you investigate what historical event (or special cause) could have caused such a change in performance.

Drawing process behavior charts or time series charts isn't difficult. The part that is trickier, however, is interpreting these charts. For that reason, the example and practice problems for this section will concentrate on interpretation rather than on the mechanics of creating the charts.

Q. A plastic injection molded housing has a critical dimension between two bosses. A series of measurements of the dimension was taken at five-minute intervals. They're plotted over time in the following time series chart:

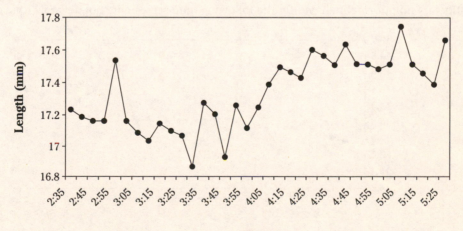

Review this time series chart and indicate if there is any evidence of special causes affecting the performance of the injection mold.

A. Two things stand out from the normal variation of the boss dimension. First, at time 2:55, a single point is observed much higher than the normal level of the rest of the variation — this is an outlier. Later, starting at about 4:00, you can see an upward trend. After the trend, from about 4:30 and on, the central level of the dimension variation seems to stay at this higher level. These out-of-the-ordinary observations — the outlier and the trend — indicate that something abnormal has affected the injection mold process.

13. A CEO is concerned about his company's recent monthly expenses. After some temporary success in reducing expenses two months ago, it's now the second month in a row since then that expenses have increased. And the expenses in this latest month are 6 percent higher than the same month a year ago. The CEO's plan is to enact a spending freeze on all departments to fix the problem. If that doesn't work, he says, "Heads are going to roll!" To check the validity of the CEO's plan, you create a time history chart of the company's expenses over the previous 21 months, as shown here:

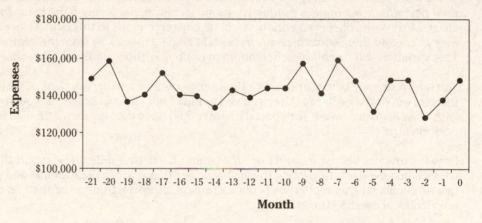

Based on the time series data, do you agree or disagree with the CEO's plan? Why?

Solve It

14. Identify any non-normal behavior in the following time series chart of delivery time data:

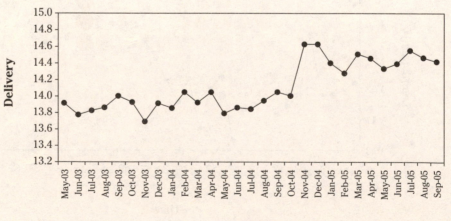

Solve It

Solutions to Exercises for Yields and Defects Problems

1 Create a 10-bucket dot plot or histogram with the purchase order data shown in the original problem earlier in the chapter.

Start by creating a horizontal line representing the dollar scale of the purchase order data. As shown in the following figure, on the left end of the line, place a tick mark for the smallest value in the data set, and on the right end, place a tick mark for the largest value:

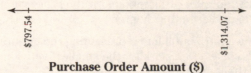

Purchase Order Amount ($)

Next, divide the horizontal scale between the max and min into 10 equal buckets. To find the width of the buckets, divide the distance between the max and the min by ten, as shown below:

$$\text{bucket width} = \frac{x_{MAX} - x_{MIN}}{\text{number buckets}} = \frac{\$1,614.07 - 797.54}{10} = \$81.65$$

Using this bucket width value, calculate and draw in the remaining tick marks along the horizontal axis to create the 10 dot plot buckets:

Purchase Order Amount ($)

Now place a dot for each data point in its corresponding bucket. Remember, if a data point falls right on a bucket division, place it in the higher of the buckets. Here's what the completed dot plot looks like:

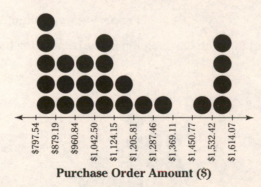

Purchase Order Amount ($)

2 Use your dot plot or histogram from Problem 1 of this chapter to describe the variation of the purchase order data. What's the shape of the variation distribution? Where's the variation centered? How spread out is the variation? Are there any outliers in the data?

This dot plot tells you about the nature of the variation in the purchase order measurements in the following ways:

➤ The shape of the variation distribution isn't bell-shaped. Most cycle time measurements are clustered on the left or lower end of the histogram with a secondary grouping occurring at the far right or higher end. This behavior may be evidence of a bi-modal distribution (two separate distributions mixed on one chart), which may have occurred due to higher spending in the last two months of the fiscal year.

✔ The mode (the tallest peak in the dot plot) is located at the far left end of the dot plot in the $797.54 – $879.19 data bucket, and the mean (the pivot point on the horizontal axis where all the dots balance) seems to be around the value of about $1,125.00. This large difference between the mode and the mean tells you that the data is clearly not normal, but is skewed.

✔ The spread of the variation is easily seen as ranging from $1,614.07 to $797.54, or a value of $816.53.

✔ No outlying data points appear away from the rest of the variation distribution other than the possible bi-modal indication.

3 Draw a 12-bucket dot plot or histogram for the processing time measurements shown in the original problem earlier in the chapter.

Start by creating a horizontal line representing the minute scale of the processing time data. On the left end, place a tick mark for the smallest value in the data set. On the right end, place a tick mark for the largest value:

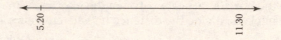

Processing Time (minutes)

Next, divide the horizontal scale between the max and min into 12 equal buckets. To find the width of the buckets, divide the distance between the max and the min by 12, as shown here:

$$\text{bucket width} = \frac{x_{MAX} - x_{MIN}}{\text{number buckets}} = \frac{11.30 - 5.20}{12} = 0.508$$

Using this bucket width value, calculate and draw in the remaining tick marks along the horizontal axis to create the 12 dot plot buckets:

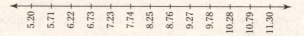

Processing Time (minutes)

Now place a dot for each data point in its corresponding bucket. Here's what the completed dot plot looks like:

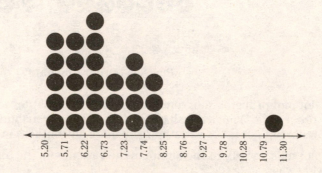

Processing Time (minutes)

4 Use your dot plot or histogram from Problem 3 of this chapter to describe the variation of the processing time measurements. What's the shape of the variation distribution? Where's the variation centered? How spread out is the variation? Are there any outliers in the data?

The dot plot of Problem 3 tells you about the nature of the variation in the processing time measurements in the following ways:

- ✔ With the exception of the two isolated points on the right, the shape of the variation distribution is somewhat bell-shaped, with most processing time measurements clustered together in a normal shape.

- ✔ The mode is located near the left end of the dot plot in the 6.22 – 6.73 minute bucket. Because of the two extreme points on the right, the mean seems to be a bit higher than the mode, at around the 6.73 – 7.23 minute bucket. This relatively small difference between the mode and the mean tells you that the data is nearly normal.

- ✔ The spread of the variation ranges from 11.30 minutes to 5.20 minutes, or a value of 6.10 minutes.

- ✔ The two extreme data points on the right are outliers. Ask yourself what caused these two measurements to be so different from all the rest.

5 Create a box plot for the set of monthly sales figures shown in the original problem earlier in the chapter.

The first step is to rank order the data, as shown here:

Order	Monthly Sales
1	$13,168
2	$13,245
3	$15,705
4	$16,151
5	$21,576
6	$22,154
7	$22,409
8	$24,036
9	$30,221
10	$32,689
11	$38,267
12	$60,231

With the data rank ordered, you can easily pick off the x_{MIN} and x_{MAX} points. For this monthly sales data, x_{MIN} = $13,168 and x_{MAX} = $60,231.

Finding the median is also easy. Because you have an even number of measurements (12), the median is the average value of the middle two points — $22,281.

To find Q_1 and Q_3, you have to calculate the average between the points that divide the four-point quarters. For Q1, you calculate the average of the third and fourth ranked points. For Q2, you calculate the average of the ninth and tenth ranked points. That leads to Q_1 being $15,928 and Q_3 being $31,455.

With the calculation of all these points prepared, your next step is to create an axis to put your box plot on. For the monthly sales dollar values, you usually settle on a vertical axis. Draw a vertical line for the axis, create tick marks along its length to indicate the scale, and plot points for each of the values — x_{MIN}, Q_1, median, Q_3, and x_{MAX}.

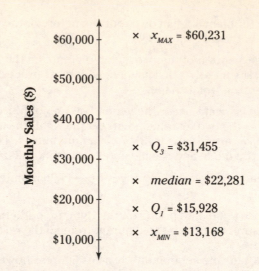

All you need to do now is draw the box between the Q_1 and Q_3 points and then draw thin whiskers from the box edges out to x_{MIN} and x_{MAX}. You complete the box plot by putting the line through the box at the point of its median, like this:

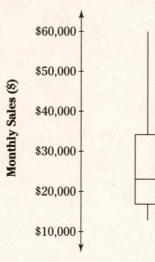

6 Describe the variation of the monthly sales data from Problem 5 of this chapter. Now suppose the monthly sales data is from the previous twelve months. What amount of sales would you expect for the next month following?

The drawn box plot shows that the monthly sales variation is mostly near the lower end, with a few months' instances rising up to high values. The median is toward the lower end of the observed range of data. All things staying the same, you'd expect future monthly sales figures to fit this same shape. So, taking a guess at what the next month's value will be, you'd have to say that it would be somewhere between about $16,000 and $30,000.

7 Three products — A, B, and C — are being compared for warranty returns. Using the data given in the original problem earlier in the chapter, which shows the monthly number of warranty returns, create box plots for all three products.

The first step is to rank order all the warranty data:

Order	Product A	Product B	Product C
1	17	24	14
2	19	27	16
3	19	28	16
4	20	30	16
5	20	30	20
6	22	31	20
7	22	31	20
8	27	31	22
9		32	24
10		32	24
11		32	29
12		32	29
13		32	
14		33	
15		34	
16		39	

After reviewing each ordered set of data, you can now find the critical values for creating box plots. Their values are shown in the table below:

Product	x_{MIN}	Q_1	Median	Q_3	x_{MAX}
A	17	18	20	22	27
B	24	30	31.5	32	39
C	14	16	20	24	29

Now, use these values to construct the box plot for each product, as shown below:

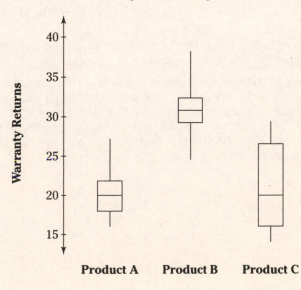

8 Using the box plots from Problem 7 of this chapter, describe the differences and similarities between the warranty performance of the three products.

Product A and Product C have nearly the same medians, but their distributions are very different. Product A has relatively little variation in its warranty performance, whereas Product C has a much wider spread. Product B stands out from the others — its level of warranty returns is significantly higher than either Product A or C. The product that has consistently lower warranty returns is Product A.

9 A company performed an experiment where glue samples were allowed to cure for different lengths of time. They then measured the force required to peel away the glue bond. Create a scatter plot by using the data from the original problem earlier in the chapter.

The *x-y* data pairs to be plotted are the cure time and peel force for each sample. Make the cure time the horizontal axis and the peel force the vertical axis and begin plotting the points. The completed plot should look something like this:

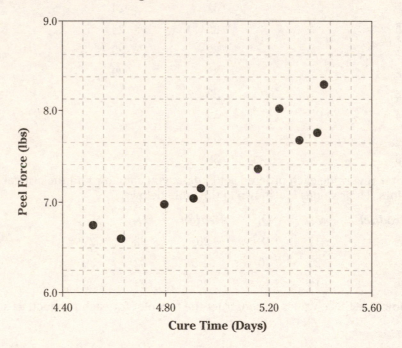

10 Describe the relationship, if any, between the cure time and the peel force variables from the scatter plot of Problem 9 of this chapter.

When looking at the plot for Problem 9, it's clear that the points aren't just randomly scattered. Instead, they roughly form a line. That means there is a relationship between the two variables. If you look more closely, you see that an increase in cure time leads to an increase in peel force. And a decrease in cure time leads to a decrease in peel strength. When the same directional changes happen in both variables, that means it's a positive relationship. If you draw a rough line through the clustered dots in the plot, as shown here, you see more about the relationship:

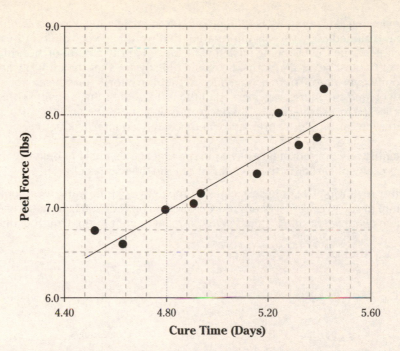

From the slope of the line, you can see that every tenth of a minute increase in cure time results in a 0.2-pound increase in peel strength and vice versa — every tenth of a minute decrease in cure time leads to a 0.2-pound reduction in peel strength.

By creating a scatter plot, you can even go as far as forecasting what the peel strength will be if you know the cure time. For example, if you cure a specimen for exactly five days, it will have a cure strength of about 7.3 pounds.

11 Describe the relationship, if any, between the Input X3 variable and the Output variable shown in the scatter plot from the original problem earlier in the chapter.

Something out of the ordinary is going on in the relationship between variables Input X3 and Output. The dots aren't randomly scattered on the plot. Note the great spread of variation on the left side of the plot. As Input X3 gets bigger though, the amount of variation reduces, which means that some mechanism in the system must be affecting the amount of variation as Input X3 changes.

12 Describe the relationship, if any, between Variable D and Variable C shown in the scatter plot from the original problem earlier in the chapter.

The scatter plot for this problem is a great example of a set of points that are randomly distributed. There aren't any trends, patterns, or groupings in the plotted points, which means that no relationship exists between the two variables — Variable D and Variable C.

13 A CEO is concerned about his company's recent monthly expenses. After some temporary success in reducing expenses two months ago, it's now the second month in a row since then that expenses have increased. And the expenses in this latest month are 6 percent higher than for the same month a year ago. The CEO's plan is to enact a spending freeze on all departments to fix the problem. If that doesn't work, he says, "Heads are going to roll!" To check the validity of the CEO's plan, you create a time series chart of the company's expenses over the previous 21 months. Based on the time series data shown in the original problem earlier in the chapter, do you agree or disagree with the CEO's plan? Why?

Reviewing raw numbers is difficult and often misleading. Plotted or charted data, on the other hand, immediately reveals information that would be very difficult to see otherwise. In this problem, the CEO is being misled. If he looked at the stream of monthly expenditures plotted over the last several months, he would quickly see that the monthly amount fluctuates randomly over time. There is no evidence that the efforts to reduce expenses have had the desired effect, and the increase observed in the last two months is easily within the typical variation expected for this variable. Therefore, nothing out of the ordinary has occurred and any special intervention would be premature and possibly counterproductive.

14 Identify any non-normal behavior in the time series chart of delivery time data (flip to the original problem earlier in the chapter to see the time series chart).

After reviewing the time series plot of the delivery time data, what looks non-normal is the jump in the average level around October-November 2004. Something out of the ordinary must have occurred to affect this type of permanent shift in the length of delivery times.

Chapter 9

Yield and Defects: Calculating the Good, the Bad, and the Ugly

● ●

In This Chapter

▶ Setting meaningful and appropriate performance specifications

▶ Calculating and interpreting Six Sigma yield metrics

▶ Determining how many defects are being created and how often

● ●

Measuring performance is at the core of Six Sigma. Fundamentally, measuring performance isn't complicated — you just count how many times things go wrong compared to how many times they go right.

Yield and defect rate are the metrics you use in Six Sigma to communicate how often things go wrong, or on the flip side, how often they go right. To be effective in Six Sigma, you need to be fluent in calculating and translating between these different yield and defect rate measurements. This chapter explains how.

Get Real: Creating Realistic Specifications

Specifications represent the specific limit values that separate good performance from poor performance — they define what's acceptable and what's not. Specifications form the basis to determine what process outputs or characteristics are either good or bad.

It's critical that you don't set your specifications arbitrarily. If a specification is set too loosely, your performance may upset or dissatisfy your customer even though it meets the specification. And, unfortunately, the excuse, "But we met our specifications," won't appease your unhappy customer. On the other hand, if a specification is set too tightly, you'll spend more time and money than you should getting the characteristic performance always inside the overly narrow goalpost.

The mind-jogging acronym, RUMBA, helps you check the appropriateness of any specification:

Reasonable: Is the specification based on a realistic assessment of the customer's actual needs? Does the specification relate directly to the performance of the characteristic?

Understandable: Is the specification clearly stated and defined so that there is no argument about its interpretation?

Measurable: Can you measure the characteristic's performance against the specification? If not, there will be a lot of debate between you and your customer as to whether the specification has been met or not.

Believable: Have you bought into the specification setting? Can you and your co-workers strive to meet the specification?

Attainable or Achievable: Can you reach the level and range of the specification?

You need to review each specification to make sure it passes the RUMBA test. If it falls short in any of the RUMBA categories, you should begin developing a plan to bring the rogue specification back under control.

You can use the following handy checklist to make sure a specification passes the RUMBA test:

RUMBA Specification Checklist

Write your specification here: _____

_____

_____

❑ **R** Is the specification realistic? If not, write what needs to be changed to make the specification realistic: _____

_____

_____

❑ **U** Is the specification understandable? If not, write what needs to be changed to make the specification understandable:

_____

_____

_____

❑ **M** Is the specification measurable? If not, write what needs to be changed to make the specification measurable: _____

_____

_____

❑ **B** Is the specification believable? If not, write what needs to be changed to make the specification believable: _____

_____

_____

❑ **A** Is the specification attainable or achievable? If not, write what needs to be changed to make the specification attainable or achievable:

_____

_____

_____

Getting It Right the First Time: Calculating First Time Yield (FTY)

With an appropriate specification in place, you can move on to calculating the yield performance of your process or characteristic. And, as you probably know, the goal of Six Sigma is to do things right the first time. Instead of comparing the number of good items that eventually come out of a process to the total number of items started (which completely misses the extra inspection, rework, and effort expended), *first time yield* (FTY) accurately measures how well your process works in its true form — without any makeup. FTY is the basic measure of a process's real capability, or ability to produce good items the first time.

The formula for first time yield (FTY) is

$$FTY = \frac{in - scrap - rework}{in}$$

where *in* is the number of items started into the process, *scrap* is the number of items that end up unusable, and *rework* is the number of items requiring additional effort to meet the specification.

Q. From the tire inflation process flow map in the following figure, what's the first time yield of the process?

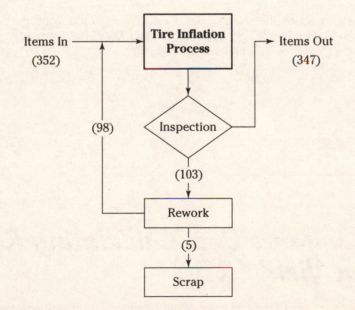

A. Even though 347 of the 352 tires that started through the inflation process eventually end up within specifications, many of them have to be reworked or repeated before they're right. From the flow map, you can see that 103 tires aren't correctly inflated the first time through (98 reworked and 5 scrapped), leaving only 249 out of 352 that the process truly produces correctly the first time. The FTY is

$$FTY = \frac{in - scrap - rework}{in} = \frac{352 - 5 - 98}{352} = \frac{249}{352} = 0.707 = 70.7\%$$

1. A study of a hospital's blood test records reveals that out of 127 samples of drawn blood, five were done incorrectly and ended up being unusable. Also, for 31 of the samples the donors had to be contacted again to correct personal information. What's the first time yield of this process?

Solve It

2. A water heater production facility is showing a 97 percent yield at the final test step in its assembly process. As you look deeper, however, you find that this yield calculation only includes the number of units that must be scrapped at the end of the test. In reality, 62 percent of all units fail final inspection on their first attempt and must be corrected before they pass. What's the true FTY of this production system?

Solve It

3. In a one-month study, an airline lost four out of 9,824 pieces of luggage. Further, 21 pieces of luggage were mishandled and were only connected with their passengers after a one- or two-day delay. What's the FTY for the 9,824 pieces of luggage?

Solve It

Rolling Many into One: Calculating Rolled Throughput Yield (RTY)

A product or process rarely consists of only a single opportunity for success or failure. Some, like an automobile, have hundreds of thousands of component specifications that must be met. More precisely, they all must be met simultaneously for the car to operate properly. Combining the yields for each of these opportunities is called *rolled throughput yield* (RTY). Whether it's a series of process steps or a collection of component parts in a product, RTY tells you how well the entire system works together.

The formula for rolled throughput yield (RTY) is

$$RTY = \prod_{i=1}^{n} FTY_i = FTY_1 \times FTY_2 \times \ldots \times FTY_n$$

where FTY_i is the first time yield of each of the *n* product or process components for $i = 1$ to *n*.

Q. The following figure illustrates a purchase order process that's made up of five individual process steps. What's the RTY of this process?

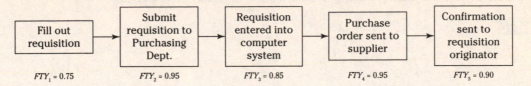

Fill out requisition	Submit requisition to Purchasing Dept.	Requisition entered into computer system	Purchase order sent to supplier	Confirmation sent to requisition originator
$FTY_1 = 0.75$	$FTY_2 = 0.95$	$FTY_3 = 0.85$	$FTY_4 = 0.95$	$FTY_5 = 0.90$

A. For this purchase order process, the rolled throughput yield is calculated as follows:

$$RTY = FTY_1 \times FTY_2 \times FTY_3 \times FTY_4 \times FTY_5$$

$$RTY = 0.75 \times 0.95 \times 0.85 \times 0.95 \times 0.90$$

$$RTY = 0.518$$

An RTY of 0.518 means that the chance of a purchase order going through the entire process correctly the first time, with no rework or scrap, is only 51.8 percent.

Like a chain only being as strong as its weakest link, an RTY can never be greater than the lowest FTY within the system. Use this mathematical fact to check your calculated answer.

---

4. A cellphone keypad has 17 specified dimensions and characteristics. If each of these specifications is met with 99 percent accuracy, what's the chance of getting a defect-free keypad?

Solve It

5. A hiring process has seven steps, each with the following first time yields:

$FTY_1 = 0.92$	$FTY_5 = 0.98$
$FTY_2 = 0.95$	$FTY_6 = 0.89$
$FTY_3 = 0.90$	$FTY_7 = 0.87$
$FTY_4 = 0.99$	

What's the rolled throughput yield for this process?

Solve It

6. A football coach is trying to improve his offense's ball possession. Looking back at game films, he finds that his offense has committed 12 turnovers through 305 plays from scrimmage, giving the team an overall probability of retaining possession at 96 percent for any single play. What's the probability of the team retaining possession for 16 consecutive plays?

"How Bad Is It, Doc?" Calculating Defect Rates

The complementary measurement to yield is defects. If your yield is 90 percent, 10 percent of your units contain one or more defects. Measuring defects and calculating the rate, or how often the defects occur, is like looking at the flip side of the yield coin.

A basic assessment of characteristic or process capability is to measure the total number of defects that occur over a known number of units produced. This number is then transformed into a calculation of how often defects occur on a single unit, which is called *defects per unit* (DPU).

When you need to compare the defect rate of one product or process to the defect rate of a different product or process, you first have to put the rates for each into comparable units — you want to compare apples to apples. You can compare the defect rates of different products or processes by counting the number of observed defects in the units inspected and compare this count to the total number of opportunities for success or failure in the inspected product or process. When you compare defect rates in this way, the metrics you use are *defects per opportunity* (DPO) and *defects per million opportunities* (DPMO).

The following equations show you how to calculate DPU, DPO, and DPMO. No order is important. Which one or ones you use depends on your situation and what you're trying to communicate:

$$DPU = \frac{number\ of\ defects\ observed}{number\ of\ units\ inspected}$$

$$DPO = \frac{total\ number\ of\ defects\ observed}{total\ number\ of\ opportunities\ inspected}$$

$$DPMO = DPO \times 1{,}000{,}000$$

Q. You process 23 loan applications during a month and find that 11 defects occurred — such things as misspelled names, missing prior residence information, and incorrect loan amounts. What's the DPU for this process?

A. The DPU for your loan process is

$$DPU = \frac{number\ of\ defects\ observed}{number\ of\ units\ inspected} = \frac{11}{23} = 0.478$$

This answer shows that you would expect to see defects in almost half the loan applications that leave your desk!

Q. If there are 7 opportunities for success or failure on each loan application (from the previous example), what is the DPO?

A. The DPO for this loan process is

$$DPO = \frac{total\ number\ of\ defects\ observed}{total\ number\ of\ opportunities\ inspected} = \frac{11}{23 \times 7} = \frac{11}{161} = 0.068$$

This answer shows that for every 100 opportunities for success or failure you encounter in this loan application, the process will produce 6 or 7 defects.

---

7. What's the DPU of a product if you find five defects on 23 units?

8. A bottle-filling process has three opportunities for success or failure — the amount of product put into the bottle, the correct assembly of the lid, and the correct application of the bottle label. Find the DPO of this process if it produces 7 defects after 40 bottles have been produced.

Solve It

9. A hospital's emergency room admittance process produces 17 defects per 500 opportunities. The radiology department produces 15 defects per 600 opportunities. Which area of the hospital has a higher defect rate? How many defects should you expect after one million patients have gone through both of these hospital departments?

What's Missing? Linking Yield to Defects

When you have an overall process with a relatively low defect rate — say, a process that produces units with a DPU less than 0.10 (or 10 percent) — you can mathematically link the process defect rate to the overall process yield:

$$RTY = e^{-DPU} \text{ and}$$

$$DPU = -\ln(RTY)$$

where *e* in the equation is a mathematical constant equal to 2.718 and *ln* is the natural logarithm function.

On your scientific calculator or spreadsheet program, you'll find a function or key for raising *e* to any number. (Look for the e^x key on your calculator.) You'll also find the same for the *ln* function.

Q. An experienced machine operator estimates that his rolled throughput yield hovers around 95 percent. What then is the DPU for a typical unit produced by this machine operator?

A. $DPU = -\ln(0.95) = 0.0513$

10. The manager of a product line with a measured DPU of 0.01 wants you to estimate the RTY for his process. What estimate do you give?

Solve It

11. If a specific model of automobile is found to have an average of four defects when purchased new, what would you expect the rolled throughput yield (RTY) of its manufacturing process to be?`

12. A hotel operator measured the first time yields for each step of the guest checkout process. The rolled throughput yield for the entire checkout process is 90 percent. How many defects should the operator expect the average guest to experience?

Solve It

13. For an RTY of 0.64, what's the corresponding DPU?

Solve It

Solutions to Yield and Defects Problems

1 A study of a hospital's blood test records reveals that out of 127 samples of drawn blood, five were done incorrectly and ended up being unusable. Also, for 31 of the samples the donors had to be contacted again to correct personal information. What's the first time yield of this process?

Recognizing that there are 5 scrapped and 31 worked samples from the 127 inspected, you can use the formula for FTY to calculate the correct answer:

$$FTY = \frac{in - scrap - rework}{in} = \frac{127 - 5 - 31}{127} = \frac{91}{127} = 0.717 = 71.7\%$$

2 A water heater production facility is showing a 97 percent yield at the final test step in its assembly process. As you look deeper, however, you find that this yield calculation only includes the number of units that must be scrapped at the end of the test. In reality, 62 percent of all units fail final inspection on their first attempt and must be corrected before they pass. What's the true FTY of this production system?

Because 97 percent of the water heaters eventually make it through the final test step, this means that the other 3 percent end up scrapped, as the problem description says. Combining this scrap number with the provided rework number of 62 percent allows you to use the FTY formula on a per 100 (percent) basis:

$$FTY = \frac{in - scrap - rework}{in} = \frac{100 - 3 - 62}{100} = \frac{35}{100} = 0.35 = 35\%$$

3 In a one-month study, an airline lost four out of 9,824 pieces of luggage. Further, 21 pieces of luggage were mishandled and were only connected with their passengers after a one- or two-day delay. What's the FTY for the 9,824 pieces of luggage?

Looking at the one-month airline study data, the total number of defects after the first try is 25 — 4 completely lost pieces of luggage (scrap) and 21 delayed deliveries (rework). Applying the formula for FTY, you have:

$$FTY = \frac{in - scrap - rework}{in} = \frac{9,824 - 4 - 21}{9,824} = \frac{9,799}{9,824} = 0.9975 = 99.75\%$$

4 A cellphone keypad has 17 specified dimensions and characteristics. If each of these specifications is met with 99 percent accuracy, what's the chance of getting a defect-free keypad?

Rolled throughput yield (RTY) is calculated by simply multiplying all the yields together for the characteristics of a system. So, for this problem, because each of the 17 characteristics runs at 99 percent, the RTY is 0.99 multiplied by itself 17 times:

$$RTY = FTY^n = 0.99^{17} = 0.843 = 84.3\%$$

5 A hiring process has seven steps, each with the following first time yields:

$FTY_1 = 0.92$ $FTY_5 = 0.98$

$FTY_2 = 0.95$ $FTY_6 = 0.89$

$FTY_3 = 0.90$ $FTY_7 = 0.87$

$FTY_4 = 0.99$

What's the rolled throughput yield for this process?

To find RTY, you multiply all the FTYs:

$$RTY = FTY_1 \times FTY_2 \times FTY_3 \times FTY_4 \times FTY_5 \times FTY_6 \times FTY_7$$

$$RTY = 0.92 \times 0.95 \times 0.90 \times 0.99 \times 0.98 \times 0.89 \times 0.87$$

$$RTY = 0.591 = 59.1\%$$

6 A football coach is trying to improve his offense's ball possession. Looking back at game films, he finds that his offense has committed 12 turnovers through 305 plays from scrimmage, giving the team an overall probability of retaining possession at 96 percent for any single play. What's the probability of the team retaining possession for 16 consecutive plays?

Even though this problem deals with sports, the math is no different. If the probability of the offense retaining possession on a single play is 0.96, or 96 percent, the chance of retaining possession for 16 consecutive plays is 0.96 multiplied by itself 16 times:

$$RTY = FTY^{16} = 0.96^{16} = 0.53 = 53\%$$

Even with a very high chance of retaining possession on a single play, you can see why coaches get gray hair when trying to get their teams to have long, sustained drives — the chances of a turnover quickly multiply!

7 What's the DPU of a product if you find five defects on 23 units?

DPU compares the number of defects found to the total number of units inspected:

$$DPU = \frac{5}{23} = 0.217$$

8 A bottle-filling process has three opportunities for success or failure — the amount of product put into the bottle, the correct assembly of the lid, and the correct application of the bottle label. Find the DPO of this process if it produces 7 defects after 40 bottles have been produced.

DPO is based on the number of defects found per opportunity. So, you have to compare the defects found to the total number of opportunities within the inspected units:

$$DPO = \frac{total\ number\ of\ defects\ observed}{total\ number\ of\ opportunities\ inspected} = \frac{7}{40 \times 3} = \frac{7}{120} = 0.058$$

9 A hospital's emergency room admittance process produces 17 defects per 500 opportunities. The radiology department produces 15 defects per 600 opportunities. Which area of the hospital has a higher defect rate? How many defects should you expect after one million patients have gone through both of these hospital departments?

If you use the DPO formula for each area of the hospital, you get:

$$DPO_{ER} = \frac{17}{500} = 0.034$$

$$DPO_{RAD} = \frac{15}{600} = 0.025$$

So, the emergency room, with its DPO of 0.034, has a slightly higher defect rate.

Putting these into defect per million opportunities (DPMO) units tells you how many defects will occur when a million patients go through each of these hospital departments:

$$DPMO_{ER} = DPO_{ER} \times 1,000,000 = 0.034 \times 1,000,000 = 34,000$$

$$DPMO_{RAD} = DPO_{RAD} \times 1,000,000 = 0.025 \times 1,000,000 = 25,000$$

So, the total DPMO for the two departments together is:

$$DPMO_{TOT} = DPMO_{ER} + DPMO_{RAD} = 34{,}000 + 25{,}000 = 59{,}000$$

10 The manager of a product line with a measured DPU of 0.01 wants you to estimate the RTY for his process. What estimate do you give?

If you know DPU, you can use the formula to find RTY:

$$RTY = e^{-DPU} = e^{-0.01} = 0.99005$$

11 If a specific model of automobile is found to have an average of four defects when purchased new, what would you expect the RTY of its manufacturing process to be?

If a car was found to have a DPU of four, the RTY is:

$$RTY = e^{-DPU} = e^{-4} = 0.0183 = 1.83\%$$

For something as complex as a car, with thousands of parts, it's not unusual to have a very low RTY.

12 A hotel operator measured the first time yields for each step of the guest checkout process. The rolled throughput yield for the checkout process is 90 percent. How many defects should the operator expect the average guest to experience?

If you know RTY, you can use the formula to find DPU:

$$DPU = -\ln(RTY) = -\ln(0.90) = 0.1054$$

13 For an RTY of 0.64, what's the corresponding DPU?

To find the corresponding DPU to an RTY of 0.64, use the following formula:

$$DPU = -\ln(RTY) = -\ln(0.64) = 0.446 = 44.6\%$$

Part IV

Assessing the Right Approach to Your Analysis

The 5th Wave By Rich Tennant

"Get ready, I think they're starting to drift."

In this part . . .

*W*hat underlies your data? What are the root causes? Which are the critical inputs? The answers to these questions come from the skills of the Analyze phase of the DMAIC process. This part exercises and builds your Six Sigma analytical muscles.

Chapter 10

Mastering Measurement System Analysis (MSA)

. . . .

In This Chapter

▶ Completing a basic measurement system audit

▶ Performing attribute measurement system analysis

▶ Interpreting the results of your continuous variable measurement systems analysis

. . . .

Measurement is the foundation of knowledge and subsequent improvement. Measurement is the tool you use to verify that you have come to the right answer, have corrected the problem, or have improved the situation. Measurement is unavoidable because you can't observe anything without the filter of some kind of measurement system — your eyes, your brain, your perception, a ruler, a stopwatch, or a laser interferometer. Everything comes to you through some kind of measurement system "lens." Because measurement is so important, you need to know whether your measurement system is giving you an accurate picture of reality.

As is always the case, no measurement system is ever perfect. Your job in Six Sigma is to start by finding out how good your measurement system is. You have to ask whether it's good enough to base decisions on and whether it's consistent. Then ask: Is it accurate? How much of the error or variation you observe is a result of the measurement system itself? A good start at answering these basic questions is to perform a measurement system audit. Read on to find out how.

Your Basic Sanity Check: Auditing Measurement Systems

An *audit* is when you compare your measurements to a known, correct standard. In an audit, your goal is to determine how often the recorded measurement hasn't matched with what it should be. Here are some points to remember when performing a basic audit on a measurement system:

✔ Experience has shown that human inspection systems detect only about 80 percent of actual defects. Remember that eyewitness accounts often are incomplete or wrong. If you want to use human inspection, you need to take precautions to try to make them accurate enough for your needs.

> ✔ If your measurement system is one that classifies problems or defects into categories, a Pareto chart (or bar chart) of the number of problems or defects placed into each category shouldn't be flat or even across the charted categories. Instead, about 80 percent of the total defects should come from a smaller subset of the possible defect categories. If the Pareto chart of your defects is flat, that means your measurement system probably isn't accurately reflecting reality. Also, if a Pareto chart of classified defects looks extremely peaked, with almost all defects in a single category, your measurement system doesn't have enough discriminating power and needs to be addressed. (Refer to *Six Sigma for Dummies* for background on creating and interpreting Pareto diagrams.)

Q. A stockroom manager uses a computer system to track inventory. The computer system is updated from production records, meaning that when a product is counted in the computer system as having been finished in production, the items in its Bill of Materials are automatically subtracted from the computer inventory. The stockroom manager wants to know how accurate this computer measure of inventory really is. So, one day he went out into the stockroom and performed a very careful physical count of all items. Here's what he found for a selection of critical inventory items:

Item	Physical Count	Computer Count
Polymer resin	20,452 kg	21,310 kg
Spindle motors	17,721 units	17,750 units
Fasteners	51,897 units	52,000 units
Adhesive	44 barrels	42 barrels
Label sets	18,366 pairs	18,370 pairs
Packaging	20,204 units	20,180 units

What is the accuracy of the computer inventory measurement system?

A. You can quickly calculate how close each computer system value is to the actual, physical count number by calculating the amount each inventory item is "off" (the difference between the computer count and the physical count) and transforming the amount "off" into a percentage (dividing each amount "off" by the actual physical count of each item). This method is accomplished by adding two columns to the table, as seen below:

Item	Physical Count	Computer Count	Amount "Off"	Percent "Off"
Polymer resin	20,452 kg	21,310 kg	858 kg	4.20%
Spindle motors	17,721 units	17,750 units	29 units	0.16%
Fasteners	51,897 units	52,000 units	103 units	0.20%
Adhesive	44 barrels	42 barrels	2 barrels	4.55%
Label sets	18,366 pairs	18,370 pairs	4 pairs	0.02%
Packaging	20,204 units	20,180 units	24 units	0.12%

The average percent that these critical items is "off" by is 1.54 percent. This average tells you how close your computer inventory is from being fully accurate. In other words, this measurement system is 98.46 percent accurate.

As a further check, you can create a Pareto or bar chart to show how "off" each of the selected inventory items is. Here's what the chart looks like:

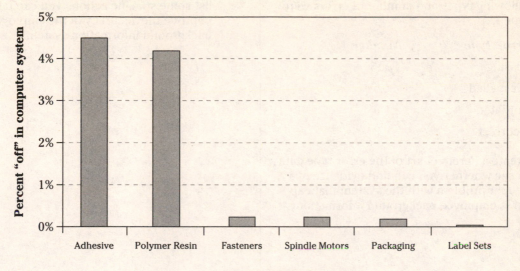

Critical Inventory Items

By looking at the Pareto chart, you can see that the accuracy of the adhesive and polymer resin is much different than the rest of the inventory items. This fact tells you that the inventory measurement system is following the Pareto principle, which states that about 80 percent of the problem is arising from about 20 percent of the items. This ratio is exactly what you'd expect when a measurement system is operating correctly. However, if the bars of the Pareto chart had all been about the same height, you'd suspect something was fishy. To improve this inventory measurement system, you'd want to start with the way the stock levels for adhesive and polymer resin are accounted for in the computer system.

1. You perform an audit of your company's employee information system. Whenever a new employee is hired, the hiring manager is required to gather specific background information for the employee, such as spouse's name, home address, emergency contact, and so on. So, you select a few random employees and pull their filed background sheets. You then have the employees review each of the 20 fields that the hiring manager filled in to verify that they're all correct. Here's what you found in your audit:

Employee	Errors in Background Info
Bob	3
John B.	4
Ruth	0
David	4
Elizabeth	3
Stacy	4
Noah	2
Sam	0
Erin	2
John M.	5

What is the average accuracy of the employee background information? Get some scrap paper to work out your calculations.

2. In the audit described in Problem 1, the following types and number of errors were found:

Error Type	Number
Missing	15
Misspelled	5
Outdated	5
Incorrect	2

Create a Pareto chart of the error type data to see whether you can find evidence of a deeper problem with the system that captures employee background information.

3. Using the scenario from Problems 1 and 2, list some specific actions you can take to improve the accuracy of the employee background information system.

Do We Agree? Performing an Attribute Measurement System Analysis

The purpose of some measurement systems is to categorize items by their attributes — to separate "good" items from "bad" ones, sort samples into "blue," "green," and "cyan" groups, and assign invoices to "engineering," "production," or "sales" departments. These types of measurement systems are called *attribute measurement systems* because they determine or measure one or more attributes of the item being inspected.

The question is, how repeatably and reliably can one of these systems determine the specific attribute you're looking for? For example, how repeatably and reliably does your attribute measurement system detect "bad" disk drives from among all the "good" ones being completed in production? To quantify how well an attribute measurement system is working, you perform an attribute measurement system analysis.

Here are the steps to complete an attribute measurement system analysis:

1. **Set aside 15 to 30 test samples of the item you're measuring.**

   Make sure these samples represent the full range of variation being encountered and make sure approximately equal amounts of each possible attribute category (for example "pass" or "fail" or "blue," "green," or "cyan") are present within the samples you've set aside.

2. **Create a "master" standard that designates each of the test samples into its true attribute category.**

3. **Select two or three typical inspectors and have them review the sample items just as they normally would in the measurement system, but in random order. Record their attribute assessment for each item.**

4. **Place the test samples in a new random order, and have the inspectors repeat their attribute assessments. (Don't reveal the new order to the inspectors!) Record the repeated measurements.**

5. **For each inspector, go through the test sample items and calculate the percentage of items where their first and second measurements agree.**

   This percentage is the *repeatability* of that inspector. To determine the repeatability of the overall attribute measurement system, calculate the average repeatability for all three inspectors.

6. **Going through each of the sample items of the study, calculate the percentage of times where all of the inspectors' attribute assessments agree for the first and second measurements for each sample.**

   This percentage is the *reproducibility* of the measurement system.

7. **You can also calculate the percent of the time all the inspectors' attribute assessments agree with each other and with the "master" standard created in Step 2.**

   This percentage, which is referred to as the *effectiveness* of the measurement system, tells you how consistently the measurement system correctly measures the true attribute it's looking for.

Q. Imagine you're starting up a Six Sigma project. It involves reducing the number of parts rejected from a manufacturing process that makes shear pins. As the pins are completed, they're reviewed by an inspector and either passed or failed (and scrapped). Before you get too far into your project, you decide to perform an attribute measurement system analysis to make sure the pass-fail assessments of the pins are reliable. How would you go about doing this analysis?

A. You specially arrange 15 random shear pin parts — about half (8) known to be good and half (7) known to be bad. Then you pick three inspectors for the study. After randomizing the order of the parts and having each inspector measure the parts two different times, you record their pass-fail measurements. A filled-out worksheet for your attribute measurement system analysis is shown in the next figure.

The worksheet helps guide you through the steps of the calculations of the analysis. Here are the actual calculation steps:

- To find the repeatability of the individual inspectors, first count the number of times each inspector's measurements agree between the two trials. Then, divide this by the number of parts inspected and multiply by 100 to get the percent repeatability.

- To find the overall repeatability, calculate the average of the three individual inspector repeatabilities.

- The overall reproducibility is calculated from a review of how many times all three inspectors agree with each other.

- The overall effectiveness of the system is calculated from a review of how many times all three inspectors agree and their agreement matches the designated "master" standard.

You can see by the worksheet that the overall repeatability of this measurement system is 84.4 percent, which means that if you repeated the measurements on the same set of pins, you'd have an 84.4 percent chance of getting the same result — a marginally acceptable level. But, the overall reproducibility, or how well this system will do given a different set of pins or different set of inspectors, is only 60 percent. This is not good enough for valid measurements. As a result of your analysis, your first project task has to be to improve the pass-fail measurement system for the shear pins. After you have valid measurement data, you can proceed if necessary.

Main item table

Item ID	True Attribute "Master"	1st Assessment Order	2nd Assessment Order
1	PASS	14	13
2	FAIL	2	15
3	FAIL	10	12
4	PASS	8	9
5	PASS	13	6
6	FAIL	7	11
7	PASS	5	8
8	FAIL	9	10
9	FAIL	1	5
10	PASS	6	1
11	FAIL	15	7
12	FAIL	4	4
13	PASS	3	2
14	PASS	12	3
15	FAIL	11	4

Appraiser 1

1st Assessment	2nd Assessment	1st and 2nd Assessment Agree? (Y/N)	1st and 2nd Assessment Agree with Master? (Y/N)
PASS	PASS	Y	Y
FAIL	FAIL	Y	Y
PASS	FAIL	N	N
PASS	PASS	Y	Y
PASS	PASS	Y	Y
FAIL	FAIL	Y	Y
PASS	FAIL	N	N
FAIL	FAIL	Y	Y
FAIL	PASS	N	N
FAIL	FAIL	Y	Y
FAIL	FAIL	Y	Y
FAIL	FAIL	Y	Y
PASS	PASS	Y	Y
PASS	PASS	Y	Y
FAIL	FAIL	Y	Y

		Agree?	Agree with Master?
A_1, Count of Agreements		13	11
B_1, Number of Items Inspected		15	15
Percent Agreement: $A_1/B_1 \times 100$		86.17	73.3
C_1, Individual *Repeatability*		86.7	73.3
Individual *Effectiveness*		86.7	73.3

Appraiser 2

1st Assessment	2nd Assessment	1st and 2nd Assessment Agree? (Y/N)	1st and 2nd Assessment Agree with Master? (Y/N)
PASS	PASS	Y	Y
FAIL	FAIL	Y	Y
FAIL	PASS	N	N
PASS	PASS	Y	Y
PASS	PASS	Y	Y
FAIL	FAIL	Y	Y
PASS	PASS	N	N
FAIL	FAIL	Y	N
FAIL	PASS	Y	N
FAIL	FAIL	Y	N
FAIL	FAIL	N	Y
PASS	FAIL	Y	N
PASS	PASS	Y	Y
PASS	PASS	Y	Y
FAIL	FAIL	Y	Y

		Agree?	Agree with Master?
A_2, Count of Agreements		11	7
B_2, Number of Items Inspected		15	15
Percent Agreement: $A_2/B_2 \times 100$		73.3	46.7
C_2, Individual *Repeatability*		73.3	46.7
Individual *Effectiveness*		73.3	46.7

Appraiser 3

1st Assessment	2nd Assessment	1st and 2nd Assessment Agree? (Y/N)	1st and 2nd Assessment Agree with Master? (Y/N)
PASS	PASS	Y	Y
FAIL	FAIL	Y	Y
FAIL	FAIL	Y	Y
PASS	PASS	Y	Y
PASS	PASS	Y	Y
FAIL	FAIL	Y	Y
PASS	PASS	Y	Y
FAIL	FAIL	Y	Y
FAIL	FAIL	N	N
PASS	PASS	Y	Y
FAIL	FAIL	Y	Y
FAIL	FAIL	Y	Y
PASS	PASS	Y	Y
PASS	PASS	Y	Y
FAIL	FAIL	Y	Y

		Agree?	Agree with Master?
A_3, Count of Agreements		14	14
B_3, Number of Items Inspected		15	15
Percent Agreement: $A_3/B_3 \times 100$		93.3	93.3
C_3, Individual *Repeatability*		93.3	93.3
Individual *Effectiveness*		93.3	93.3
Overall *Repeatability*: $(C_1+C_2+C_3)/3$			84.4

Combined

1st and 2nd Assessment Agree? (Y/N)	1st and 2nd Assessment Agree with Master? (Y/N)
Y	Y
Y	Y
N	N
Y	Y
Y	Y
N	Y
N	N
Y	Y
Y	N
Y	Y
N	N
Y	Y
Y	Y
N	Y
Y	Y

	Agree?	Agree with Master?
A_z, Count of Agreements	9	8
B_z, Number of Items Inspected	15	15
Percent Agreement: $A_z/B_z \times 100$	30.0	53.3
C_z, Individual *Repeatability*	60.0	53.3
Individual *Effectiveness*		53.3

Using the example from this section as a guideline, perform an attribute measurement system analysis on a measurement system from your own work, or better yet, from your own Six Sigma project. Use this template, or print it from www.dummies.com/go/sixsigmaworkbook.

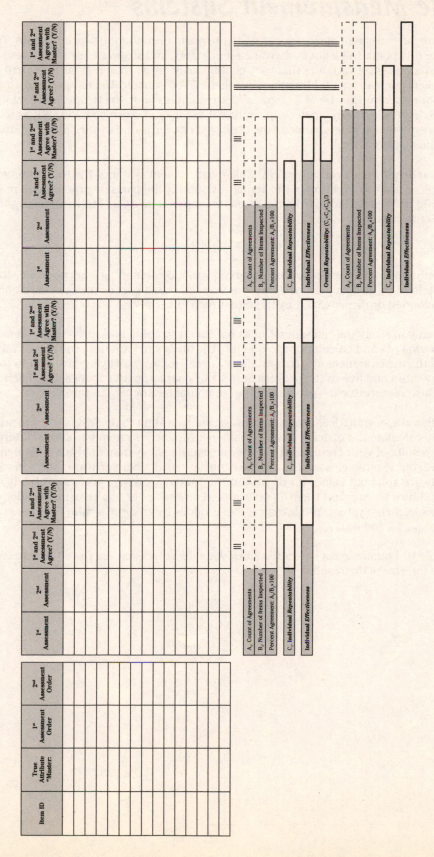

Gauging Gages: Analyzing Continuous Variable Measurement Systems

Many measurement systems operate in the realm of continuous variable data. To illustrate this point, think about thermometers, rulers, and stopwatches — all these are used to measure variables that vary continuously rather than just fall into attribute buckets such as "small," "medium," or "large." For example, the temperature in your room right now may be 71.2 degrees. Thirty minutes later, the temperature may be 70.8 degrees. A thermometer can capture these up and down changes. But as with all measurement systems, some of the observed change is due to variation from the measurement system itself.

When dealing with continuous variable measurement systems, the total variation you observe is a combination of the actual variation of the parts or process you're investigating and the variation from the measurement system itself. Mathematically, this can be written as

$$\sigma^2_{OBSERVED} = \sigma^2_{ACTUAL} + \sigma^2_{MEASUREMENTS}$$

Ideally, you want the part of the observed variation stemming from your measurement system to be as small as possible. That way the actual part or process variation won't be clouded or drowned out by the measurement variation.

When you study the "goodness" of a continuous variable measurement system, you do experiments and calculations to quantify the observed variation, the actual variation, and the measurement system variation. These studies usually involve two to three inspectors and five to ten process outputs or characteristics to measure. Each inspector also measures each process output or characteristic two to three times.

At this stage, statistical analysis software, such as Minitab or JMP, is used to automatically calculate the observed, actual, and measurement system variations. Interpreting the results of your continuous variable measurement system analysis *is* straightforward, but is often glossed over in the explanations of your software tool. After your software spits out values for $\sigma_{OBSERVED}$, σ_{ACTUAL}, and $\sigma_{MEASUREMENTS}$, you must clearly understand how to interpret them if you want to know whether you're using an adequate measurement system. You interpret these values by creating a ratio between $\sigma_{MEASRUEMENTS}$ and $\sigma_{OBSERVED}$.

Table 10-1 summarizes the ratio values you may get, describes the situation, and helps you interprets the results.

Table 10-1	Measurement-to-Observed Variation Ratio Values and Interpretation	
Calculated Variance Ratio	**Diagnosis**	**Prescription**
$\dfrac{\sigma_{MEASUREMENTS}}{\sigma_{OBSERVED}} \leq 0.1$	This is an effective measurement system. Contribution of the measurement system itself to the overall observed variation is small enough to enable good decisions from the measurements.	Use the measurement system as it is now. Look for opportunities to simplify or make the measurement system less expensive or more efficient.
$0.1 \leq \dfrac{\sigma_{MEASUREMENTS}}{\sigma_{OBSERVED}} \leq 0.3$	This is a marginal measurement system. Contribution of the measurement system itself to the overall observed variation is beginning to cloud results. You risk making a wrong decision due to the extra variation of the measurement system.	Use this system with caution and only if no better measurement alternative exists. Begin to improve the measurement system by training operators, standardizing measurement procedures, and investigating new measurement equipment.
$\dfrac{\sigma_{MEASUREMENTS}}{\sigma_{OBSERVED}} \geq 0.3$	This is an unacceptable measurement system. Guessing is probably just as precise. Don't base important decisions on information compiled from a measurement system that's in this condition.	This measurement system needs to be corrected before any valid information can be derived from the system. Investigate causes of gross inconsistency.

Go through the example and practice exercises that follow to become proficient at interpreting the results of a continuous variable measurement system analysis.

Q. You just performed a measurement system study on the temperature sensor used in the oven of your shrink-wrap process. Here are the results that your computer software spit out:

$$\sigma^2_{OBSERVED} = 0.0325$$

$$\sigma^2_{MEASUREMENTS} = 0.0007$$

What is your assessment of this situation? Is the temperature measurement system effective?

A. The first thing to do with the output of your computer calculations is to create a ratio of the standard deviation of the measurement system to the standard deviation of the total observed variation:

$$\frac{\sigma_{MEASUREMENTS}}{\sigma_{OBSERVED}} = \frac{\sqrt{\sigma^2_{MEASUREMENTS}}}{\sqrt{\sigma^2_{OBSERVED}}} = \frac{\sqrt{0.0007}}{\sqrt{0.0325}} = \frac{0.0265}{0.1803} = 0.147$$

After you achieve this number and look at Table 10-1, you can see that this system falls into the marginal category between 0.1 and 0.3, which means that the temperature sensor system in the shrink-wrap oven has some limitations but is still good enough to use if no other system is available. If more reliable measurements are necessary, you need to make changes to the temperature measurement system.

4. An analysis of a length measurement system — that is, a ruler — produces the following breakdown of the variation in the system:

$$\sigma^2_{OBSERVED} = 0.250$$

$$\sigma^2_{MEASUREMENTS} = 0.042$$

What is your diagnosis of the measurement system?

Solve It

5. The results of your measurement system analysis on the method you use to measure sliding friction on a conveyor system reveal that:

$$\sigma^2_{OBSERVED} = 178$$

$$\sigma^2_{ACTUAL} = 121$$

Is this measurement system reliable?

Solve It

Solutions to MSA Problems

1 You perform an audit of your company's employee information system. Whenever a new employee is hired, the hiring manager is required to gather specific background information for the employee, such as spouse's name, home address, emergency contact, and so on. So, you select a few random employees and pull their filed background sheets. You then have the employees review each of the 20 fields that the hiring manager filled in to verify they're all correct. Check the original question earlier in the chapter to see what you found in your audit.

Each background form has 20 fields, so the accuracy as a percentage of any form would be the number of correct fields (20 minus the number of errors) divided by the total number of fields (20). The table below shows the calculated accuracy percentage for each background form audited:

Employee	Errors in Background Info	Correct Fields	Accuracy (% Correct)
Bob	3	17	85%
John B.	4	16	80%
Ruth	0	20	100%
David	4	16	80%
Elizabeth	3	17	85%
Stacy	4	16	80%
Noah	2	18	90%
Sam	0	20	100%
Erin	2	18	90%
John M.	5	15	75%

The average accuracy is just the average of all the individual accuracies, which is 86.5 percent.

2 Create a Pareto chart of the error type data from Problem 1 to see whether you can find evidence of a deeper problem with the system that captures employee background information (see original question earlier in the chapter for more details).

The Pareto chart for the types of errors with their stated quantities would look like the following figure:

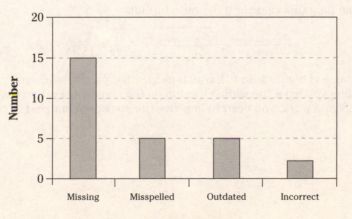

You can see that the Pareto diagram looks just as it should — about 20 percent of the categories accounting for about 80 percent of all the errors. This tells you that the variation in the measurement system is normal and that there is no cause for alarm.

3 Using the scenario from Problems 1 and 2, list some specific actions you can take to improve the accuracy of the employee background information system.

Here's a list of some immediate actions that can be taken to improve the employee background information (you may have thought of others):

- ✔ Have the new employee, instead of the hiring manger, fill out the form.

- ✔ Send a copy of each employee's background form to the employee annually for review. Doing so gives the employee a chance to update addresses, phone numbers, or other information that may be obsolete.

- ✔ Have the appropriate background information copied over from the same information already recorded on the official company job application.

4 An analysis of a length measurement system — that is, a ruler — produces a breakdown of the variation in the system (see the original question earlier in the chapter for details). What is your diagnosis of the measurement system?

Start by calculating the ratio of the standard deviation of the measurement system to the standard deviation of the total observed variation.

This ratio shows that the variation from the length measurements accounts for only a small portion of the observed variation. In fact, this is better than the 0.10 rule of thumb. You can trust the measurements from this ruler and can go forward knowing that your work is based on a sound foundation of data.

5 The results of your measurement system analysis of the method you use to measure sliding friction on a conveyor system are revealed (see the original problem earlier in the chapter for details). Is the measurement system reliable?

The way you can tell whether this is a reliable measurement system is to construct the ratio of the standard deviation of the measurement system to the standard deviation of the entire system.

The standard deviation for the measurements themselves isn't given. But, you can calculate it just by knowing the other two components:

$$\sigma^2_{OBSERVED} = \sigma^2_{ACTUAL} + \sigma^2_{MEASUREMENTS}$$
$$\sigma^2_{MEASUREMENTS} = \sigma^2_{OBSERVED} - \sigma^2_{ACTUAL} = 178 - 151 = 27$$

Now you can plug this value into the ratio formula:

$$\frac{\sigma_{MEASUREMENTS}}{\sigma_{OBSERVED}} = \frac{\sqrt{\sigma^2_{MEASUREMENTS}}}{\sqrt{\sigma^2_{OBSERVED}}} = \frac{\sqrt{27}}{\sqrt{178}} = \frac{5.20}{13.34} = 0.39$$

This ratio value is higher than 0.3, which means that your measurement system isn't capable of reliably telling you what the sliding friction on the conveyor system really is. Before you do any further Six Sigma work, you need to improve the measurement part of the system.

Chapter 11

Capability: Matching Performance to Need

. . . .

In This Chapter

▶ Discovering how to calculate sigma (Z) scores

▶ Understanding the shift between short- and long-term performance

▶ Using capability indices (C_P, C_{PK}, P_P, P_{PK}) to apply an improvement plan

. . . .

Capability is a measure of how well a product or process is able to meet a specific requirement. If PGA Tour fairways are 30 yards wide, the capability of a golfer's tee shot is his or her measured ability to stay within this 30-yard width. Does the golf ball stay on the fairway all of the time? Part of the time? How capable is the golfer? "Poor," "pretty good," or "Tiger Woods good" are basically useless measures of capability in Six Sigma because they're too vague. They offer no improvement traction. In this chapter, you practice how to calculate the precise capability of a process or characteristic. With a proper capability metric in hand, you can compare the performance of one process to another, you can determine how many items will end up outside the required performance limits, and you'll have a basis for measuring performance improvement.

Many of the formulas for capability rely on measures of the average and short- and long-term standard deviation. Flip to Chapter 7 to find out how to calculate these average and standard deviation values.

Calculating and Interpreting Sigma (Z) Scores

The *sigma (Z) score* is one of the most basic ways to describe the capability of a process or characteristic (see Table 11-1). For example, if you know the Z score, you can quickly look up the corresponding level of defect rate performance.

Calculating a sigma score is straightforward. A small Z is the number of short-term standard deviations you can fit between the mean value of the process's or characteristic's performance and its nearest specification limit (*SL*).

$$Z = \frac{|SL - \overline{x}|}{\sigma_{ST}}$$

Table 11-1	Sigma (Z) Score Defects Per Million Opportunities (*DPMO*)
Z_{ST}	$DPMO_{LT}$
0.0	933,193
0.5	841,345
1.0	691,462
1.5	500,000
2.0	308,538
2.5	158,655
3.0	66,807
3.5	22,750
4.0	6,210
4.5	1,350
5.0	233
5.5	32
6.0	3.4

An example will help illustrate how to calculate and interpret a sigma (Z) score.

EXAMPLE

Q. A plastic housing part has a critical length dimension of 32.30 ± 0.10 mm. You've measured a short-term sample of housings and calculated the following about the variation in this characteristic:

$$\overline{x} = 32.34$$

$$\sigma_{ST} = 0.017$$

What is the sigma (Z) score for this critical characteristic? What is its expected long-term defect rate?

A. The sigma (Z) score is how many short-term standard deviations you can fit between the mean and the nearest specification limit. In this example, the measured mean of 32.34 mm is slightly closer to the upper specification limit of 32.40 mm. So the formula is:

$$Z = \frac{|SL - \overline{x}|}{\sigma_{ST}} = \frac{|32.4 - 32.34|}{0.017} = 3.53$$

This characteristic is operating at a sigma level of 3.53 — not quite Six Sigma level. What is the defect rate? You find this by finding the calculated Z value and then looking up the corresponding *DPMO* value. From Table 11-1, you can see that the Z entry for 3.50 has a *DPMO* of 22,750. This characteristic has a slightly higher Z value than that, which means that its performance will be slightly better. So, roughly estimating, the characteristic's *DPMO* will be about 21,000.

1. Your company has payment terms of net 30 days on its accounts receivables. Any payment received later than 30 days is considered late. You've measured a sample of payment data and found the average payment time to be 25 days with a standard deviation of 2 days. Calculate the sigma (Z) score and estimate the *DPMO* for this process.

2. A fill-volume setting for a 1-liter bottle filling process is set at 1.1 liters, which provides a small cushion against the bottle being filled too low. A sample shows that the average fill volume is actually 1.15 liters with a standard deviation of 0.10 liters. Calculate the sigma (Z) score and indicate about how many bottles will have a fill volume lower than the 1.1-liter production limit.

Solve It

3. Your preferred plastic injection molder tells you that when all things are carefully controlled, he can operate his process to a standard deviation of 0.001 inches for critical dimensions. In the plastic part you're designing, there is a screw boss that must be positioned 5.010 inches from a datum feature on the part. If your engineering department's policy is that all dimensions must have a sigma (Z) value of 6, at what plus or minus value do you set the specifications for this dimension?

4. The reaction time of a certain chemical process is, on average, 145 minutes with a standard deviation of 3⅓ minutes. The requirement for the reaction to be completed is between 135 and 150 minutes. Anything shorter or longer than this results in a defect. What change in defect rate will you get if you adjust the process average to be centered at 137½ minutes?

Solve It

Shift Happens: Transforming Between Short- and Long-Term Performance

The calculation of a process's or characteristic's sigma (Z) score is a based off its short-term standard deviation. Short-term standard deviations are easy to measure; you just go out and quickly capture a data sample from the process or characteristic.

But in the sigma (Z) value look-up tables, like in Table 11-1, the defect rate or yield listed is for the corresponding long-term performance. For example, a process with a short-term sigma (Z) value of 6 will have a *short-term* defect rate of 0.001 *DPMO*. But as you can see from Table 11-1, it will have a long-term defect rate of 3.4 *DPMO*.

Why all the mixing of short- and long-term values? The reason is that early Six Sigma practitioners found it easier and more practical to gather a short-term sample and calculate a short-term standard deviation and Z score, but at the same time they wanted to convey the loss of capability that always occurs over the long-term. To accomplish this, the early practitioners contrived the now-famous 1.5-sigma shift and built it right into all of their sigma (Z) score tables.

$$Z_{LT} = Z_{ST} - 1.5 \text{ or}$$
$$Z_{ST} = Z_{LT} + 1.5$$

The 1.5 value in the equations is called the 1.5-sigma shift. An example shows you how to use the idea of the 1.5-sigma shift to easily transform between the short- and long-term domains.

Q. An engineering design manager has just been told that the most recent set of prototypes for a soon-to-be-launched product has a defect rate of 0.621 percent, or 6,210 per million. The manager turns to you and remarks, "This is great! At this rate, we'll be able to launch full-scale production overseas rather than proving things out first here." Do you agree with the manager's assessment?

A. Prototypes are always treated with special care: They're carefully crafted and assembled and tuned and maintained. And usually only a few are made. What this means is that prototypes provide short-term data because they don't capture all the variation effects that occur over the long-term. So, the key point to keep in mind in this example is that the 6,210 *DPMO* reported for the prototypes is a short-term measure of the product's defect rate.

In the long-term, however, the sigma (Z) score for the product will degrade. Referring to Table 11-1, a *DPMO* of 6,210 corresponds to a short-term sigma (Z) value of 4. In the long-term, the Z score will be 1.5 less than this, or 2.5. This value corresponds to the true long-term *DPMO* of 158,655. As real production for the product ramps up, specialized prototype tooling will be replaced by multi-cavity production tooling, multiple suppliers will begin producing raw materials, and full production staffs will be used for assembly. All these changes lead to extra sources of variation that the prototype never encountered. So, you can tell your manager that with a defect rate of 158,655 per million, the soon-to-be-launched product isn't quite ready for off-shore production.

5. You calculate the short-term sigma (Z) score for a packaging process to be 5.12. What will the long-term Z value be?

6. The long-term sigma (Z) score for a critical characteristic is 2.5. What will the defect rate for this characteristic be in the long-term?

7. The short-term sigma (Z) value for correctly filling out a loan application form is 3.7. What is the short-term defect rate for this application form?

8. When you measure one car's fuel efficiency, you find that the sigma (Z) score for it meeting your company's minimum fuel efficiency requirement is 2.2. What will the Z score and defect rate be for the company's entire fleet of cars?

Calculating and Interpreting Capability Indices

Six Sigma practitioners use indices to communicate the capability of a process or characteristic. These indices, C_P, C_{PK}, P_P, P_{PK}, each compare the width of the process's or characteristic's specification requirement to its short- or long-term variation width. Knowing these index values, you can quickly figure out how the process or characteristic is performing and you can compare the capabilities of different processes to each other. See Table 11-2 for an outline of the formulas and descriptions for each capability index.

Table 11-2	Short- and Long-Term Capability Indices	
Index Name	**Formula**	**Description**
Short-term capability index (C_p)	$C_P = \dfrac{USL - LSL}{6\sigma_{ST}}$	Compares the width of the specification to the short-term width of the process
Adjusted short-term capability index (C_{pk})	$C_{PK} = \min\left(\dfrac{USL - \overline{x}}{3\sigma_{ST}}, \dfrac{\overline{x} - LSL}{3\sigma_{ST}}\right)$	Compares the width of the specification to the short-term width of the process AND accounts for off-centering of the process from the specification
Long-term capability index (P_p)	$P_P = \dfrac{USL - LSL}{6\sigma_{LT}}$	Compares the width of the specification to the long-term width of the process
Adjusted long-term capability index (P_{pk})	$P_{PK} = \min\left(\dfrac{USL - \overline{x}}{3\sigma_{LT}}, \dfrac{\overline{x} - LSL}{3\sigma_{LT}}\right)$	Compares the width of the specification to the long-term width of the process AND accounts for off-centering of the process from the specification

Note: "USL" stands for Upper Specification Limit; "LSL" stands for Lower Specification Limit.

Prescribing an Improvement Plan

Having calculated each of the four capability indices for a process or characteristic, you can use these values to determine a plan for improvement. Table 11-3 shows you how.

Table 11-3	Prescriptive Capability Improvement Plan	
Symptom	**Diagnosis**	**Prescription**
$C_P \neq C_{PK} \neq P_P \neq P_{PK}$	Your process or characteristic isn't centered and you find special causes are expanding the long-term variation.	Begin by eliminating special causes. Later focus on centering the process.

Symptom	Diagnosis	Prescription
$C_P = C_{PK}$ and $P_P = P_{PK}$	Overall, your process or characteristic is centered within its specifications.	As needed, focus on reducing the long-term variation in your process or characteristic while maintaining on-center performance.
$C_P = P_P$ and $C_{PK} = P_{PK}$	Your process or characteristic suffers from a consistent offset in its center location.	Focus on correcting the set point of your process or characteristic until it's centered.
$C_P = P_{PK}$	Your process is operating at its entitlement level of variation.	Continue to monitor the capability of your process. Redesign your process to improve its entitlement level of performance.

TIP

You can link the C_{PK} back to the sigma (Z) score and the corresponding defect rate with the formula:

$$Z = 3C_{PK}$$

EXAMPLE

Q. A progressive pizza chain has studied the preferences of its customers. The findings are that each small, individual pizza must have at least 8 pepperonis and that having more than 12 pepperonis adds extra cost with no benefit. The manager of the pizza chain wants to know how capable the chain is at meeting this requirement, so over a period of time she counts the number of pepperonis on small pizzas. From her data, this is what she finds:

$$\overline{x} = 9$$

$$\sigma_{ST} = 0.33$$

$$\sigma_{LT} = 0.50$$

Calculate C_P, C_{PK}, P_P, and P_{PK} and describe the current situation at the pizza chain. How many pizzas will end up being outside the required range of 8 to 12 pepperonis? Then, based on the calculated capability indices, devise an improvement strategy for the pizza chain.

A. Recognizing that the upper specification limit (USL) is 12 and the lower specification limit (LSL) is 8, you can plug the average and standard deviation values from the manager's measurements into the formulas from Table 11-2 to calculate all the capability indices, like this:

$$C_P = \frac{USL - LSL}{6\sigma_{ST}} = \frac{12 - 8}{6 \cdot 0.33} = \frac{4}{2} = 2.00$$

$$C_{PK} = \min\left(\frac{USL - \overline{x}}{3\sigma_{ST}}, \frac{\overline{x} - LSL}{3\sigma_{ST}}\right) = \min\left(\frac{12 - 9}{3 \cdot 0.33}, \frac{9 - 8}{3 \cdot 0.33}\right) = \min\left(\frac{3}{1}, \frac{1}{1}\right) = (3, 1) = 1.00$$

$$P_P = \frac{USL - LSL}{6\sigma_{LT}} = \frac{12 - 8}{6 \cdot 0.50} = \frac{4}{3} = 1.33$$

$$P_{PK} = \min\left(\frac{USL - \overline{x}}{3\sigma_{LT}}, \frac{\overline{x} - LSL}{3\sigma_{LT}}\right) = \min\left(\frac{12 - 9}{3 \cdot 0.5}, \frac{9 - 8}{3 \cdot 0.5}\right) = \min\left(\frac{3}{1.5}, \frac{1}{1.5}\right) = \min(2, 0.67) = 0.67$$

The long-term defect rate for the current situation at the pizza chain can be found by multiplying the calculated C_{PK} by 3 to get the sigma (Z) value and then looking up the corresponding defect rate in Table 11-1:

$$Z = 3C_{PK} = 3 \cdot 1.00 = 3.00$$

At a Z of 3, Table 11-1 shows that the long-term defect rate will be 66,807 per million. That's about 6.7 percent of customers who will think that their pizza has either too many or too few pepperonis.

How should the pizza chain improve its capability? Because $C_P \neq C_{PK} \neq P_P \neq P_{PK}$, this situation falls into the first listed scenario in Table 11-3. The improvement step for this diagnosis is to eliminate the special, out-of-the-ordinary causes of variation. By doing so, the short-term and long-term standard deviations will be equal, making $C_P = P_P$ and $C_{PK} = P_{PK}$. The improvement plan for this diagnosis is to center the process variation between the 8 and 12 specification limits. With this accomplished, $C_P = C_{PK} = P_P = P_{PK}$ and the pizza chain is operating at its entitlement level.

---

9. For a manufacturing process with an upper specification limit of 40 mm, a lower specification limit of 37.5 mm, and a short-term standard deviation of 0.97, calculate the C_P.

Solve It

10. An accounting firm takes, on average, 39 days with a short-term standard deviation of 3 days to prepare a client's taxes. They want to have all clients' taxes prepared within 45 days. Calculate the C_{PK} for this process at the accounting firm. Also, calculate the Z score and determine the percentage of clients who will wait longer than 45 days for their taxes to be completed.

Solve It

11. What is going on in a process when the calculated C_P is the same as the C_{PK}?

Solve It

12. You've performed a lot of measurements on a new adhesive application process. Here are the statistics you've determined from the process:

$$\bar{x} = 105.3$$

$$\sigma_{ST} = 5.12$$

$$\sigma_{LT} = 5.28$$

To be successful, the result of this adhesive process must be between 90 and 130. Calculate the C_P for this process.

Solve It

13. Calculate the C_{PK} for the scenario described in Problem 12.

Solve It

14. Calculate the P_P for the scenario described in Problem 12.

Solve It

15. Calculate the P_{PK} for the scenario described in Problem 12.

16. What's the defect rate for the scenario described in Problem 12?

17. Outline an improvement strategy for the scenario described in Problem 12.

Solutions to Capability Problems

1 Your company has payment terms of net 30 days on its accounts receivables. Any payment received later than 30 days is considered late. You've measured a sample of payment data and found the average payment time to be 25 days with a standard deviation of 2 days. Calculate the sigma (Z) score and estimate the *DPMO* for this process.

The specification limit in this problem is the 30-day limit on accounts receivables. Knowing the average or mean (25 days) and the standard deviation (2 days), you can plug these into the formula to calculate the sigma (Z) score:

$$Z = \frac{|SL - \bar{x}|}{\sigma_{ST}} = \frac{|30 - 25|}{2} = \frac{5}{2} = 2.5$$

Referring to Table 11-1, the *DPMO* corresponding to this Z score is 158,655. That's how many accounts out of a million that will end up taking longer than the 30-day limit.

2 A fill-volume setting for a 1-liter bottle filling process is set at 1.1 liters, which provides a small cushion against the bottle being filled too low. A sample shows that the average fill volume is actually 1.15 liters with a standard deviation of 0.10 liters. Calculate the sigma (Z) score and indicate about how many bottles will have a fill volume lower than the 1.1-liter production limit.

Knowing the 1.1-liter specification level, the average (1.15 liters), and the standard deviation (0.1 liters), you can plug these values into the formula to calculate the Z value:

$$Z = \frac{|SL - \bar{x}|}{\sigma_{ST}} = \frac{|1.1 - 1.15|}{0.1} = \frac{0.05}{0.1} = 0.5$$

This is a low Z value. From Table 11-1, you can see that the defect rate for this Z value is very high: 841,345 defects per million opportunities.

3 Your preferred plastic injection molder tells you that when all things are carefully controlled, he can operate his process to a standard deviation of 0.001 inches for critical dimensions. In the plastic part you're designing, there is a screw boss that must be positioned 5.010 inches from a datum feature on the part. If your engineering department's policy is that all dimensions must have a sigma (Z) value of 6, at what plus or minus value do you set the specifications for this dimension?

In this problem, you're not solving for Z. Instead, you're solving for the plus or minus tolerance ($\pm Tol$) that needs to be specified around the target design nominal of 5.010 inches. The first thing, then, is to use some basic algebra to rearrange the formula into a form that will calculate the $\pm Tol$ value:

$$Z = \frac{|SL - \bar{x}|}{\sigma_{ST}} = \frac{\pm Tol}{\sigma_{ST}}$$
$$\pm Tol = Z\sigma_{ST}$$

Now, plugging the provided values into the rearranged equation, you get:

$$\pm Tol = Z\sigma_{ST} = 6 \cdot 0.001 = 0.006$$

With the plus or minus tolerance value being 0.006 inches, the specification limits for the design will have to be between 5.016 and 5.004 inches in order to meet your 6 sigma design goal.

4 The reaction time of a certain chemical process is, on average, 145 minutes with a standard deviation of 3⅓ minutes. The requirement for the reaction to be completed is between 135 and 150 minutes. Anything shorter or longer than this results in a defect. What change in defect rate will you get if you adjust the process average to be centered at 137½ minutes?

The closest specification limit to the process average is 150 minutes. So, plug this value, together with the stated process mean and standard deviation, into the formula for the sigma (Z) score:

$$Z = \frac{|SL - \overline{x}|}{\sigma_{ST}} = \frac{|150 - 145|}{3.333} = \frac{5}{3.333} = 1.5$$

From Table 11-1, the defect rate at this Z level is 500,000 *DPMO*.

Now calculate the Z value if the process average were shifted to the centered value of 137.5 minutes:

$$Z = \frac{|SL - \overline{x}|}{\sigma_{ST}} = \frac{|150 - 137.5|}{3.333} = \frac{12.5}{3.333} = 3.75$$

Using Table 11-1, the defect rate for this Z value between 3.5 and 4.0 can be estimated to be about 13,000 to 15,000. What an improvement just centering the process made!

5 You calculate the short-term sigma (Z) score for a packaging process to be 5.12. What will the long-term Z value be?

$$Z_{LT} = Z_{ST} - 1.5 = 5.12 - 1.5 = 3.62$$

6 The long-term sigma (Z) score for a critical characteristic is 2.5. What will the defect rate for this characteristic be in the long-term?

$$Z_{ST} = Z_{LT} + 1.5 = 2.5 + 1.5 = 4.0$$

Table 11-1 lists long-term *DPMOs* for short-term Z scores. The long-term *DPMO* associated with the short-term Z score of 4.0 is 6,210.

7 The short-term sigma (Z) value for correctly filling out a loan application form is 3.7. What is the short-term defect rate for this application form?

Because Table 11-1 gives long-term defect rates for short-term sigma (Z) scores, you have to adjust the Z value you look up by 1.5. By looking at the table, you can see that the long-term defect rate for the short-term sigma (Z) value of 3.7 is about 14,000 *DPMO*. The short-term defect rate will be found at a sigma (Z) value of 1.5 sigma higher than this, or 5.2. At a Z of 5.2, Table 11-1 shows that the defect rate is about 100, which is the short-term defect rate for the short-term sigma (Z) value of 3.7.

8 When you measure one car's fuel efficiency, you find that the sigma (Z) score for it meeting your company's minimum fuel efficiency requirement is 2.2. What will the Z score and defect rate be for the company's entire fleet of cars?

Measuring one car provides a short-term estimate of the sigma (Z) value of the company's entire fleet. The long-term Z for the fleet will be 1.5 sigmas less than this, which in this case is a value of 0.7. But in Table 11-1, you can only look up the short-term Z value to find the long-term defect rate. In this case, the long-term defect rate corresponds to the look-up value of 2.2 in Table 11-1, or about 250,000 *DPMO*.

Estimating a value between two entries in a table is called *interpolating*. For example, a Z value of 2.2 falls between 2.0 and 2.5 in Table 11-1, but not exactly in between; 2.2 is a little closer to 2.0 than it is to 2.5. In fact, the value of 2.2 is located exactly two-fifths of the way from 2.0 to 2.5. So, the corresponding DPMO value for 2.2 will be two-fifths of the way from 308,538 to 158,655. You can solve for this value mathematically with the following expression:

$$308,538 - \frac{2}{5}\left(308,538 - 158,655\right) = 248,585 = 250,000$$

9 For a manufacturing process with an upper specification limit of 40 mm, a lower specification limit of 37.5 mm, and a short-term standard deviation of 0.97, calculate the C_P.

$$C_P = \frac{USL - LSL}{6\sigma_{ST}} = \frac{40.0 - 37.5}{0.97} = 0.43$$

10 An accounting firm takes, on average, 39 days with a short-term standard deviation of 3 days to prepare a client's taxes. They want to have all clients' taxes prepared within 45 days. Calculate the C_{PK} for this process at the accounting firm. Also, calculate the Z score and determine the percentage of clients who will wait longer than 45 days for their taxes to be completed.

First calculate the adjusted short-term capability index C_{PK}. In this exercise, you only have an upper specification limit (USL), so the C_{PK} is:

$$C_{PK} = \frac{USL - \overline{x}}{3\sigma_{ST}} = \frac{45 - 39}{3 \cdot 3} = \frac{6}{9} = 0.67$$

The Z for this scenario is calculated from:

$$Z = 3C_{PK} = 3 \cdot 0.67 = 2.00$$

Now, looking up this Z value in Table 11-1, you get a _DPMO_ of 308,538, or 30.8 percent. So, in the long-run, nearly one in three clients will have their taxes take longer than the 45-day goal of the company.

11 What is going on in a process when the calculated C_P is the same as the C_{PK}?

When the calculated C_P is the same as the calculated C_{PK}, the process or product characteristic is centered between the specification limits such that no "discounting" of the capability index occurs.

12 You've performed a lot of measurements on a new adhesive application process. Here are the statistics you've determined from the process:

$$\overline{x} = 105.3$$

$$\sigma_{ST} = 5.12$$

$$\sigma_{LT} = 5.28$$

To be successful, the result of this adhesive process must be between 90 and 130. Calculate the C_P for this process.

The C_P is found from the formula:

$$C_P = \frac{USL - LSL}{6\sigma_{ST}} = \frac{130 - 90}{6 \cdot 5.12} = \frac{40}{30.72} = 1.30$$

13 Calculate the C_{PK} for the scenario described in Problem 12.

$$C_{PK} = \min\left(\frac{USL - \overline{x}}{3\sigma_{ST}}, \frac{\overline{x} - LSL}{3\sigma_{ST}}\right) = \min\left(\frac{130 - 105.3}{3 \cdot 5.12}, \frac{105.3 - 90}{3 \cdot 5.12}\right) =$$

$$\min\left(\frac{24.7}{15.36}, \frac{15.3}{15.36}\right) = \min(1.61, 1.00) = 1.00$$

14 Calculate the P_P for the scenario described in Problem 12.

$$P_P = \frac{USL - LSL}{6\sigma_{LT}} = \frac{130 - 90}{6 \cdot 5.28} = \frac{40}{31.68} = 1.26$$

15 Calculate the P_{PK} for the scenario described in Problem 12.

$$P_{PK} = \min\left(\frac{USL - \bar{x}}{3\sigma_{LT}}, \frac{\bar{x} - LSL}{3\sigma_{LT}}\right) = \min\left(\frac{130 - 105.3}{3 \cdot 5.28}, \frac{105.3 - 90}{3 \cdot 5.28}\right) =$$

$$\min\left(\frac{24.7}{15.84}, \frac{15.3}{15.84}\right) = \min(1.56, 0.97) = 0.97$$

16 What's the defect rate for the scenario described in Problem 12?

The defect rate is calculated by finding the sigma (Z) value and then looking up the corresponding *DPMO* value in Table 11-1:

$$Z = 3C_{PK} = 3 \cdot 1.00 = 3.00$$

Looking up this value in Table 11-1 gives you the *DPMO* value of 66,807.

17 Outline an improvement strategy for the scenario described in Problem 12.

Reviewing the answers from Exercises 12 through 16, you can see that both of the following are true:

$$C_P \approx P_P$$
$$C_{PK} \approx P_{PK}$$

Fitting this into the various scenarios of Table 11-3, you can see that the prescription to this diagnosis is to first work on centering the process average, which needs to be set as closely as possible to the middle of the specification, at a value of 110.

Subsequently, if more improvement is still needed, you would begin to eliminate common causes, which would reduce the short- and long-term standard deviations of the process.

Chapter 12

Narrowing Your Inputs with Confidence

- -

- -

What the wheel is to transportation, sampling is to statistics. *Statistical sampling* allows you to understand an entire population that's too large to measure individually by inspecting only a few, representative samples of the population. For example, what's the average height of European males? If answering that question required you to locate and measure every man on the continent, you'd never finish! However, the invention of statistical sampling allows you to find the answer by measuring only a small representative sample of the population. (Next time you meet a statistician, be sure to stop and thank him for his contribution to humanity!)

There's one catch to using samples though: When you work with a sample instead of the entire population, you may discover that your sample doesn't exactly represent the population. In fact, the smaller your sample, the greater this potential for error becomes. (Can you honestly say that the average of Pierre's and Hans' heights accurately represents the average height of all men in Europe?)

Statisticians have studied sampling to an almost sickening extreme. They use the Greek symbols, such as μ and σ, to represent the exact population parameters and the Roman symbols, such as $\bar{x}$ and s, to represent the calculated parameters of a sample. What they've found is that each time you take a different sample from the same population and calculate the sample's mean or its standard deviation — or any other statistical measure — you end up with a slightly different calculation result. When you collect the repeated sample calculations together, they form what's called a *sampling distribution*. And statisticians know exactly how wide this variation will be depending on how many data points are in your sample.

A *confidence interval* quantifies the potential variation around your calculated metrics, such as the mean or the standard deviation. If, for example, you're basing your mean calculation off of a sample rather than off of the entire population (which is almost always the case), a confidence interval allows you to say, "With 95 percent confidence, I know the average height of the European male population is between 1.75 and 1.78 meters."

Because in the real world you almost always work with calculated values from samples instead of entire populations, it's important that you know how to quantify the potential error in your measurements and how this quantification affects your decisions. This chapter provides examples and practice problems that help you become an expert in creating confidence intervals around your calculations.

Creating Confidence Intervals for Means

Whenever you use the calculated average of a sample ($\bar{x}$) to infer what the average of the entire population (μ) is, you have a potential for error. Confidence intervals for means allow you to quantify how much your inference may be off based on the number of data points in your sample.

When your sample has 30 or more data points, the confidence interval for the calculated mean is:

$$\mu = \bar{x} \pm Z \frac{s}{\sqrt{n}}$$

where

- μ is the true population mean
- $\bar{x}$ is the calculated sample mean
- Z is the sigma value corresponding to the desired level of confidence you want to have
- s is the sample standard deviation
- n is the number of data points in your sample

On the other hand, when your sample has fewer than 30 data points, the confidence interval for the calculated mean must instead be based on an adjusted t value, which depends on the size of your sample. Here's the equation:

$$\mu = \bar{x} \pm t \frac{s}{\sqrt{n}}$$

Table 12-1 provides t and Z values for various levels of desired confidence.

Table 12-1	t and Z Values for Mean Confidence Levels				
Confidence	**t ($n = 2$)**	**t ($n = 5$)**	**t ($n = 10$)**	**t ($n = 25$)**	**Z ($n \geq 30$)**
68%	1.837	1.142	1.059	1.021	1
95%	13.968	2.869	2.320	2.110	2
99.7%	235.811	6.620	4.094	3.345	3

EXAMPLE

Q. You've taken 32 parts at random from a shipment of 10,000 switches. The plating thickness measurements for the 32 parts are given below. With 95 percent confidence, what's the mean plating thickness for the entire 10,000-part shipment?

0.068	0.075	0.067	0.069
0.064	0.065	0.068	0.067
0.071	0.067	0.071	0.080
0.076	0.062	0.068	0.074
0.076	0.061	0.068	0.082
0.079	0.065	0.068	0.067
0.059	0.066	0.077	0.078
0.069	0.059	0.070	0.062

A. The first thing you must recognize is that your sample is large enough (greater than 30 data points) that you can use the Z formula for calculating the confidence interval for the mean. Reviewing that formula, you need to know values for the sample mean ($\overline{x}$), Z for a confidence level of 95 percent, the sample standard deviation (s), and the number of data points in your sample (n). $\overline{x}$ and s can be calculated quickly from the 32 measurements (refer to Chapter 7 if necessary). From Table 12-1, the Z value for 95 percent confidence is 2. Now, just plug these values into the formula:

$$\mu = \overline{x} \pm Z \frac{s}{\sqrt{n}} = 0.069 \pm 2 \frac{0.006}{\sqrt{32}} =$$

$$0.069 \pm 0.002 = [0.067, 0.071]$$

Even though the calculated mean for the sample is exactly 0.069, you haven't measured every switch in the 10,000-part population, which means that you don't have exact certainty in estimating the population mean. What you can say with 95 percent confidence, though, is that the true population mean lies between 0.067 and 0.071.

Q. Suppose now that you've received a second 10,000-part shipment of the same type of switches as in the last example problem. This time, you take a 25-piece sample and find the sample mean ($\overline{x}$) to be 0.074 and the sample standard deviation (s) to be 0.005. With a 95 percent level of confidence, can you tell whether a difference exists between the average plating thickness for the two 10,000-part shipments?

A. For an $n = 25$ sample, you have to use the t formula to calculate the confidence interval for the population mean. From Table 12-1, the t value for a 25-point sample at 95 percent confidence is 2.11. So, you can figure the confidence interval for the mean as follows:

$$\mu = \overline{x} \pm t \frac{s}{\sqrt{n}} = 0.074 \pm 2.110 \frac{0.005}{\sqrt{25}}$$

$$= 0.074 \pm 0.002 = [0.072, 0.076]$$

Comparing the confidence intervals for the two shipments, you can see that they don't overlap — the predicted range for the first shipment is completely different from the predicted range for the second shipment. This indicates that, with 95 percent confidence, you can say that a difference does exist between the average plating thickness of the two shipments, with the second shipment being 0.004 thicker on average than the first.

If the two confidence intervals in the example had overlapped, you would have had to conclude that no difference existed between the averages of the two shipments. Overlap in the confidence intervals is what you look for when comparing means.

1. You have received material samples from four different suppliers — A, B, C, and D. The compiled data on the density of each supplier's samples is summarized below:

Supplier	Sample Size (n)	Sample Mean ($\bar{x}$)	Sample Std. Dev. (s)
A	60	10.7	0.950
B	10	12.0	0.048
C	25	9.8	0.220
D	34	10.0	0.300

Calculate the 99.7 percent confidence interval for each population mean and identify any differences in average density between the suppliers.

Solve It

2. You've developed two alternative curing processes for an adhesive. Now you need to determine which one results in a higher shear strength for the adhesive. Knowing that you'll conduct 25 tests using each process and estimating that the standard deviation of both processes will be 1.2 pounds, how large must the difference be between the sample means of each of the 25 tests before you declare with 95 percent confidence that one process is better than the other?

Solve It

3. Calculate the 99.7 percent confidence interval for the population mean from the following sample data set:

4.76	3.73	6.99	4.68
5.98			

Solve It

4. You receive an e-mail from a colleague stating that Process A is better than Process B because the average cycle time of Process A is better than the average cycle time of Process B. What other information do you need to know to verify your colleague's claim?

Solve It

Calculating Confidence Intervals for Standard Deviations

Just as with the mean of a sample, the standard deviation of a sample (s) doesn't exactly tell you what the true population standard deviation (σ) is. But, you can bind your calculation with a confidence interval surrounding the true value. And just as with confidence intervals for means, the more data points you have in your sample, the tighter your confidence interval for the population standard deviation will be.

Confidence intervals for standard deviations are based on the χ^2 distribution:

$$\sigma = \left[\sqrt{\frac{(n-1)s^2}{\chi^2_{LOWER}}}, \sqrt{\frac{(n-1)s^2}{\chi^2_{UPPER}}} \right]$$

Table 12-2 provides χ^2 values for common sample sizes and confidence levels.

Table 12-2	χ^2 Values for Standard Deviation Confidence Intervals			
Confidence	**n = 2**	**n = 5**	**n = 10**	**n = 25**
68%	1.987	6.599	13.088	30.833
	0.040	1.416	4.919	17.169
95%	5.187	11.365	19.301	39.749
	0.001	0.460	2.628	12.225
99.7%	10.273	17.800	27.093	50.163
	0.000	0.106	1.241	8.382

Note: The first value listed in each table cell is χ^2_{LOWER}. The second value listed in each cell is χ^2_{UPPER}.

When comparing two sample standard deviations, you can determine which population standard deviation is larger by creating a confidence interval around the ratio of their corresponding sample variances. If the confidence interval includes the value of 1, no detectable difference exists between the population standard deviations. But, if the range of the confidence interval ends up being greater than 1, the population standard deviation from the numerator of your ratio is greater than the population standard deviation from the denominator. And the reverse is also true: If the range of the confidence interval ends up being less than 1, the population standard deviation from the numerator of your ratio is smaller than the population standard deviation from the denominator.

Confidence intervals for the ratio of two variances are based on the F distribution:

$$\frac{\sigma_1^2}{\sigma_2^2} = \left[\frac{1}{F(c=n_2, r=n_1)} \frac{s_1^2}{s_2^2}, F(c=n_1, r=n_2) \frac{s_1^2}{s_2^2} \right]$$

Table 12-3 provides F distribution values for common sample sizes at a confidence level of 95 percent.

Table 12-3		*F* Distribution Values for 95% Confidence Intervals with Various Sample Sizes		
	c = 2	*c = 5*	*c = 10*	*c = 25*
r = 2	161.446	224.583	240.543	249.052
r = 5	7.709	6.388	5.999	5.774
r = 10	5.117	3.633	3.179	2.900
r = 25	4.260	2.776	2.300	1.984

REMEMBER

When you're given an *F* value to look up, it will be in the form of $F(c, r)$, which helps you determine which column and row to look in. For example, the first value given for looking up *F* — the "*c*" in $F(c, r)$ — tells you which *column* to look in. The second value given — the "*r*" in $F(c, r)$ — tells you which *row* to look in. So $F(10, 25)$ would be in the column corresponding to $c = 10$ and the row corresponding to $r = 25$, giving a value of 2.300.

EXAMPLE

Q. You have a 10-point sample of purchase order data from a longtime supplier to your company, ACME Engineering Services, Ltd. Here's the data:

$29,309.46	$32,935.89	$24,977.75	$32,518.55
$27,061.33	$32,756.21	$29,461.38	$27,500.59
$30,561.79	$33,986.21		

Calculate the 95 percent confidence interval for the population standard deviation of this data.

A. Reviewing the formula for the confidence interval for a standard deviation, you need to know the sample standard deviation (s), the size of the sample (n), and the correct χ^2_{LOWER} and χ^2_{UPPER} values corresponding to your sample size and to 95 percent confidence. The calculated sample standard deviation (refer to Chapter 7 if necessary) is $2,972.53. You need to look up the χ^2 values from Table 12-2. For 95 percent confidence and a sample size of $n = 10$, the values are $\chi^2_{LOWER} = 19.301$ and $\chi^2_{UPPER} = 2.628$. Now just plug these values into the formula as follows:

$$\sigma = \left[\sqrt{\frac{(n-1)s^2}{\chi^2_{LOWER}}}, \sqrt{\frac{(n-1)s^2}{\chi^2_{UPPER}}} \right] = \left[\sqrt{\frac{(10-1)\,\$2,972.53^2}{19.301}}, \sqrt{\frac{(10-1)\,\$2,972.53^2}{2.628}} \right] =$$

$$[\$2,029.82, \$5,500.91]$$

So, from your 10-point sample, you can say with 95 percent confidence that the true population standard deviation lies somewhere between $2,029.82 and $5,500.91.

Don't be surprised if your calculated confidence interval for a standard deviation looks very wide. Unless you have a lot of data points in your sample, your confidence interval will be wide because estimates of standard deviations are always less accurate than estimates of means.

Q. Now, in addition to the supplier from the previous example, suppose that you have a second supplier, Jones Brothers, LLC, with a standard deviation from a 25-point sample of their historical purchase orders of $3,500. With 95 percent confidence, is there a difference in the variation of these two suppliers?

A. To compare the width of the populations of these two suppliers, you create a confidence interval for the ratio of their variances. You need to know the sample standard deviations for each supplier (s_1 and s_2), the size of the sample for each supplier (n_1 and n_2), and the F statistics following the pattern in the formula for the confidence interval. After you have all of the required numbers, you can plug them into the formula like this:

$$\frac{\sigma_1^2}{\sigma_2^2} = \left[\frac{1}{F(c=n_2, r=n_1)} \frac{s_1^2}{s_2^2}, F(c=n_1, r=n_2) \frac{s_1^2}{s_2^2} \right] = \left[\frac{1}{F(c=25, r=10)} \frac{s_1^2}{s_2^2}, F(c=10, r=25) \frac{s_1^2}{s_2^2} \right] =$$

$$\left[\frac{1}{2.900} \frac{\$2,972.53^2}{\$3,500.00^2}, 2.300 \frac{\$2,972.53^2}{\$3,500.00^2} \right] = [0.249, 1.659]$$

Reviewing the calculated limits of the confidence interval, you can say that with a confidence of 95 percent that the ratio includes the value of 1. So, you know that the width of the variation of the first supplier is no different than the width of the second supplier.

---

5. Calculate a 99.7 percent confidence interval for the population standard deviation of the following cycle time data:

20.2	15.3	13.7	16.9
18.1	18.0	16.5	16.4
17.0	17.7	15.1	17.4
18.3	18.2	18.4	20.9
14.8	17.2	18.2	15.6
14.2	16.9	17.3	16.2
21.5			

Solve It

6. Calculate the 95 percent confidence interval for the population standard deviation of the following cycle time data:

16.91	16.94	17.12	16.94
16.96	17.13	16.97	16.93
17.00	16.93		

Solve It

7. Create a 95 percent confidence interval for the ratio of the variance from Problem 5 to the variance from Problem 6.

 Solve It

8. At a 95 percent confidence level, is there a difference in the population variances of the data in Problems 5 and 6?

 Solve It

Four Out of Five Recommend: Using Confidence Intervals for Proportions

Sometimes, the data you've collected creates a *proportion,* such as 8 "good" disk drives out of 10 disk drives inspected. The group of 10 disk drives inspected in this example is a sample of the larger population of total disk drive items produced. So, you can create a confidence interval. You can also create confidence intervals around the difference between two proportions.

If y is the number of items identified out of the total number inspected (n), the proportion is written mathematically as

$$\frac{y}{n}$$

The confidence interval around the true population proportion (p) is written as

$$p = \frac{y}{n} \pm Z \sqrt{\frac{(y/n)(1-y/n)}{n}}$$

REMEMBER

To compute p, all you need to know is y (the number of items identified out of your sample), n (the actual number of items in your sample), and Z (the sigma value corresponding to the level of confidence you want your interval to have).

The confidence interval for the difference between two proportions is written as:

$$\frac{y_1}{n_1} - \frac{y_2}{n_2} \pm Z \sqrt{\frac{(y_1/n_1)(1-y_1/n_1)}{n_1} + \frac{(y_2/n_2)(1-y_2/n_2)}{n_2}}$$

In reality, proportions can never be less than zero or greater than one. So, if the calculated confidence interval for your proportion exceeds these natural limits, just adjust the confidence interval to the natural limit.

Q. You do a quick survey of five of your department colleagues as to whether they like the new organization structure that your company has just announced. You find that three out of five of the colleagues think that the new organization structure will work better. Create a $Z = 1.64$ (90 percent) confidence interval for the true proportion of the company's entire workforce population thinking the same way.

A. Recognizing that $y = 3$, $n = 5$, and $Z = 1.64$, you plug these values into the equation:

$$p = \frac{y}{n} \pm Z\sqrt{\frac{(y/n)(1-y/n)}{n}} = \frac{3}{5} \pm 1.64\sqrt{\frac{(3/5)(1-3/5)}{5}} = 0.6 \pm 0.36$$

Q. A survey of a different department at the same company explained in the previous example results in 7 colleagues out of 8 sampled thinking that the new organization structure will be better. With 90 percent confidence ($Z = 1.64$) is there really any difference between the feelings of these two departments?

A. To find out, just plug the values into the confidence interval equation for the difference of two proportions:

$$p_1 - p_2 = \frac{y_1}{n_1} - \frac{y_2}{n_2} \pm Z\sqrt{\frac{(y_1/n_1)(1-y_1/n_1)}{n_1} + \frac{(y_2/n_2)(1-y_2/n_2)}{n_2}} =$$

$$\frac{3}{5} - \frac{7}{8} \pm 1.64\sqrt{\frac{(3/5)(1-3/5)}{5} + \frac{(7/8)(1-7/8)}{8}} = -0.275 \pm 0.407$$

Because this confidence interval spans the value of zero, with 90 percent confidence, you can say that even though the sample proportions look different, no difference exists between the true population proportions.

---

9. You review 17 purchase order forms from the previous year. Out of the 17 forms, 12 have no mistakes. Calculate the 95 percent confidence interval for the true population proportion of correct purchase orders for the previous year.

10. You've just received a shipment of 2,000 shock sensors. Your plan is to place these sensors into some of your own shipments to see whether they're exceeding the 10g shock limit your customers require of you. The shock sensors work like this: Capsules inside the sensors break when they experience any shock above 10g's, which causes a viewing tube to fill with dye. So, you take 12 shock sensors from your shipment and give them a known shock of 15g's. Eleven of the shock sensors properly break, which indicates that the 10g shock level was exceeded. Calculate the 95 percent confidence interval for the proportion of the entire shipment that will work properly.

11. Your marketing team has conducted two focus group sessions to evaluate a new product design. The first focus group consisted of teenagers and resulted in four out of five of the teens liking the new product. The second group was made up of parents of young children. Only one out of five people in this group said they liked the same new product as the teens. With 90 percent confidence ($Z = 1.64$), can you say that there is a difference between the views of these two populations?

12. Four out of five and 40 out of 50 are the same proportion. So why should you treat these proportions differently?

Solutions to Narrowing Inputs Problems

1 You have received material samples from four different suppliers — A, B, C, and D. The compiled data on the density of each supplier's samples is summarized below:

Supplier	Sample Size (n)	Sample Mean ($\bar{x}$)	Sample Std. Dev. (s)
A	60	10.7	0.950
B	10	12.0	0.048
C	25	9.8	0.220
D	34	10.0	0.300

Calculate the 99.7 percent confidence interval for each population mean and identify any differences in average density between the suppliers.

Start with Supplier A. Its sample has 60 data points, so it's large enough that you can use the Z formula for the confidence interval for the mean. All the values needed for the calculation are given in the problem statement. Plug the numbers into the formula like this:

$$\mu_A = \bar{x}_A \pm Z \frac{s_A}{\sqrt{n_A}} = 10.7 \pm 3 \frac{0.501}{\sqrt{60}} = 10.7 \pm 0.37 = [10.33, 11.07]$$

Suppliers B and C both have too few samples to use the Z formula. Instead you have to use the t formula. With a 99.7 percent confidence level, you have to look up the t value for a sample size of 10 for Supplier B and a sample size of 25 for Supplier C. Here are the calculations:

$$\mu_B = \bar{x}_B \pm t_{0.997, n=10} \frac{s_B}{\sqrt{n_B}} = 12.0 \pm 4.094 \frac{0.048}{\sqrt{10}} = 12.0 \pm 0.06 = [11.94, 12.06]$$

$$\mu_C = \bar{x}_C \pm t_{0.997, n=25} \frac{s_C}{\sqrt{n_C}} = 9.8 \pm 3.345 \frac{0.22}{\sqrt{25}} = 9.8 \pm 0.15 = [9.65, 9.95]$$

Supplier D has enough points in its sample to use the Z formula. Here are the calculations:

$$\mu_D = \bar{x}_D \pm Z \frac{s_D}{\sqrt{n_D}} = 10.0 \pm 3 \frac{0.300}{\sqrt{34}} = 10.0 \pm 0.15 = [9.85, 10.15]$$

Compare these confidence intervals graphically by lining up each of the confidence intervals on a chart, as in the following figure:

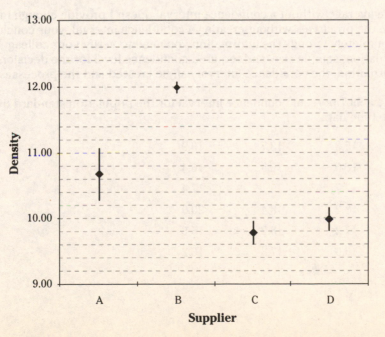

Whenever confidence intervals overlap, you can say that no significant difference exists between the populations. Suppliers C and D, for example, overlap, meaning they're the same. Suppliers A and B, on the other hand, have obvious gaps between them. So, they're different from each other and from Suppliers C and D.

2 You've developed two alternative curing processes for an adhesive. Now you need to determine which one results in a higher shear strength for the adhesive. Knowing that you'll conduct 25 tests using each process and estimating that the standard deviation of both processes will be 1.2 pounds, how large must the difference be between the sample means of each of the 25 tests before you declare with 95 percent confidence that one process is better than the other?

The average performance of the adhesives will be statistically different if their confidence intervals don't overlap. With the same standard deviation, the same number of samples, and the same t value, the minimum difference between the means would have to be as follows:

$$2t_{0.997,\, n=25} \frac{s}{\sqrt{n}} = 2 \cdot 2.110 \frac{1.2}{\sqrt{25}} = 1.013$$

If the sample averages of the adhesives are different by 1.013 or more, the gap between the confidence intervals will verify that the populations are truly different.

3 Calculate the 99.7 percent confidence interval for the population mean from the following sample data set:

4.76	3.73	6.99	4.68
5.98			

With a small sample size of only five data points, simply follow the t formula for calculating the confidence interval for the population mean. First calculate the sample mean and standard deviation, and then plug them into the formula like this:

$$\mu = \overline{x} \pm t_{0.997,\, n=5} \frac{s}{\sqrt{n}} = 5.23 \pm 6.620 \frac{1.271}{\sqrt{5}} = 5.23 \pm 3.76 = [1.46, 8.99]$$

4 You receive an e-mail from a colleague stating that Process A is better than Process B because the average cycle time of Process A is better than the average cycle time of Process B. What other information do you need to know to verify your colleague's claim?

A sample average without a confidence interval doesn't provide enough information. When you compare the processes without creating a confidence interval, your conclusions may end up being completely wrong. The information you need to verify your colleague's claim is the standard deviation, sample size, and required confidence level for the decision being made. With this information, the confidence interval can be created and the processes validly compared.

5 Calculate a 99.7 percent confidence interval for the population standard deviation of the following cycle time data:

20.2	15.3	13.7	16.9
18.1	18.0	16.5	16.4
17.0	17.7	15.1	17.4
18.3	18.2	18.4	20.9
14.8	17.2	18.2	15.6
14.2	16.9	17.3	16.2
21.5			

The χ^2 distribution formula is used to calculate the confidence interval around the standard deviation. Just plug the values into the formula like this:

$$\sigma = \left[\sqrt{\frac{(n-1)\,s^2}{\chi^2_{LOWER}}},\ \sqrt{\frac{(n-1)\,s^2}{\chi^2_{UPPER}}}\right] = \left[\sqrt{\frac{(25-1)\cdot 1.912^2}{50.163}},\ \sqrt{\frac{(25-1)\cdot 1.912^2}{8.382}}\right] = [1.323, 3.236]$$

With this confidence interval, you know with 99.7 percent confidence that the true population standard deviation lies between these values.

6 Calculate the 95 percent confidence interval for the population standard deviation of the following cycle time data:

16.91	16.94	17.12	16.94
16.96	17.13	16.97	16.93
17.00	16.93		

The χ^2 distribution formula is used to calculate the confidence interval around the standard deviation. Just plug the values into the formula as follows:

$$\sigma = \left[\sqrt{\frac{(n-1)\,s^2}{\chi^2_{LOWER}}},\ \sqrt{\frac{(n-1)\,s^2}{\chi^2_{UPPER}}}\right] = \left[\sqrt{\frac{(10-1)\cdot 0.080^2}{19.301}},\ \sqrt{\frac{(10-1)\cdot 0.080^2}{2.628}}\right] = [0.054, 0.147]$$

With this confidence interval, you know with 95 percent confidence that the true population standard deviation lies between these values.

7 Create a 95 percent confidence interval for the ratio of the variance from Problem 5 to the variance from Problem 6.

A confidence interval for the ratio of variances is based on the F distribution. You need to know the variances for each of the two samples and you need to know the correct F value based on the sizes of the two samples.

For this problem, the sample size from Problem 5 is $n_1 = 25$ and the sample size from Problem 6 is $n_2 = 10$. Using the previously calculated values for the sample standard deviations from Problems 5 and 6, you can plug these values into the F value equation like this:

$$\frac{\sigma_1^2}{\sigma_2^2} = \left[\frac{1}{F(c=n_2),r=n_1}\frac{s_1^2}{s_2^2},\ F(c=n_1,r=n_2)\frac{s_1^2}{s_2^2}\right] = \left[\frac{1}{2.300}\frac{1.912^2}{0.080^2},\ 2.900\frac{1.912^2}{0.080^2}\right] = [250.6,\ 1{,}671.7]$$

8 At a 95 percent confidence level, is there a difference in the population variances of the data in Problems 5 and 6?

The ratio of these two variances and the surrounding confidence interval show that the width of the variation from Problem 5 is much larger than the width of the variation in Problem 6.

If the two variations were the same, the confidence interval of their ratio would have included the value of 1.

9 You review 17 purchase order forms from the previous year. Out of the 17 forms, 12 have no mistakes. Calculate the 95 percent confidence interval for the true population proportion of correct purchase orders for the previous year.

To create this confidence interval for the true population proportion, you just need to plug the values into the formula. Remember that a confidence level of 95 percent corresponds to a Z value of 2. Here are the calculations:

$$p = \frac{y}{n} \pm Z\sqrt{\frac{(y/n)(1-y/n)}{n}} = \frac{12}{17} \pm 2\sqrt{\frac{(12/17)(1-12/17)}{17}} = 0.71 \pm 0.22 = [0.48, 0.93]$$

10 You've just received a shipment of 2,000 shock sensors. Your plan is to place these sensors into some of your own shipments to see whether they're exceeding the 10g shock limit your customers require of you. The shock sensors work like this: Capsules inside the sensors break when they experience any shock above 10g's, which causes a viewing tube to fill with dye. So, you take 12 shock sensors from your shipment and give them a known shock of 15g's. Eleven of the shock sensors properly break, which indicates that the 10g shock level was exceeded. Calculate the 95 percent confidence interval for the proportion of the entire shipment that will work properly.

In this exercise, the total number inspected (n) is equal to 12 and the number of successes (y) is equal to 11. So, the 95 percent ($Z = 2$) confidence interval for the true proportion is as follows:

$$p = \frac{y}{n} \pm Z \sqrt{\frac{(y/n)(1 - y/n)}{n}} = \frac{11}{12} \pm 2 \sqrt{\frac{(11/12)(1 - 11/12)}{12}} = 0.92 \pm 0.16 = [0.76, 1.00]$$

Notice that on the high end of the confidence interval, the value is capped at the theoretical limit for proportions at 1.00.

11 Your marketing team has conducted two focus group sessions to evaluate a new product design. The first focus group consisted of teenagers and resulted in four out of five of the teens liking the new product. The second group was made up of parents of young children. Only one out of five people in this group said that they liked the same new product as the teens. With 90 percent confidence ($Z = 1.64$), can you say that there is a difference between the views of these two populations?

This exercise requires you to use the formula for calculating the confidence interval around the difference of two proportions. It's just a matter of plugging in the right values for the first and second proportions. Here's the formula:

$$p_1 - p_2 = \frac{y_1}{n_1} - \frac{y_2}{n_2} \pm Z \sqrt{\frac{(y_1/n_1)(1 - y_1/n_1)}{n_1} + \frac{(y_2/n_2)(1 - y_2/n_2)}{n_2}} =$$

$$\frac{4}{5} - \frac{1}{5} \pm 1.64 \sqrt{\frac{(4/5)(1 - 4/5)}{5} + \frac{(1/5)(1 - 1/5)}{5}} = 0.60 \pm 0.41 = [0.19, 1.00]$$

Because the calculated confidence interval for the difference is positive, you know that there is, in fact, a difference between the teenager and the young parent populations. (Not that you needed a statistical study to tell you something that obvious!)

12 Four out of five and 40 out of 50 are the same proportion. So why should you treat these proportions differently?

The answer to this problem is all in the size of the samples. Four out of five produces a much less confident measure of the true proportion than 40 out of 50 does.

Part V
Improving and Controlling

In this part . . .

The final stages of DMAIC are Improve and Control. Skills for synthesizing improvements can be mastered by anyone through the exercises and worksheets provided in this part. And, finally, you learn Control — you become proficient in the skills of maintaining and sustaining the improvements you've implemented.

Chapter 13

Quantifying Variable Relationships

● ●

In This Chapter

▶ Calculating how much correlation there is between variables

▶ Determining equations with curve fitting

▶ Making sure fitted lines are valid

● ●

After you've defined your most important process or product outputs (*Y*s) and those process or product inputs most likely to affect them (*X*s), you need to understand and quantify the relationship between them. The first step is to identify which *X*s are correlated to *Y*. You can get hints about correlations by looking at scatter plots, discussed in Chapter 8. But to be sure, you need to quantify the correlation and test for statistical significance. You can also develop an actual line equation mathematically relating *X* to *Y*. This chapter covers these topics.

Quantifying Correlation between Variables

Correlation is a frequent and popular subject of the news: "High income linked to schooling outcomes," "Low-fat diets correlated with reduced heart disease," and "Sodas contribute to obesity." Almost every day a headline reports on a new study linking two variables together in a cause-effect relationship.

Correlation is all about quantifying the strength of the relationship between two variables. You want to know whether it's a loose relationship or whether it's so strong that by knowing one variable, you can predict the other confidently.

To quantify the linear relationship between two variables (*x* and *y*), you use the following formula to calculate their *correlation coefficient* (*r*). The equation may seem complicated, but it's actually quite simple when you break it down:

$$r = \frac{1}{n-1} \sum_{i=1}^{n} \left(\frac{x_i - \overline{x}}{\sigma_x} \right) \left(\frac{y_i - \overline{y}}{\sigma_y} \right)$$

where *n* is the number of data pair measurements,

x_i and y_i are the individual *x*-variable and *y*-variable measurements, taken at the same time or within the same subject to create a data pair,

$\overline{x}$ and $\overline{y}$ are the averages of the *x*- and *y*-variable measurements, respectively,

σ_x and σ_y are the standard deviations of the *x*- and *y*-variable measurements, respectively, and

Σ is the Greek letter telling you to sum up all the $\left(\frac{x_i - \overline{x}}{\sigma_x} \right) \left(\frac{y_i - \overline{y}}{\sigma_y} \right)$ terms from 1 to *n*.

The calculated correlation coefficient value has some interesting properties:

- The calculated r will always be between –1 and 1.

- The sign of r tells you the direction of the relationship between the variables.

    If r is positive, then when one variable increases in value, the other variable will also increase. The opposite is also true: If one variable decreases, the other variable will also decrease. This is called a *positive correlation*.

    If r is negative, then when one variable increases in value, the other variable will decrease, and vice versa. This is called a *negative correlation*.

- The absolute value of r tells you how strong the relationship between the variables is.

    The closer r gets to its theoretical limits of –1 or 1, the stronger the correlation is. An r equal to –1 or 1 indicates a *perfect linear relationship,* with all the *x-y* points lying exactly on a straight line.

    An r close to 0 indicates an absence of a linear fit, or correlation to the data.

Q. An HR manager has just finished a Six Sigma training course. She's been working on understanding the perception among new hires that the hiring process the company uses "stinks." Over the last year, the HR manager has had all new hires complete a survey rating their hiring experience. A score of 20 on the survey means that a new hire thought the hiring experience was wonderful, whereas a survey score of 0 means that the new hire thought the process was awful. On a hunch, the HR manager has created data points for each employee hired over the last year, combining how many days it took the person to be hired with the person's new-hire survey score. The tabulated and plotted forms of the following data pairs are shown in the accompanying figure:

Number of days to hire	Hiring process satisfaction
38	9
32	15
41	13
48	12
47	7
50	4
27	15
39	9
47	7
33	16
36	7
30	11

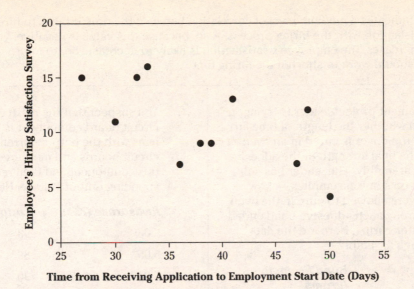

Do you find a correlation between the number of days from when the employees submitted their applications to the start date of their employment and their perceived satisfaction with the hiring process?

A. Calculating the correlation coefficient (r) between the two variables will quantify the strength of their relationship. See Table 13-1.

Table 13-1   **Table Used to Calculate the Correlation Coefficient for the Example Problem**

x_i	y_i	$\dfrac{x_i - \bar{x}}{\sigma_x}$	$\dfrac{y_i - \bar{y}}{\sigma_y}$	$\left(\dfrac{x_i - \bar{x}}{\sigma_x}\right)\left(\dfrac{y_i - \bar{y}}{\sigma_y}\right)$
38	9	−0.13	−0.37	0.05
32	15	−0.91	1.19	−1.08
41	13	0.26	0.67	0.17
48	12	1.17	0.41	0.48
47	7	1.04	−0.89	−0.92
50	4	1.43	−1.67	−2.38
27	15	−1.56	1.19	−1.85
39	9	0.00	−0.37	0.00
47	7	1.04	−0.89	−0.92
33	16	−0.78	1.45	−1.13
36	7	−0.39	−0.89	0.35
30	11	−1.17	0.15	−0.18
Averages ($\bar{x}, \bar{y}$) 39.00	10.42		$\displaystyle\sum_{i=1}^{12}\left(\dfrac{x_2 - \bar{x}}{\sigma_x}\right)\left(\dfrac{y_i - \bar{y}}{\sigma_y}\right)$	−7.41
Standard Deviations (σ_x, σ_y) 7.71	3.85		$r = \dfrac{1}{n-1}\displaystyle\sum_{i=1}^{12}\left(\dfrac{x_i - \bar{x}}{\sigma_x}\right)\left(\dfrac{y_i - \bar{y}}{\sigma_y}\right)$	−0.67

An *r* of –0.67 indicates a medium level of correlation between the time it takes to hire the employees and their satisfaction with the hiring process. Also, because this value is negative, you know that if the hiring time increases, the employee's satisfaction is likely to decrease. So, to improve satisfaction, the HR manager should work to shorten the hiring time.

1. An improvement project leader is trying to understand whether the length of time an assembled top cover is cured in an oven relates to the final strength of the adhesive bond of its assembly. The leader has collected data on some assemblies — how long they were allowed to cure in the oven and how strong each adhesive bond ended up being after curing. Here are the data pairs for each assembly:

Cure Time (minutes)	Bond Strength (grams)
24	150
23	140
21	150
17	109
26	143
22	146
22	124
22	141
20	127
22	122
15	88
21	128
17	100
10	82
20	127

Quantify the correlation and describe the relationship between these two variables. Get your scrap paper ready!

Solve It

2. You suspect that the resistance of a certain circuit board component is leading to problems with the output current. You grab 10 circuit boards and measure the resistance of this component and then record their corresponding output voltage. Here is your data:

Resistance (KΩ)	Output Current (A)
5.06	93
5.05	89
5.01	90
5.11	96
5.22	90
5.09	96
5.17	90
5.03	94
5.18	94
4.99	91

Is the resistance of the component correlated with the output current of the circuit?

 Solve It

3. A production manager believes that the quality of machined parts, defined by the number of defects found out of 100 parts inspected, is related to the hours of training the machine operator has had. Here are data pairs for 18 machine operators:

Training (Hours)	Defects (Per 100)
8.1	5
8.4	3
7.6	3
8.2	7
8.6	9
8.9	6
9.6	3
7.5	6
8.3	7
7.7	7
9.5	1
9.7	1
7.9	7
7.9	5
8.3	7
9.7	5
9.9	7
8.5	11

Calculate the correlation between these two variables and describe their relationship.

4. A news story reports that reading comprehension has been found to be correlated to a person's height. What's your response to this reported cause-effect relationship?

Fitting Lines to Variable Relationships

Curve fitting goes a step beyond correlation. In curve fitting, you actually determine the equation for the curve that best fits your *x-y* data. Armed with this information, you can quantitatively predict what effect one variable will have on another.

The most basic curve to fit to your data is a straight line. The equation for a line fitting your data can be written as $\hat{y} = \beta_0 + \beta_1 x + \varepsilon$ where β_0 defines the intercept where the line crosses the *y* axis and β_1 defines the slope of the line. ε represents all the variation that isn't due to the linear relationship (meaning what the fitted line doesn't capture — flip to the next section for more about ε). You calculate β_0 and β_1 from these equations:

$$\beta_1 = \frac{\sum_{i=1}^{n}(x_i - \bar{x}) y_i}{\sum_{i=1}^{n}(x_i - \bar{x})^2}$$

$$\beta_0 = \bar{y} - \beta_1 \bar{x}$$

where x_i and y_i are the paired data points and $\bar{x}$ and $\bar{y}$ are the calculated averages for all the *x* data points and all the *y* data points, respectively.

Q. The HR manager from the example problem in the previous section now wants to fit a line to the hiring time – satisfaction data. Find the equation for this line.

A. A calculation table, like Table 13-2, helps in computing the values for β_0 and β_1.

Table 13-2		Table Used To Calculate β_0 and β_1 For Example Problem			
	x_i	y_i	$x_i - \bar{x}$	$(x_i - \bar{x})y_i$	$(x_i - \bar{x})^2$
	38	9	−1	−9	1
	32	15	−7	−105	49
	41	13	2	26	4
	48	12	9	108	81
	47	7	8	56	64
	50	4	11	44	121
	27	15	−12	−180	144
	39	9	0	0	0
	47	7	8	56	64
	33	16	−6	−96	36
	36	7	−3	−21	9
	30	11	−9	−99	81
Averages $(\bar{x}, \bar{y})$	39.00	10.42	Σ	−220	654
				β_1	−0.34
				β_0	23.54

You start the calculation table by computing the mean or average for both the x and y data. After the mean and average are calculated, they feed into the calculation of the other columns. At the end, you sum up the $(x_i - \overline{x})y_i$ and $(x - \overline{x})^2$ columns. As a final step, you divide the sum of the $(x_i - \overline{x})y_i$ column by the sum of the $(x - \overline{x})^2$ column. This calculation gives you the β_1 term. Knowing β_1, you use the formula $\beta_0 = \overline{y} - \beta_1\overline{x}$ to solve for β_0.

By plugging in the values you calculated, you find that the equation for the best-fit line through the data is: $y = 23.54 - 0.34x$.

You can plot this line through the set of points to see how it fits, as in the following figure. As you can see by the figure, the line does in fact fit.

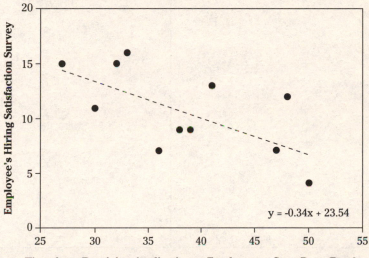

y = -0.34x + 23.54

Time from Receiving Application to Employment Start Date (Days)

5. Calculate the equation for a line fitting the cure time – bond strength data in Problem 1. Plot the line on a graph along with the original data. Make sure you have extra paper on hand!

Solve It

6. Using the line equation you created in Problem 5, calculate the expected bond strength for an assembly that had a cure time of 17 minutes.

Solve It

7. Calculate the equation for the line fitting the training hours – part quality data in Problem 3. Plot the line on a graph along with the original data. Keep that scrap paper handy!

8. Using the line equation you created in Problem 7, calculate the expected defects per 100 parts for an operator with 9 hours of training.

Assessing the Adequacy of a Fitted Line

Fitting a line to your data isn't always statistically valid. Sometimes no significant relationship exists, and sometimes a line isn't the right type of curve to fit your data. So each time you fit a line to your data, you need to check to make sure that the result is statistically valid.

You need to remember several things about checking the adequacy of your fitted line model:

✔ *Residuals* are the errors between your actual data and the prediction of your fitted line model. Each point in your data set has a residual (e_i), which can be written mathematically as:

$$e_i = y_i - \hat{y}_i$$

where y_i are the actual, observed data values and $\hat{y}_i$ are the predicted values from your fitted line equation.

To determine whether your fitted line equation is statistically valid, you need to plot the residuals in several different ways to make sure they appear normally distributed, which is the criteria for your line equation to be statistically valid. Using your residuals, create the following plots:

- A scatter plot of the residuals (e_i) versus the predicted values ($\hat{y}_i$) from your line equation

- A scatter plot of the residuals (e_i) versus the observed x_i data

- If you collected your observed x_i, y_i data sequentially over time, a run order chart of each of the residuals (e_i) versus their preceding residuals (e_{i-1})

- Additional scatter plots of the residuals (e_i) versus other x variables that you didn't include in your equation

✔ Calculate the *coefficient of determination* (R^2) for your fitted line using this formula:

$$R^2 = \frac{\sum_{i=1}^{n} \left(\hat{y}_i - \bar{y} \right)^2}{\sum_{i=1}^{n} \left(y_i - \bar{y} \right)^2}$$

R^2 should generally be greater than 0.8 for a strong linear fit. Lesser values of R^2 should be used with caution for predictions.

✔ Calculate the F statistic with the following equation to test the statistical significance of the fitted line:

$$\frac{\sum_{i=1}^{n} \left(\hat{y}_i - \bar{y} \right)^2}{\frac{1}{n-2} \left[\sum_{i=1}^{n} \left(y_i - \bar{y} \right)^2 - \sum_{i=1}^{n} \left(\hat{y}_i - \bar{y} \right)^2 \right]} \geq F\left(1, n-2 \right)$$

If the left side of this equation is greater than the right side F statistic from the look-up table in Chapter 12 (Table 12-3), you can say that the line you fitted to your data is statistically significant with 95 percent confidence.

✔ ε represents a random, normal distribution centered at a value of zero. This value is an inherent part of your predictive linear equation. An estimate of the standard deviation of the ε distribution can be calculated using the following equation:

$$\hat{\sigma}_\varepsilon = \sqrt{\frac{1}{n-2} \left[\sum_{i=1}^{n} \left(y_i - \bar{y} \right)^2 - \sum_{i=1}^{n} \left(\hat{y}_i - \bar{y} \right)^2 \right]}$$

The estimate of the standard deviation of the ε distribution comes in handy when you want to mimic what might happen in reality. You use your derived linear model to predict the average or expected performance of the output $\hat{y}$ and then add to it a random number generated from the ε distribution — with a mean of zero and standard deviation equal to $\hat{\sigma}_\varepsilon$. In this way, you can simulate what would happen if your process or characteristic were repeated over and over again.

Q. The HR manager from the previous examples in this chapter wants to determine whether the line equation she has fitted to her hiring time – satisfaction data is statistically valid. Perform all the checks to make sure her fitted line is valid.

A. In setting up to check the validity of a fitted line, use a table to lay out all of the values and calculations. See Table 13-3, which was created for this hiring example.

Table 13-3	Table for Calculating Standard Deviation of the Unexplained Variation in Your Line Model				
x_i	y_i	$\hat{y}_i$	e_i	$(\hat{y}_i - \bar{y})^2$	$(y_i - \bar{y})^2$
38	9	10.75	−1.75	0.11	2.01
32	15	12.77	2.23	5.54	21.01
41	13	9.74	3.26	0.45	6.67
48	12	7.39	4.61	9.17	2.51
47	7	7.73	−0.73	7.24	11.67

(continued)

Table 13-3 (continued)

	x_i	y_i	$\hat{y}_i$	e_i	$(\hat{y}_i - \bar{y})^2$	$(y_i - \bar{y})^2$
	50	4	6.72	−2.72	13.69	41.17
	27	15	14.45	0.55	16.29	21.01
	39	9	10.42	−1.42	0.00	2.01
	47	7	7.73	−0.73	7.24	11.67
	33	16	12.44	3.56	4.07	31.17
	36	7	11.43	−4.43	1.02	11.67
	30	11	13.44	−2.44	9,17	0.34
Averages $(\bar{x}, \bar{y})$	39.00	10.42		Σ	74.01	162.92

The $\hat{y}_i$ values used in the above calculation table are found by plugging the x_i values into the fitted line equation.

Now plot the residuals (e_i) versus the predicted fit values ($\hat{y}_i$). In this plot, you're checking to make sure the residuals look normally distributed around a center of zero. Take a look at the following figure and determine whether the residuals look normally distributed:

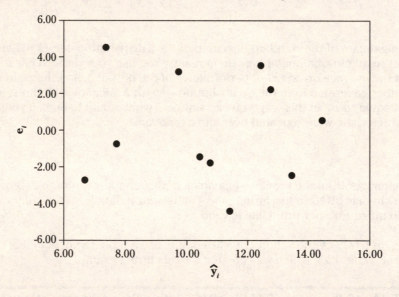

The residuals indeed look normally distributed. There's no clumping or patterns in the plotted data — it all looks randomly scattered. So far, so good. Now check the plot of the residuals versus the x_i data values, as in the following figure:

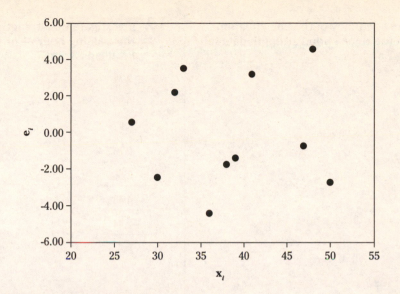

Again, these residuals all look normal and random, with no clumps, trends, or patterns. Because this example includes no other *x* variables, and because the data measurements weren't taken sequentially, you don't need to check any other residual plots.

Next calculate the coefficient of determination R^2 for the fitted line. You calculate R^2 by dividing the sum of the $(\hat{y}_i - \bar{y})^2$ column by the sum of the $(y_i - \bar{y})^2$ column, located at the right side of the calculation table. The result looks like this:

$$R^2 = \frac{\sum_{i=1}^{n}\left(\hat{y}_i - \bar{y}\right)^2}{\sum_{i=1}^{n}\left(y_i - \bar{y}\right)^2} = \frac{74.01}{162.92} = 0.45$$

An R^2 of 0.45 means that only 45 percent of the observed variation of the data is explained by the fitted line. That percentage is not so hot. If you used the equation of the fitted line to predict employee satisfaction with the hiring process, most of the time you wouldn't be very close.

A final test of validity can be done by calculating the *F* statistic with the following formula:

$$\frac{\sum_{i=1}^{n}\left(\hat{y}_i - \bar{y}\right)^2}{\frac{1}{n-2}\left[\sum_{i=1}^{n}\left(y_i - \bar{y}\right)^2 - \sum_{i=1}^{n}\left(\hat{y}_i - \bar{y}\right)^2\right]} = \frac{74.01}{\frac{1}{12-2}[162.92 - 74.01]} = 8.32 \geq 4.96 = F(1,10) = F(1, n-2)$$

The story here is that because your calculated *F* statistic is greater than the look-up test statistic of $F(1,10)$ from Table 12-3 (flip to Chapter 12), a weak linear relationship exists that is statistically valid for your fitted line. However, the line only accounts for 45 percent of the total variation, so there may be errors or other factors that weaken the relationship. This low percentage is a signal to investigate further before making predictions.

A final piece of information you can glean from the fitted line is an estimate of the standard deviation of ε, which is the portion of the line equation that's unaccounted-for variation. You just plug the values from the calculation table into the formula like this:

$$\hat{\sigma}_\varepsilon = \sqrt{\frac{1}{n-2}\left[\sum_{i=1}^{n}\left(y_i - \bar{y}\right)^2 - \sum_{i=1}^{n}\left(\hat{y}_i - \bar{y}\right)^2\right]} = \sqrt{\frac{1}{12-2}[162.92 - 74.01]} = 2.98$$

So, the full equation for the fitted line ends up looking like this:

$$y = 23.54 - 0.34x + N(0, 2.98)$$

Overall, you can say that the HR manager definitely has a statistically significant fitted line for the hiring data. But, she has to consider that fitted line only explains 45 percent of the observed variation. The rest is unaccounted-for random variation with a standard variation of 2.98.

9. Assess the adequacy of the line equation from the cure time – bond strength data in Problems 1 and 5.

10. Investigate the strength of the fitted line for the training hours – product quality data in Problems 3 and 7.

Solve It

Solutions to Quantifying Variable Relationships Problems

1 An improvement project leader is trying to understand whether the length of time an assembled top cover is cured in an oven relates to the final strength of the adhesive bond of its assembly. The leader has collected data on some assemblies — how long they were allowed to cure in the oven and how strong each adhesive bond ended up being after curing. Here are the data pairs for each assembly:

Cure Time (minutes)	Bond Strength (grams)
24	150
23	140
21	150
17	109
26	143
22	146
22	124
22	141
20	127
22	122
15	88
21	128
17	100
10	82
20	127

Quantify the correlation and describe the relationship between these two variables.

To find the correlation coefficient, you create a table that guides you through the calculations. See Table 13-4 to check your own table.

Table 13-4		Table Used for Calculating Correlation Coefficient			
x_i	y_i	$\frac{x_i - \bar{x}}{\sigma_x}$	$\frac{y_i - \bar{y}}{\sigma_y}$		$\left(\frac{x_i - \bar{x}}{\sigma_x}\right)\left(\frac{y_i - \bar{y}}{\sigma_y}\right)$
24	150	0.97	1.14		1.11
23	140	0.72	0.68		0.49
21	150	0.22	1.14		0.25
17	109	−0.79	−0.74		0.58
26	143	1.47	0.82		1.21
22	146	0.47	0.96		0.45
22	124	0.47	−0.05		−0.02

(continued)

Table 13-4 (continued)

	x_i	y_i	$\frac{x_i - \overline{x}}{\sigma_x}$	$\frac{y_i - \overline{y}}{\sigma_y}$	$\left(\frac{x_i - \overline{x}}{\sigma_x}\right)\left(\frac{y_i - \overline{y}}{\sigma_y}\right)$
	22	141	0.47	0.73	0.34
	20	127	−0.03	0.09	0.00
	22	122	0.47	−0.14	−0.07
	15	88	−1.29	−1.71	2.20
	21	128	0.22	0.13	0.03
	17	100	−0.79	−1.16	0.91
	10	82	−2.55	−1.98	5.05
	20	127	−0.03	0.09	0.00
Averages $(\overline{x}, \overline{y})$	20.13	125.13		$\sum_{i=1}^{12}\left(\frac{x_i - \overline{x}}{\sigma_x}\right)\left(\frac{y_i - y}{\sigma_y}\right)$	12.53
Standard Deviations (σ_x, σ_y)	3.98	21.75		$r = \frac{1}{n-1}\sum_{i=1}^{12}\left(\frac{x_i - \overline{x}}{\sigma_x}\right)\left(\frac{y_i - y}{\sigma_y}\right)$	0.90

After going through all of the calculations, you should determine that the correlation coefficient r is 0.90. This value indicates that a strong, positive correlation between the two variables exists. When cure time goes up, bond strength goes up too. When cure time goes down, bond strength also goes down.

2 You suspect that the resistance of a certain circuit board component is leading to problems with the output current. You grab 10 circuit boards and measure the resistance of this component and then record their corresponding output voltage. Here is your data:

Resistance (KΩ)	Ouput Current (A)
5.06	93
5.05	89
5.01	90
5.11	96
5.22	90
5.09	96
5.17	90
5.03	94
5.18	94
4.99	91

Is the resistance of the component correlated with the output current of the circuit?

To calculate r, create a calculation table and compare it to Table 13-5.

Table 13-5		Table Used to Calculate the Correlation Coefficient			
	x_i	y_i	$\dfrac{x_i-\bar{x}}{\sigma_x}$	$\dfrac{y_i-\bar{y}}{\sigma_y}$	$\left(\dfrac{x_i-\bar{x}}{\sigma_x}\right)\left(\dfrac{y_i-\bar{y}}{\sigma_y}\right)$
	5.06	93	−0.40	0.27	−0.11
	5.05	89	−0.53	−1.26	0.66
	5.01	90	−1.04	−0.88	0.91
	5.11	96	0.24	1.41	0.34
	5.22	90	1.66	−0.88	−1.45
	5.09	96	−0.01	1.41	−0.02
	5.17	90	1.02	−0.88	−0.89
	5.03	94	−0.79	0.65	−0.51
	5.18	94	1.15	0.65	0.74
	4.99	91	−1.30	−0.49	0.64
Averages $(\bar{x}, \bar{y})$	5.09	92.30		$\displaystyle\sum_{i=1}^{12}\left(\dfrac{x_i-\bar{x}}{\sigma_x}\right)\left(\dfrac{y_i-y}{\sigma_y}\right)$	0.33
Standard Deviations (σ_x, σ_y)	0.08	2.63		$r=\dfrac{1}{n-1}\displaystyle\sum_{i=1}^{12}\left(\dfrac{x_i-\bar{x}}{\sigma_x}\right)\left(\dfrac{y_i-\bar{y}}{\sigma_y}\right)$	0.04

TIP

As you can see by Table 13-5, the correlation coefficient r for this set of data is 0.04, which isn't a good correlation between the variables.

The next step would be to look for other, stronger correlations, test for statistical significance, or investigate higher-order relationships.

3 A production manager believes that the quality of machined parts, defined by the number of defects found out of 100 parts inspected, is related to the hours of training the machine operator has had. Here are data pairs for 18 machine operators:

Training (Hours)	Defects (Per 100)	Training (Hours)	Defects (Per 100)
8.1	5	7.7	7
8.4	3	9.5	1
7.6	3	9.7	1
8.2	7	7.9	7
8.6	9	7.9	5
8.9	6	8.3	7
9.6	3	9.7	5
7.5	6	9.9	7
8.3	7	8.5	11

Calculate the correlation between these two variables and describe their relationship.

Use a table, like Table 13-6, to calculate all the intermediate steps in the calculation.

Table 13-6			Table for Calculating the Correlation Coefficient		
	x_i	y_i	$\dfrac{x_i - \overline{x}}{\sigma_x}$	$\dfrac{y_i - \overline{y}}{\sigma_y}$	$\left(\dfrac{x_i - \overline{x}}{\sigma_x}\right)\left(\dfrac{y_i - \overline{y}}{\sigma_y}\right)$
	8.1	5	−0.30	−0.29	0.09
	8.4	3	0.17	−1.26	−0.22
	7.6	3	−1.08	−1.26	1.36
	8.2	7	−0.14	0.68	−0.10
	8.6	9	0.48	1.65	0.80
	8.9	6	0.95	0.19	0.18
	9.6	3	2.05	−1.26	−2.58
	7.5	6	−1.23	0.19	−0.24
	8.3	7	0.02	0.68	0.01
	7.7	7	−0.92	0.68	−0.62
	9.5	1	1.89	−2.23	−4.21
	9.7	1	2.20	−2.23	−4.90
	7.9	7	−0.61	0.68	−0.41
	7.9	5	−0.61	−0.29	0.18
	8.3	7	0.02	0.68	0.01
	9.7	5	2.20	−0.29	−0.64
	9.9	7	2.51	0.68	1.70
	8.5	11	0.33	2.61	0.86
Averages $(\overline{x}, \overline{y})$	8.29	5.60	$\displaystyle\sum_{i=1}^{12}\left(\dfrac{x_i - \overline{x}}{\sigma_x}\right)\left(\dfrac{y_i - y}{\sigma_y}\right)$		−1.32
Standard Deviations (σ_x, σ_y)	0.64	2.07	$r = \dfrac{1}{n-1}\displaystyle\sum_{i=1}^{12}\left(\dfrac{x_i - \overline{x}}{\sigma_x}\right)\left(\dfrac{y_i - y}{\sigma_y}\right)$		−0.15

In this example, the correlation coefficient r ends up being −0.15. Here the correlation between the two variables is weak. The correlation is also negative, which means that when the x value increases, the y values decrease, and vice versa.

4 A news story reports that reading comprehension has been found to be correlated to a person's height. What's your response to this reported cause-effect relationship?

In this practice problem, you can see that someone has misunderstood the tool of correlation. Even though a correlation exists numerically between a person's height and his or her reading comprehension, it's probably due to the fact that in general, older, taller individuals naturally have learned to read better than those people who are younger and shorter — height isn't the causing factor, but instead is just an indicating factor.

Correlation doesn't automatically indicate cause.

5 Calculate the equation for a line fitting the cure time – bond strength data in Problem 1. Plot the line on a graph along with the original data.

To help in computing the values for β_0 and β_1 you should have created a calculation table. Compare your table to Table 13-7.

Table 13-7		Table of Intermediate Values Used in Calculating β_0 and β_1		
x_i	y_i	$x_i - \overline{x}$	$(x_i - x)y_i$	$(x_i - \overline{x})^2$
24	150	3.87	580.00	14.95
23	140	2.87	401.33	8.22
21	150	0.87	130.00	0.75
17	109	−3.13	−341.53	9.82
26	143	5.87	838.93	34.42
22	146	1.87	272.53	3.48
22	124	1.87	231.47	3.48
22	141	1.87	263.20	3.48
20	127	−0.13	−16.93	0.02
22	122	1.87	227.73	3.48
15	88	−5.13	−451.73	26.35
21	128	0.87	110.93	0.75
17	100	−3.13	−313.33	9.82
10	82	−10.13	−830.93	102.68
20	127	−0.13	−16.93	0.02
Averages $(\overline{x}, \overline{y})$ 20.13	125.13	Σ	1,084.73	221.73

From the calculation table, you can plug the intermediate sums into the formulas for β_0 and β_1:

$$\beta_1 = \frac{\sum_{i=1}^{n}(x_i - \overline{x})y_i}{\sum_{i=1}^{n}(x_i - \overline{x})^2} = \frac{1084.73}{221.73} = 4.89 \text{ and}$$

$$\beta_0 = \overline{y} - \beta_i \overline{x} = 125.13 - 4.89 \cdot 20.13 = 26.64$$

The equation for the fitted line is:

$$\hat{y} = \beta_0 + \beta_1 x = 26.64 + 4.89x$$

The next step is to plot the original data and add this line to the plot, like in the following figure:

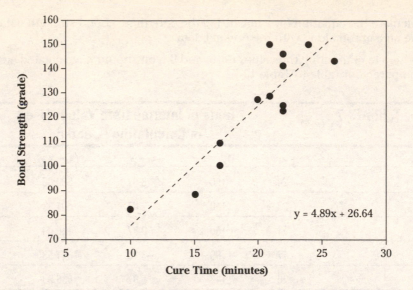

You can see that the calculated line equation does indeed fit the data.

6 Using the line equation you created in Problem 5, calculate the expected bond strength for an assembly that had a cure time of 17 minutes.

To estimate the bond strength for a 17-minute cure time, you simply plug the value of 17 minutes into the derived equation and calculate what the resulting bond strength output is. Here's the calculation:

$$\hat{y} = 26.64 + 4.89x = 26.84 + 4.89 \times 17 = 109.8$$

7 Calculate the equation for the line fitting the training hours – part quality data in Problem 3. Plot the line on a graph along with the original data.

A calculation table helps in computing the values for β_0 and β_1. See Table 13-8 to check your own table.

Table 13-8		Table of Intermediate Values Used in Calculating β_0 and β_1		
x_i	y_i	$x_i - \overline{x}$	$(x_i - \overline{x})y_i$	$(x_i - \overline{x})^2$
8.1	5	−0.47	−2.36	0.22
8.4	3	−0.17	−0.52	0.03
7.6	3	−0.97	−2.92	0.95
8.2	7	−0.37	−2.61	0.14
8.6	9	0.03	0.25	0.00
8.9	6	0.33	1.97	0.11
9.6	3	1.03	3.08	1.06
7.5	6	−1.07	−6.43	1.15
8.3	7	−0.27	−1.91	0.07
7.7	7	−0.87	−6.11	0.76
9.5	1	0.93	0.93	0.86

	x_i	y_i	$x_i - \overline{x}$	$(x_i - \overline{x})y_i$	$(x_i - \overline{x})^2$
	9.7	1	1.13	1.13	1.27
	7.9	7	−0.67	−4.71	0.45
	7.9	5	−0.67	−3.36	0.45
	8.3	7	−0.27	−1.91	0.07
	9.7	5	1.13	5.64	1.27
	9.9	7	1.33	9.29	1.76
	8.5	11	−0.07	−0.79	0.01
Averages $(\overline{x}, \overline{y})$	8.29	5.60	Σ	−11.32	10.64

From the calculation table, you can plug the intermediate sums into the formulas for β_0 and β_1. Here are the calculations:

$$\beta_1 = \frac{\sum_{i=1}^{n}(x_i - \overline{x})y_i}{\sum_{i=1}^{n}(x_i - \overline{x})^2} = \frac{-11.32}{10.64} = -1.06 \text{ and}$$

$$\beta_0 = \overline{y} - \beta_1 \overline{x} = 5.60 + 1.06 \cdot 8.29 = 14.68$$

The equation for the fitted line is:

$$\hat{y} = \beta_0 + \beta_1 x = 14.68 - 1.06x$$

The next step is to plot the original data and add this line to the plot, like in the next figure.

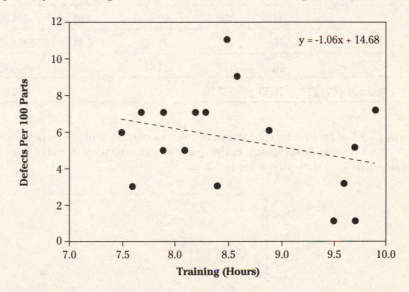

8 Using the line equation you created in Problem 7, calculate the expected defects per 100 parts for an operator with 9 hours of training.

To estimate what the defects per 100 parts will be for an operator with 9 hours of training, you simply plug the input of 9 hours into the equation for the line like this:

$$\hat{y} = 14.68 - 1.06x = 14.68 - 1.06 \times 9 = 5.1$$

9   Assess the adequacy of the line equation from the cure time – bond strength data in Problems 1 and 5.

In setting up to check the validity of a fitted line, it's good to use a table to lay out all the values and calculations. See Table 13-9 to check your own table.

Table 13-9	Table for Calculating Residuals				
x_i	y_i	$\hat{y}_i$	e_i	$(\hat{y}-\bar{y})^2$	$(y_i-\bar{y})^2$
24	150	144.05	5.95	357.81	618.35
23	140	139.16	0.84	196.67	221.02
21	150	129.37	20.63	17.98	618.35
17	109	109.80	−0.80	234.96	260.28
26	143	153.83	−10.83	823.70	319.22
22	146	134.27	11.73	83.39	435.42
22	124	134.27	−10.27	83.39	1.28
22	141	134.27	6.73	83.39	251.75
20	127	124.48	2.52	0.43	3.48
22	122	134.27	−12.27	83.39	9.82
15	88	100.02	−12.02	630.64	1378.88
21	128	129.37	−1.37	17.98	8.22
17	100	109.80	−9.80	234.96	631.68
10	82	75.56	6.44	2457.47	1860.48
20	127	124.48	2.52	0.43	3.48
Averages $(\bar{x}, \bar{y})$ 20.13	125.13		Σ	5306.58	6621.73

Now plot the residuals (e_i) column of the calculation table versus the predicted fit values ($\hat{y}_i$) column (see the next figure). In this plot, you're checking to make sure the residuals look normally distributed around a center of zero.

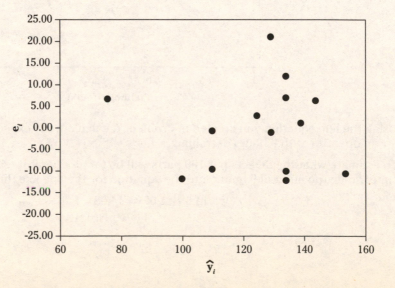

The scattering of the residuals versus the predicted values looks randomly distributed. No problems here. Now plot the residuals (e_i) column of the calculation table versus the observed x values (x_i) (see the next figure).

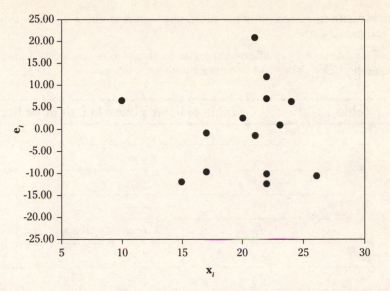

Still, after studying the plot in the figure, everything appears normally and randomly distributed. The residuals don't point to any problems with the fitted line equation.

Now calculate the coefficient of determination (R^2) for the fitted line by dividing the sum of the $(\hat{y}_i - \overline{y})^2$ column by the sum of the $(y_i - \overline{y})^2$ column, which is located at the right side of the calculation table. The calculations look like this:

$$R^2 = \frac{\sum_{i=1}^{n}\left(\hat{y}_i - \overline{y}\right)^2}{\sum_{i=1}^{n}\left(y_i - \overline{y}\right)^2} = \frac{5306.58}{6621.73} = 0.80$$

An R^2 of 0.80 means that 80 percent of the observed variation of the data is explained by the fitted line. That's just enough to have confidence in your predictions from the line. If you use the equation of the fitted line to predict employee satisfaction with the hiring process, you'll be fairly close to the right answer.

A final test of validity can be done by calculating the F statistic. Use the following formula:

$$\frac{\sum_{i=1}^{n}\left(\hat{y}_i - \overline{y}\right)^2}{\frac{1}{n-2}\left[\sum_{i=1}^{n}\left(y_i - \overline{y}\right)^2 - \sum_{i=1}^{n}\left(\hat{y}_i - \overline{y}\right)^2\right]} = \frac{5306.58}{\frac{1}{15-2}\left[6621.73 - 5306.58\right]} =$$

$$52.45 \geq 4.67 = F(1, 13) = F(1, n-2)$$

Your calculated F statistic is greater than the look-up test statistic of $F(1,13)$ from Table 12-3 (see Chapter 12), so your fitted line is also statistically valid.

A final piece of information you can glean from the fitted line is an estimate of the standard deviation of ε, which is the portion of the line equation that's unaccounted-for variation. You just plug the values from the calculation table into the formula like this:

$$\hat{\sigma}_\varepsilon = \sqrt{\frac{1}{n-2}\left[\sum_{i=1}^{n}\left(y_i - \overline{y}\right)^2 - \sum_{i=1}^{n}\left(\hat{y}_i - \overline{y}\right)^2\right]} = \sqrt{\frac{1}{15-2}\left[6621.73 - 5306.58\right]} = 10.06$$

So, the full equation for the fitted line ends up being:

$$y = 26.44 + 4.89x + N(0, 10.06)$$

Overall, you can say that you definitely have a statistically significant fitted line for the cure time – bond strength data, and you know that the fitted line explains 80 percent of the observed variation. The rest is unaccounted-for, random variation with a standard variation of 10.06.

10 Investigate the strength of the fitted line for the training hours – product quality data in Problems 3 and 7.

Use a table to lay out all the values and calculations you need to assess the adequacy of the fitted line. See Table 13-10 to check your own table.

Table 13-10	Table of Values Used to Calculate Residuals				
x_i	y_i	$\hat{y}_i$	e_i	$(\hat{y}_i - \bar{y})^2$	$(y_i - \bar{y})^2$
17	100	109.80	−9.80	234.96	631.68
8.1	5	6.06	−1.06	0.25	0.31
8.4	3	5.74	−2.74	0.03	6.53
7.6	3	6.59	−3.59	1.07	6.53
8.2	7	5.95	1.05	0.16	2.09
8.6	9	5.53	3.47	0.00	11.86
8.9	6	5.21	0.79	0.12	0.20
9.6	3	4.46	−1.46	1.20	6.53
7.5	6	6.70	−0.70	1.30	0.20
8.3	7	5.85	1.15	0.08	2.09
7.7	7	6.48	0.52	0.86	2.09
9.5	1	4.57	−3.57	0.98	20.75
9.7	1	4.36	−3.36	1.44	20.75
7.9	7	6.27	0.73	0.51	2.09
7.9	5	6.27	−1.27	0.51	0.31
8.3	7	5.85	1.15	0.08	2.09
9.7	5	4.36	0.64	1.44	0.31
9.9	7	4.14	2.86	2.00	2.09
8.5	11	5.63	5.37	0.01	29.64
Averages ($\bar{x}$, $\bar{y}$) 8.29	5.60		Σ	12.05	116.44

Now plot the residuals (e_i) column of the calculation table versus the predicted fit values ($\hat{y}_i$) column. In this plot, you're checking to make sure the residuals look normally distributed around a center of zero (see the following figure).

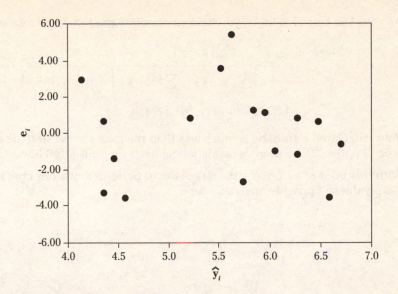

These residuals look normally scattered with no patterns or trends. Now plot the observed x values (x_i) versus the residuals (see the next figure).

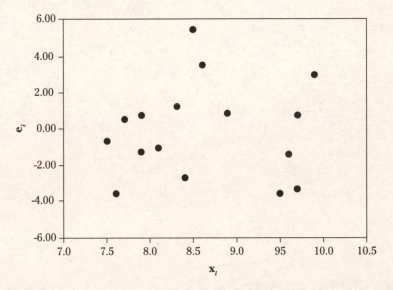

After studying this figure, you can see that no apparent problems exist in this residual plot. Now calculate the coefficient of determination (R^2) for the fitted line by dividing the sum of the column $(\hat{y}_i - \overline{y})^2$ by the sum of the $(y_i - \overline{y})^2$ column, which is located at the right side of the calculation table. The calculations look like this:

$$R^2 = \frac{\sum_{i=1}^{n}\left(\hat{y}_i - \overline{y}\right)^2}{\sum_{i=1}^{n}\left(y_i - \overline{y}\right)^2} = \frac{12.05}{116.44} = 0.10$$

An R^2 of 0.10 means that only 10 percent of the observed variation of the data is explained by the fitted line. Almost all of the variation is unaccounted for by the fitted line. Even though the math works to provide you an equation for a line fitting the data, the fitted line really serves no practical purpose.

As your last test of validity, you have to calculate the F statistic by using the following formula:

$$\frac{\sum_{i=1}^{n}\left(\hat{y}_i - \overline{y}\right)^2}{\frac{1}{n-2}\left[\sum_{i=1}^{n}\left(y_i - \overline{y}\right)^2 - \sum_{i=1}^{n}\left(\hat{y}_i - \overline{y}\right)^2\right]} = \frac{12.05}{\frac{1}{18-2}\left[116.44 - 12.05\right]} =$$

$$1.85 \geq 4.49 = F(1, 16) = F(1, n-2)$$

Your calculated F statistic is much less than the look-up test statistic of $F(1,16)$ from Table 12-3 (see Chapter 12), so there is no statistical basis for your fitted line.

With this poor of a fit, you have no reason to perform any other checks — your fitted line simply doesn't provide any value here.

Chapter 14

Planning and Conducting 2^k Factorial Experiments

. . . .

In This Chapter

▶ Setting up and implementing 2^k factorial experiments

▶ Blocking and randomizing variables

▶ Calculating effects

▶ Eliminating insignificant effects

▶ Forming $Y = f(X)$ equations

. . . .

Chapter 13 shows how Xs are related to the critical Ys. Now you have to determine what causes these effects. The questions you have to ask yourself are, "What can I adjust or change to improve my Ys?" and "What's the ideal adjustment to make?"

The answer to all of these questions is simply: You have to experiment. Experimenting is at the heart of Six Sigma. We're not talking about trial-and-error or knee-jerk experiments — we're talking about thoughtfully planned and designed experiments. *Design of experiments* (DOE) is a topic large enough to fill an entire *For Dummies* book by itself. To give you immediate proficiency, however, this chapter gives you practice in planning, conducting, and analyzing the most common type of experiment used in Six Sigma — the 2^k *factorial*. 2^k factorial experiments can be adapted to provide screening, characterization, or optimization information.

Don't Be a Frankenstein: Planning Experiments

Every experiment in Six Sigma targets a better understanding of the $Y = f(X)$ relationship between the input Xs and the output Ys of the process or system being improved. Better understanding from experimentation includes:

✔ Knowing which input Xs have a significant effect on the output Y and knowing which Xs are insignificant

✔ Formulating and quantifying the mathematical relationship between the significant Xs and the output Y

✔ Discovering where to set the values of the significant Xs so that they combine to produce the optimal output value of Y

Fight the urge to rush into an experiment. You can never spend too much time planning and designing your experiment. In fact, shifting some time up front to the planning and design phase of experimentation almost always saves time later, and it ensures that the resources you expend provide viable information.

When planning your 2^k factorial experiment, take the following items into consideration:

✔ **2^k factorial experiments are best suited to studying two to five input variables.** So, first narrow your investigation down to this smaller subset of likely suspects. Typically, these are factors that have already been found to have a statistically significant impact on the output variable of interest. Your *selected variables,* or factors as they're often called, can be either continuous or attribute variables. (In case you're wondering, the "k" in 2^k represents the number of factors in your experiment.)

✔ **Select exactly two experimental levels for each input variable — one "high" and one "low" — which span the range you want to investigate for each variable.** (The "2" in 2^k represents the number of levels for each factor in your experiment.)

✔ **Your factorial experiment will have 2^k experimental runs.** For example, if you have three factors, you will have $2^3 = 2 \times 2 \times 2 = 8$ experimental runs. Each run represents a unique setting of the factors at their high and low levels.

✔ **Create a coded experiment design matrix that captures each of the 2^k unique experiment settings by creating a column for each of the factors and a row for each of the 2^k runs.** Using –1's as codes for the "low" variable settings and +1's as codes for the "high" settings, start with the left-most factor column. Fill in this column's cells with alternating –1's and +1's. With the left-most column filled in, move on to the next column to the right and repeat the process — but this time fill the column in with alternating *pairs* of –1's and +1's. Fill in the next column to the right with alternating *quadruplets* of –1's and +1's, and so on, repeating this process from left to right until, in the right-most column, you have the first half of the runs marked as –1's and the bottom half as +1's. This table of patterned +1's and –1's is called the *coded design matrix* and represents the experimental settings for each of the 2^k experimental runs.

Q. An engineer at a food processing plant is getting ready to conduct an experiment. With this experiment, she wants to understand how the input variables of the caustic cleaning process reduce the pressure differential across the plant's filter system. The input variables are

• **The temperature of the caustic cleaning solution.** In the past, solution temperatures ranging from 65 to 85 degrees Celsius have been used successfully.

• **The time the caustic cleaning solution is allowed to contact and flow through the filter surfaces.** The duration of the cleaning is sometimes as low as 10 minutes and sometimes as high as 45 minutes.

• **The concentration of the acid in the caustic cleaning solution.** Records show that concentrations of 4 to 8 percent have been used.

Help the engineer select the levels for the experiment factors and create a coded design matrix for a 2^k factorial experiment.

A. Three factors will be included in the engineer's experiment. A good practice is to select the high and low experimental levels for each factor by reviewing what operating ranges have been used in the past. So, going through each factor:

• X_1: **Temperature:** The high level could be set at 85 degrees Celsius and the low level could be set at 65 degrees Celsius.

• X_2: **Time:** The high level could be set at 45 minutes and the low level could be set at 10 minutes.

• X_3: **Concentration:** The high level could be set at 8 percent and the low level could be set at 4 percent.

Now, you have to put these factors and their levels into a coded design matrix. This experiment, which has three factors, will have $2^3 = 8$ unique runs. You lay out the coded design matrix by creating a table with a row for each run (eight in this case) and columns for each of the factors. In the Temperature column you fill in the values for each row with alternating –1's and +1's. In next column to the right, you fill in alternating pairs of –1's and +1's. Finally, in the right-most column, you fill in alternating quadruplets of –1's and +1's. When completed, your table should look like this:

Run	X_1: Temperature	X_2: Time	X_3: Concentration
1	–1	–1	–1
2	+1	–1	–1
3	–1	+1	–1
4	+1	+1	–1
5	–1	–1	+1
6	+1	–1	+1
7	–1	+1	+1
8	+1	+1	+1

This coded design matrix shows you what the factor settings will be for each run in your experiment. For example, run Number 6 will have a temperature at its +1 "high" setting (85 degrees Celsius), time at its –1 "low" setting (10 minutes), and concentration at its +1 "high" setting (8 percent).

1. How many unique runs will a 2^k factorial experiment that investigates four factors have?

Solve It

2. Create a coded design matrix for a 2^2 factorial experiment.

Solve It

3. Create a coded design matrix for a 2^k factorial experiment that's investigating five factors. Make sure you have plenty of scrap paper to use.

4. A project leader wants to set up an experiment to explore two production variables: production line and shift. The company has two duplicate production lines — Line A and Line B. And it has two shifts — day shift and afternoon shift. Create a coded design matrix for this 2^2 factorial experiment.

Solve It

Managing Those Pesky Nuisance Variables

In almost every experiment, you have variables that can affect the Y outputs that aren't explicitly included in your experiment design plan. For example, an experiment studying the effect of depth of cut and cutting speed on a machined surface finish doesn't include the variable of the machinist: Whether the machining operation is performed by Bob or Hank may affect the results of the surface finish. The experiment also doesn't include cutting tool sharpness: Meaning that as the cutting tool dulls during the experiment runs, it may begin to have an impact on your results. In a well-designed experiment, these influential factors are addressed and managed so that the results of the experiment remain valid.

A simple, catchy phrase can help you remember how to manage potential nuisance variables that aren't included in your experiment: *Block what you can and randomize against what you can't block.*

The following descriptions show you how to apply this catch phrase:

- **Blocking:** When you *know* the source of a potential nuisance variable, you can purposely remove its influence completely or include its effect evenly through all of your experimental runs. By blocking, you guarantee that you won't have an unfair bias on only a portion of your experimental settings.

- **Randomizing:** To inoculate your experiment against the detrimental effects of *unknown* nuisance variables, you need to randomize all the variables that aren't directly part of your experiment. You randomize such things as the order of the experimental runs, the materials being used, the operators performing the work, the time of day the experiment runs are made, and so on. Randomizing spreads out the otherwise concentrated or confounding potential for unknown nuisance effects evenly and fairly over all of the experimental runs and preserves the accuracy of your results.

Q. An improvement leader is planning an experiment to explore the effect of temperature and pressure on the quality of molded parts. The leader has determined several variables he knows will have an effect on his results unless he does something about them. These variables include the difference between the mold presses typically used for the process (three different presses are typically used) and the time allowed for the machine to warm up to operating conditions. He also suspects that other variables will influence his experiment, but he isn't sure what those variables might be. Give some suggestions for what the improvement leader might do to manage the effects of these extraneous variables.

A. For the known nuisance variables of mold press and warm-up time, the improvement leader should do something to block their effects. The best way to block the extra variation from the three different mold presses is to conduct the experiment on just one of the presses. By using only one press, the typical variation that's observed from press to press will be eliminated from the experiment.

To block the effect of the warm-up time, the experimental runs could be conducted rapidly, at approximately the same point in the warm-up cycle. Or, if each run requires a lot of time, a different way to block the warm-up time variable would be to conduct one run each day, at precisely the same time in the warm-up cycle.

The most basic thing to do about the lurking, unknown nuisance variables is to randomize the order of the experiment runs so that all of the runs will have an equal likelihood of experiencing the unknown influences.

5. Using the food plant caustic filter cleaning example from the "Don't Be a Frankenstein: Planning Experiments" section earlier in this chapter, determine some of the non-experiment factors that you think may exert unwanted influence on the experiment.

Solve It

6. For each of the non-experiment factors you identify in Problem 5, explain how you might manage its effect on the experiment.

Solve It

7. What should you always do to mitigate the effect of unknown variable influences?

8. An investigator of car quality decides to test four newly manufactured cars. What are some of the blocking and randomizing strategies the investigator could use to make sure his selection of newly manufactured cars is valid?

Calculating Main Effects

Main effects are the quantitative influences each single experiment factor (X) has individually on the output response (Y). Each factor in your experiment has a main effect.

To explore and quantify the main effect of each factor in your experiment, follow these steps:

1. **Create a main effects plot for each factor.**

   You create this plot by plotting the line between the point representing the average of the responses with the factor at its high level and the point representing the average of the responses with the factor at its low level.

   The steeper the line, the stronger the effect.

2. **Quantify the main effect for each factor E_i using this formula:**

$$E_i = \frac{1}{2^{k-1}} \sum_{j=1}^{2^k} c_{i,j} y_j$$

EXAMPLE

Q. The engineer from the food plant caustic filter cleaning example described earlier in the chapter ran the experiment and recorded the following results:

Run	Order	X_1: Temperature Coded Value: c_1	X_2: Time Coded Value: c_2	X_3: Concentration Coded Value: c_3	Y: Pressure Differential Reduction (%)
1	3	−1	−1	−1	60.8
2	7	+1	−1	−1	85.0
3	4	−1	+1	−1	68.6
4	2	+1	+1	−1	90.6
5	8	−1	−1	+1	67.8
6	6	+1	−1	+1	78.2
7	1	−1	+1	+1	75.3
8	5	+1	+1	+1	86.6

Plot, quantify, and compare the main effects for each factor.

A. The main effect for the X_1 temperature factor can be seen graphically by plotting the line between the point representing the average of the responses with the factor at its "high" level and the point representing the average of the responses with the factor at its "low" level. The responses for this factor at its "high" level are those runs where the coded value for temperature c_1 is at +1. These runs include 2, 4, 6, and 8. The average response at the "high" level for this factor is calculated like this:

$$\frac{y_2 + y_4 + y_6 + y_8}{4} = \frac{85.0 + 90.6 + 78.2 + 86.6}{4} = \frac{340.4}{4} = 85.1$$

The responses for the X_1 temperature factor at its low level are those runs with the coded value c_1 at a value of −1. These runs include 1, 3, 5, and 7. The average response at the "low" level for this factor is calculated like this:

$$\frac{y_1 + y_3 + y_5 + y_7}{4} = \frac{60.8 + 68.6 + 67.8 + 75.3}{4} = \frac{272.5}{4} = 68.1$$

Plotting these two points and drawing a straight line between them using standard statistical software shows you a graph of the X_1 main effect, like in the following figure.

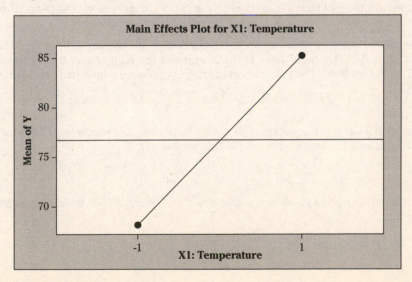

The main effect plot for the X_1 temperature factor shows a positive slope, which means that as the temperature of the caustic cleaning solution is increased, the percent reduction in pressure also increases.

The main effect plot for the X_2 time factor is found in a similar way by plotting the line between the point of the average response from the runs with X_2 at its "high" level and the point of the average response from the runs with X_2 at its "low" level. Referring to the coded design matrix created at the beginning of this example, the runs with X_2 at its "high" level are those where c_2 is equal to +1. These runs include 3, 4, 7, and 8. The calculation for the average response at the "high" level is:

$$\frac{y_3 + y_4 + y_7 + y_8}{4} = \frac{68.6 + 90.6 + 75.3 + 86.6}{4} = \frac{321.1}{4} = 80.3$$

The runs with X_2 at its "low" level are those where c_2 is set at −1. These runs include 1, 2, 5, and 6. The calculation for the average response at the "low" level is:

$$\frac{y_1 + y_2 + y_5 + y_6}{4} = \frac{60.8 + 85.0 + 67.8 + 78.2}{4} = \frac{291.8}{4} = 73.0$$

Plotting these two points and drawing a straight line between them gives you a graph of the X_2 main effect. The graph ends up looking something like the next figure.

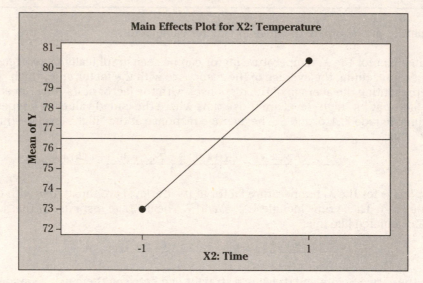

Like with X_1, the main effect plot for the X_2 time factor shows a positive slope, which means that as the exposure time of the caustic cleaning solution is increased, the percent reduction in pressure also increases.

To create the main effect plot for the X_3 concentration factor, you go through the same process. The point with X_3 at its "high" level is the average of the runs where c_3 is set at +1. These runs include 5, 6, 7, and 8. So, the calculation for the average response from these runs is:

$$\frac{y_5 + y_6 + y_7 + y_8}{4} = \frac{67.8 + 78.2 + 75.3 + 86.6}{4} = \frac{307.9}{4} = 77.0$$

The point with X_3 at its "low" level is the average of the runs where c_3 is set at −1. These runs include 1, 2, 3, and 4. The calculation for this average is:

$$\frac{y_1 + y_2 + y_3 + y_4}{4} = \frac{60.8 + 85.0 + 68.6 + 90.6}{4} = \frac{305.0}{4} = 76.3$$

Plotting these two points gives you a graph of the X_3 main effect, which looks like the one in the following figure.

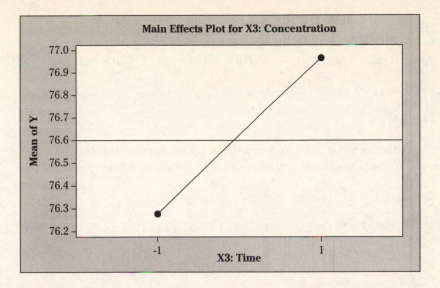

Like with the other two main effects, the main effect for the X_3 concentration factor is also positive, which means that the higher the concentration of the caustic solution, the greater the pressure reduction.

A very important step in reviewing the main effects plots is to place them side by side, all on the same vertical scale, which allows you to compare the relative slopes of the lines visually. Check out the next figure to see what your plots for this example should look like.

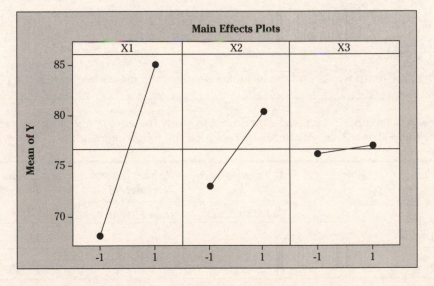

After examining the figure, you can immediately see that X_1 has a much stronger main effect than either X_2 or X_3. In fact, even though you can calculate a number for the X_3 main effect, by comparison to the others it really is nearly flat!

A quantitative value E_i can be calculated for each main effect. This value is simply the difference between the high-setting average and the low-setting average for the factor you're calculating. But, the standard formula using the coded design matrix values produces this exact value in every case. You just plug the c values in from the coded design matrix and plug them into the formula. For the X_1 temperature factor, the quantitative main effect E_1 is calculated like this:

$$E_1 = \frac{1}{2^{k-1}} \sum_{j=1}^{2^k} c_{1,j} y_j = \frac{1}{2^{k-1}} \left[c_{1,1} y_1 + c_{1,2} y_2 + \ldots + c_{1,8} y_8 \right]$$

$$E_1 = \frac{1}{2^{3-1}} \left[(-1)60.8 + (+1)85.0 + (-1)68.6 + (+1)90.6 + (-1)67.8 + (+1)78.2 + (-1)75.3 + (+1)86.6 \right]$$

$$E_1 = \frac{1}{4} \left[-60.8 + 85.0 - 68.6 + 90.6 - 67.8 + 78.2 - 75.3 + 86.6 \right]$$

$$E_1 = \frac{1}{4} \left[67.8 \right] = 16.9$$

The same formula can be used to quantify the main effect for the second and third experiment factors, E_2 and E_3. Here are the calculations for the quantitative main effect E_2.

$$E_2 = \frac{1}{2^{k-1}} \sum_{j=1}^{2^k} c_{2,j} Y_j = \frac{1}{2^{k-1}} \left[c_{2,1} Y_1 + c_{2,2} Y_2 + \ldots + c_{2,8} Y_8 \right]$$

$$E_2 = \frac{1}{2^{3-1}} \left[(-1)60.8 + (-1)85.0 + (+1)68.6 + (+1)90.6 + (-1)67.8 + (-1)78.2 + (+1)75.3 + (+1)86.6 \right]$$

$$E_2 = \frac{1}{4} \left[-60.8 - 85.0 + 68.6 + 90.6 - 67.8 - 78.2 + 75.3 + 86.6 \right]$$

$$E_2 = \frac{1}{4} \left[29.3 \right] = 7.3$$

And, finally, here are the calculations for E_3:

$$E_3 = \frac{1}{2^{k-1}} \sum_{j=1}^{2^k} c_{3,j} y_j = \frac{1}{2^{k-1}} \left[c_{3,1} y_1 + c_{3,2} y_2 + \ldots + c_{3,8} y_8 \right]$$

$$E_3 = \frac{1}{2^{3-1}} \left[(-1)60.8 + (-1)85.0 + (-1)68.6 + (-1)90.6 + (+1)67.8 + (+1)78.2 + (+1)75.3 + (+1)86.6 \right]$$

$$E_3 = \frac{1}{4} \left[-60.8 - 85.0 - 68.6 - 90.6 + 67.8 + 78.2 + 75.3 + 86.6 \right]$$

$$E_3 = \frac{1}{4} \left[2.8 \right] = 0.7$$

Sure enough, the math works and the formula quantifies the main effects from the plots perfectly!

---

9. An engineer has set up a 2^2 factorial experiment to study the effects of heat treatment temperature on the yield strength of a material. He recorded the following results:

Run	Order	X₁: Supplier	X₂: Heat Treatment Temperature	Y: Yield Strength (ksi)
		Coded Value: c_1	Coded Value: c_2	
1	2	−1	−1	27,800
2	4	+1	−1	28,740
3	1	−1	+1	32,150
4	3	+1	+1	31,240

Plot and calculate the main effect for the X_1 supplier factor.

Solve It

10. Using the information from the experiment in Problem 9, plot and calculate the main effect for the X_2 heat treatment temperature factor.

11. Using the information from Problems 9 and 10, create a side-by-side main effects plot for X_1 and X_2 and compare the relative strengths of the two.

Calculating Interaction Effects

Sometimes a variable has an effect on an outcome when it combines and interacts with another variable. For example, think of baking a cake: A delicious-tasting outcome (the Y) is a function of several input Xs, such as "amount of flour," "number of eggs," "oven temperature," "baking time," and so on. Obviously, the right value for the variable of "baking time" depends on the setting for "oven temperature." How hot the oven is and how long you leave the cake in the oven are two input variables that interact with each other.

A properly designed and conducted 2^k factorial experiment allows you to identify and quantify all *interaction effects* among your experimental factors. You'll have a potential interaction effect for each possible factor combination.

To explore and quantify the interaction effect of each factor combination in your experiment, follow these steps:

1. **Create a two-way interaction effect plot for each two-factor combination by creating a plot with the following two lines:**

    • The first line is drawn between the point created by the average response of the runs where the first-listed factor is at its "high" level and the second-listed factor is also at its "high" level and the point created by the average response of the runs where the first-listed factor is still at its "high" level and the second-listed factor is at its "low" level.

    • The second line is drawn between the point created by the average response of the runs where the first-listed factor is at its "low" level and the second-listed factor is at its "high" level and the point created by the average response of the runs where the first-listed factor is at its "low" level and the second-listed factor is also at its "low" level.

The greater the difference in the slope of the two lines, the stronger the interaction effect between the two factors.

2. Quantify the interaction effect for any factor combination $E_{ab...z}$ using the following formula:

$$E_{ab...z} = \frac{1}{2^{k-1}} \sum_{j=1}^{2^k} \left(c_{a,j} \times c_{b,j} \times ... \times c_{z,j} \right) y_j$$

Q. Using the information from the food plant caustic filter cleaning example described earlier in the chapter, plot the two-way interaction effects and quantify and compare all of the interaction effects for each factor.

A. In this 2^3 factorial experiment, you have the following three two-way interaction effects:

- E_{12} is the interaction effect between X_1: Temperature and X_2: Time

- E_{13} is the interaction effect between X_1: Temperature and X_3: Concentration

- E_{23} is the interaction effect between X_2: Time and X_3: Concentration

The interaction effect between X_1: Temperature and X_2: Time can be seen graphically by creating a plot with the following two lines:

- The first line on the plot is drawn between the point created by the average response of the runs where the X_1 temperature factor is at its "high" level and the X_2 time factor is also at its "high" level and the point created by the average response of the runs where the X_1 temperature factor is still at its "high" level and the X_2 time factor is at its "low" level.

- The second line is drawn between the point created by the average response of the runs where the X_1 temperature factor is at its "low" level and the X_2 time factor is at its "high" level and the point created by the average response of the runs where the X_1 temperature factor is at its "low" level and the X_2 time factor is also at its "low" level.

Start by calculating the first point for the first line. Looking back at the coded design matrix, the runs where c_1 is at its coded "high" level of +1 and c_2 is also at its coded "high" level of +1 are 4 and 8. So, the average response of these runs is:

$$\frac{y_4 + y_8}{2} = \frac{90.6 + 86.6}{2} = \frac{177.2}{2} + 88.6$$

The second point for the first line is the average of the runs where the c_1 is still at its "high" level of +1 and c_2 is at its "low" level of –1. After referring to the coded design matrix, you'll see that runs 2 and 6 are at these levels. The average response of these runs is:

$$\frac{y_2 + y_6}{2} = \frac{85.0 + 78.2}{2} = \frac{163.2}{2} = 81.6$$

Now calculate the first point for the second line. The runs where c_1 is at its coded "low" level of –1 and c_2 is at its coded "high" level of +1 are 3 and 7. The average response of these runs is:

$$\frac{y_3 + y_7}{2} = \frac{68.6 + 75.3}{2} = \frac{143.9}{2} = 72.0$$

Next, calculate the second point for the second line. The runs where c_1 is at its coded "low" level of –1 and c_2 is also at its coded "low" level of –1 are 1 and 5. The average response of these runs is:

$$\frac{y_1 + y_5}{2} = \frac{60.8 + 67.8}{2} = \frac{128.6}{2} = 64.3$$

Now plot the two lines formed by these two pairs of calculated points, as shown in the next figure. You have successfully created the two-way interaction effect plot for X_1: Temperature and X_2: Time.

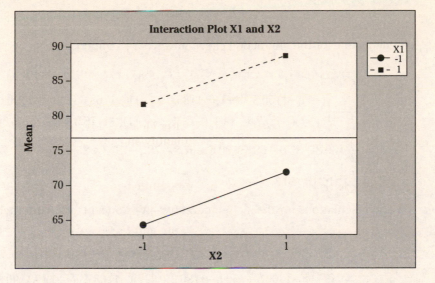

You can see that the slopes of these two lines are graphically identical — the lines are nearly parallel — which means that no interaction exists between the X_1 temperature and X_2 time factors.

Follow the same process to create two-way interaction plots for the X_1: Temperature – X_3: Concentration and the X_2: Time – X_3: Concentration interactions. Lay out all of the two-way interaction plots for review and inspection by plotting them on the same vertical scale and placing them in a matrix pattern, like in the following figure.

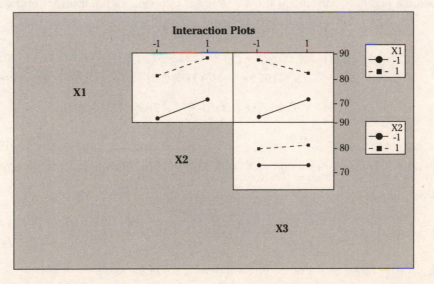

When looking at all of the two-way interactions, you see that only the plot for the X_1: Temperature – X_3: Concentration and the X_2: Time – X_3: Concentration interaction shows lines with significantly different slopes. This indicates an interaction between these two variables.

You quantify the interaction effect values by plugging the coded design matrix values and the experiment run responses into the following formula:

$$E_{ab \cdots z} = \frac{1}{2^{k-1}} \sum_{j=1}^{2^k} \left(c_{a,j} \times c_{b,j} \times \dots \times c_{z,j} \right) y_j$$

So, the quantified value for the interaction effect between X_1: Temperature and X_2: Time is as follows:

$$E_{12} = \frac{1}{2^{k-1}} \sum_{j=1}^{2^k} c_{1,j} c_{2,j} y_j = \frac{1}{2^{k-1}} \left[c_{1,1} c_{2,1} y_1 + c_{1,2} c_{2,2} y_2 + \dots + c_{1,8} c_{2,8} y_8 \right]$$

$$E_{12} = \frac{1}{2^{3-1}} \left[\begin{array}{l} (-1)(-1)\,60.8 + (+1)(-1)\,85.0 + (-1)(+1)\,68.66\,(+1)(+1)\,90.6 + \\ (-1)(-1)\,67.8 + (+1)(-1)\,78.2 + (-1)(+1)\,75.3 + (+1)(+1)\,86.6 \end{array} \right]$$

$$E_{12} = \frac{1}{2^2} \left[60.8 - 85.0 - 68.6 + 90.6 + 67.8 - 78.2 - 75.3 + 86.6 \right]$$

$$E_{12} = \frac{1}{4} \left[-1.3 \right] = -0.3$$

The formula and calculations for the X_1: Temperature – X_3: Concentration interaction E_{13} look like this:

$$E_{13} = \frac{1}{2^{k-1}} \sum_{j=1}^{2^k} c_{1,j} c_{3,j} y_j = \frac{1}{2^{k-1}} \left[c_{1,1} c_{3,1} y_1 + c_{1,2} c_{3,2} y_2 + \dots + c_{1,8} c_{3,8} y_8 \right]$$

$$E_{13} = \frac{1}{2^{3-1}} \left[\begin{array}{l} (-1)(-1)\,60.8 + (+1)(-1)\,85.0 + (-1)(-1)\,68.6 + (+1)(-1)\,90.6 + \\ (-1)(+1)\,67.8 + (+1)(+1)\,78.2 + (-1)(+1)\,75.3 + (+1)(+1)\,86.6 \end{array} \right]$$

$$E_{13} = \frac{1}{2^2} \left[60.8 - 85.0 + 68.6 - 90.6 - 67.8 + 78.2 - 75.3 + 86.6 \right]$$

$$E_{13} = \frac{1}{4} \left[-24.5 \right] = -6.1$$

The formula and calculations for the X_2: Time – X_3: Concentration interaction E_{23} look like this:

$$E_{23} = \frac{1}{2^{k-1}} \sum_{j=1}^{2^k} c_{2,j} c_{3,j} y_j = \frac{1}{2^{k-1}} \left[c_{2,1} c_{3,1} y_1 + c_{2,2} c_{3,2} y_2 + \dots + c_{2,8} c_{3,8} y_8 \right]$$

$$E_{23} = \frac{1}{2^{3-1}} \left[\begin{array}{l} (-1)(-1)\,60.8 + (-1)(-1)\,85.0 + (+1)(-1)\,68.6 + (+1)(-1)\,90.6 + \\ (-1)(+1)\,67.8 + (-1)(+1)\,78.2 + (+1)(+1)\,75.3 + (+1)(+1)\,86.6 \end{array} \right]$$

$$E_{23} = \frac{1}{2^2} \left[60.8 + 85.0 - 68.6 - 90.6 - 67.8 - 78.2 + 75.3 + 86.6 \right]$$

$$E_{23} = \frac{1}{4} \left[2.5 \right] = 0.6$$

For the one three-way interaction of X_1-X_2-X_3, E_{123}, the formula and calculations look like this:

$$E_{123} = \frac{1}{2^{k-1}} \sum_{j=1}^{2^k} c_{1,j} c_{2,j} c_{3,j} y_j = \frac{1}{2^{k-1}} \left[c_{1,1} c_{2,1} c_{3,1} y_1 + c_{1,2} c_{2,2} c_{3,2} y_2 + \dots + c_{1,8} c_{2,8} c_{3,8} y_8 \right]$$

$$E_{123} = \frac{1}{2^{3-1}} \left[\begin{array}{l} (-1)(-1)(-1)\,60.8 + (+1)(-1)(-1)\,85.0 + (-1)(+1)(-1)\,68.6 + (+1)(+1)(-1)\,90.6 + \\ (-1)(-1)(+1)\,67.8 + (+1)(-1)(+1)\,78.2 + (-1)(+1)(+1)\,75.3 + (+1)(+1)(+1)\,86.6 \end{array} \right]$$

$$E_{123} = \frac{1}{2^2} \left[-60.8 + 85.0 + 68.6 - 90.6 + 67.8 - 78.2 - 75.3 + 86.6 \right]$$

$$E_{123} = \frac{1}{4} \left[3.1 \right] = 0.8$$

12. List all of the possible interaction effects for a 2^4 factorial experiment.

Solve It

13. Create a two-way interaction plot for the 2^2 factorial experiment from Problem 9. After you create the plot, calculate the E_{12} value for this interaction effect.

Solve It

14. For the two-way plots in the accompanying figure, which ones display evidence of an interaction effect?

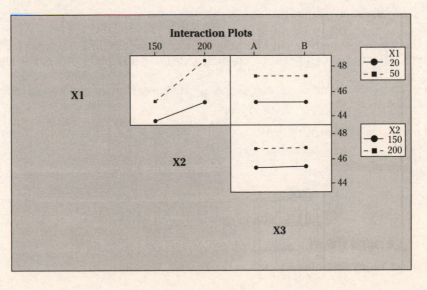

Solve It

Determining Which Effects Are Significant

Unfortunately, just because you can calculate the main effects and the interaction effects for an experiment doesn't mean that all of the values are statistically significant. The Pareto Principle (see Chapter 6) indicates that only a relatively small minority of all the possible effects will explain the majority of the changes in the response. After calculating all the possible main and interaction effects, you have to test them to see which few you should keep and which you should discard.

To find out which calculated effects are significant, you plot the calculated effects against their normal Z scores. If the effects are insignificant, the plotted points will fall into the shape of a line. Any effect in which a corresponding point falls far off the line, however, is significant.

You create the plotted points by following these steps:

1. **Rank order the calculated estimates from lowest to highest.**

2. **Calculate the probability for each of the ranked estimates using this formula:**

$$P_i = \frac{i - 0.5}{2^k - 1}$$

3. **Look up the normal, or Z_i, score corresponding to each calculated P_i.**

   You can look up the Z_i score in the Standard Normal Distribution Table at `www.dummies.com/go/sixsigmaworkbook`.

4. **Plot each calculated effect versus its Z_i.**

5. **Identify the significant effects from those that are far off the line created by the plotted points.**

Q. Using the food plant caustic filter cleaning example from earlier in the chapter, determine which calculated effects are significant by creating a normal probability plot of the effects.

A. The first step is to list all of the calculated effects in rank order and assign them their rank order (i), like this:

Effect	Calculated Value	Rank(i)$_i$
E_{13}	−6.1	1
E_{12}	−0.3	2
E_{23}	0.6	3
E_3	0.7	4
E_{123}	0.8	5
E_2	7.3	6
E_1	16.9	7

The next step is to calculate the probability for each ranked effect using this formula:

$$P_i = \frac{i - 0.5}{2^k - 1}$$

As an example, P_1, for the lowest rank ordered effect, is calculated like this:

$$P_1 = \frac{1 - 0.5}{2^3 - 1} = \frac{0.5}{7} = 0.0714$$

You repeat this calculation for the P_i for each ranked effect. The P_i column on the table of values can now be updated:

Effect	Calculated Value	Rank(i)	P_i
E_{13}	−6.1	1	0.0714
E_{12}	−0.3	2	0.2143
E_{23}	0.6	3	0.3571
E_3	0.7	4	0.5000
E_{123}	0.8	5	0.6429
E_2	7.3	6	0.7857
E_1	16.9	7	0.9286

You can find similar Standard Normal Distribution tables online or in virtually every statistics and Six Sigma book. Maybe that's why they're called "standard" — because they're a standard way for authors to fill up the pages of their statistics books! The final value to find for the ranked effect is its normal score, or the Z value, which you can find in any Standard Normal Distribution table. You can find one at this book's bonus material Web page: www.dummies.com/go/sixsigmaworkbook.

For E_{13}, the calculated P_i is 0.0714. This value is a probability value in the half of the Standard Normal Distribution Table that's not listed. You have to first figure its symmetrical probability. Here are the calculations:

$$1 - 0.0714 - 0.9286$$

After looking up the probability of 0.9286 in a Standard Normal Distribution Table, you find that the Z value corresponding to this probability is 1.46 and 1.47. So, a value of 1.465 is probably close. But, don't forget that because you've used symmetry to look up this Z value, you have to use a negative Z value (−1.465).

By repeating this same look-up process, you can find Z values for each of the rank ordered effects. Your table of values should now look like this:

Effect	Calculated Value	Rank(i)	P_i	Z_i
E_{13}	−6.1	1	0.0714	−1.465
E_{12}	−0.3	2	0.2143	−0.792
E_{23}	0.6	3	0.3571	−0.366
E_3	0.7	4	0.5000	0
E_{123}	0.8	5	0.6429	0.366
E_2	7.3	6	0.7857	0.792
E_1	16.9	7	0.9286	1.657

With these values all calculated, you're ready to draw a normal probability plot to test the significance of the effects. You simply plot the points created by each effect and its corresponding Z value, like in the next figure.

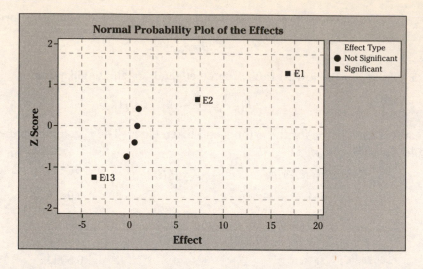

The points created by effects E_1, E_2, and E_{13} are far off the line that was created by the rest of the effects. These off-line points signal that these effects aren't just random chance, but are significant. You now have evidence that allows you to dismiss the other calculated effects.

15. In the normal probability plot for the effects in the accompanying figure, circle which effects appear significant:

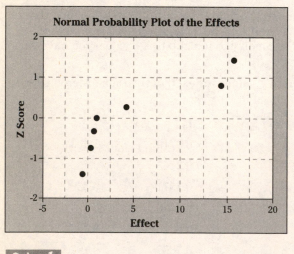

Solve It

16. Plot the normal probabilities for the 2^2 factorial experiment in Problem 9. Indicate which effects are significant.

Solve It

The Ultimate Power Trip: Forming Y = f(X) Equations

2^k factorial experiments not only reveal which factors affect the output Y, but they also allow you to understand the form of the $Y = f(X)$ equation for the system or process you're improving. At the start, a 2^k experiment investigates the possibility of *all* main and interaction effects being significant. Later, you whittle this list down to just the significant effects. What you do next is create a $Y = f(X)$ equation for your system, which allows you to predict future outputs from known inputs.

The equation has a constant term (β_0) and also potential terms for each main and interaction effect (Xs). These terms each have a corresponding coefficient, labeled β.

For a three-factor system, the general form of the equation with all its potential terms looks like this:

$$Y = \beta_0 + \beta_1 X_1 + \beta_2 X_2 + \beta_3 X_3 + \beta_{12} X_1 X_2 + \beta_{13} X_1 X_3 + \beta_{23} X_2 X_3 + \beta_{123} X_1 X_2 X_3$$

For a two-factor system, the general form of the equation with all its potential terms looks like this:

$$Y = \beta_0 + \beta_1 X_1 + \beta_2 X_2 + \beta_{12} X_1 X_2$$

To create the specific equation for your process or system, you start with its general form and then remove all but the constant term β_0 and the terms corresponding to the effects that were found to be significant. You calculate the β coefficients from these equations:

$$\beta_0 = \overline{y}$$

$$\beta_{ab\cdots z} = \frac{1}{2} E_{ab\cdots z}$$

Q. Create the specific $Y = f(X)$ equation for the food plant caustic filter cleaning example in this chapter.

A. The experiment for this example is a 2^3 factorial. So, the general form of the $Y = f(X)$ equation, with all its potential terms will look like this:

$$Y = \beta_0 + \beta_1 X_1 + \beta_2 X_2 + \beta_3 X_3 + \beta_{12} X_1 X_2 + \beta_{13} X_1 X_3 + \beta_{23} X_2 X_3 + \beta_{123} X_1 X_2 X_3$$

However, only the E_1, E_2, and E_{13} effects were found to be significant, which means that you can reduce the form of the equation so that it looks like this:

$$Y = \beta_0 + \beta_1 X_1 + \beta_2 X_2 + \beta_{13} X_1 X_3$$

To find the specific values for the βs in the reduced equation, simply use the formulas:

$$\beta_0 = \overline{y} = \frac{1}{2^k} \sum_{i=1}^{2^k} y_i = \frac{1}{2^3}[60.8 + 85.0 + 68.6 + 90.6 + 67.8 + 78.2 + 75.3 + 86.6] = \frac{1}{8}[612.9] = 76.6$$

$$\beta_1 = \frac{1}{2} E_1 = \frac{1}{2}(16.9) = 8.5$$

$$\beta_2 = \frac{1}{2} E_2 = \frac{1}{2}(7.3) = 3.7$$

$$\beta_{13} = \frac{1}{2} E_{13} = \frac{1}{2}(-6.1) = -3.1$$

Plugging these β values back into the reduced $Y = f(X)$ equation, you get this equation:

$$Y = 76.6 + 8.5X_1 + 3.7X_2 - 3.1X_1X_3$$

17. Write out the general form of the $Y = f(X)$ equation, with all of its potential terms, for a 2^4 factorial experiment.

18. For the experiment in Problem 9, write out the general form of the equation, including all of its potential terms.

Solve It

19. For the experiment in Problem 9, write out the specific form of the equation using only the significant terms.

Solve It

Solutions to 2^k Factorial Experiment Problems

1 How many unique runs will a 2^k factorial experiment that investigates four factors have?

For 2^k factorial experiments, k represents the number of factors. The number of runs is equal to 2^k, or in this case, $2^4 = 16$ runs.

2 Create a coded design matrix for a 2^2 factorial experiment.

For a 2^2 factorial experiment, you'll have two levels for each of the two factors — a "high" level and a "low" level — and you'll have $2^2 = 4$ runs. Each run represents a unique combination of the levels of the two factors. Using the alternating pattern of +1's to represent the "high" factor levels and −1's to represent the "low" factor levels shown in this pattern, you create a list of the four unique experiment runs. This is what your coded design matrix for the experiment should look like:

Run	X_1	X_2
1	−1	−1
2	+1	−1
3	−1	+1
4	+1	+1

3 Create a coded design matrix for a 2^k factorial experiment that's investigating five factors.

A 2^5 factorial experiment will have 32 unique runs. You use the alternating −1, +1 pattern shown in this chapter to create the coded design matrix. It should look like this:

Run	X_1	X_2	X_3	X_4	X_5
1	−1	−1	−1	−1	−1
2	+1	−1	−1	−1	−1
3	−1	+1	−1	−1	−1
4	+1	+1	−1	−1	−1
5	−1	−1	+1	−1	−1
6	+1	−1	+1	−1	−1
7	−1	+1	+1	−1	−1
8	+1	+1	+1	−1	−1
9	−1	−1	−1	+1	−1
10	+1	−1	−1	+1	−1
11	-1	+1	−1	+1	−1
12	+1	+1	−1	+1	−1
13	−1	−1	+1	+1	−1
14	+1	−1	+1	+1	−1
15	−1	+1	+1	+1	−1
16	+1	+1	+1	+1	−1

17	−1	−1	−1	−1	+1
18	+1	−1	−1	−1	+1
19	−1	+1	−1	−1	+1
20	+1	+1	−1	−1	+1
21	−1	−1	+1	−1	+1
22	+1	−1	+1	−1	+1
23	−1	+1	+1	−1	+1
24	+1	+1	+1	−1	+1
25	−1	−1	−1	+1	+1
26	+1	−1	−1	+1	+1
27	−1	+1	−1	+1	+1
28	+1	+1	−1	+1	+1
29	−1	−1	+1	+1	+1
30	+1	−1	+1	+1	+1
31	−1	+1	+1	+1	+1
32	+1	+1	+1	+1	+1

4 A project leader wants to set up an experiment to explore two production variables: production line and shift. The company has two duplicate production lines — Line A and Line B. And it has two shifts — day shift and afternoon shift. Create a coded design matrix for this 2^2 factorial experiment.

With two factors and two levels for each factor, you'll have $2^2 = 4$ experiment runs. For the X_1: production line factor you have two levels: Line A represented by −1 and Line B represented by +1. For the X_2: shift factor you have two levels: day shift represented by −1 and afternoon shift represented by +1. The coded design matrix should look like this:

Run	X_1: Line	X_2: Shift
1	−1	−1
2	+1	−1
3	−1	+1
4	+1	+1

5 Using the food plant caustic filter cleaning example from the "Don't Be a Frankenstein: Planning Experiments" section earlier in this chapter, determine some of the non-experiment factors that you think may exert unwanted influence on the experiment.

The factors included in the experiment are temperature, time, and concentration. Other influencing factors include:

- Flow rate of the caustic solution through the filter
- Pressure differential measurement system being used
- Length of time since the last caustic cleaning of the filters
- Shelf life of caustic chemicals

Your list may include some of the many other variables that influence the system. Remember to consult your list of Xs that have previously been identified as correlated when constructing your experimental definition.

6 For each of the non-experiment factors you identify in Problem 5, explain how you might manage its effect on the experiment.

Below, for each of the identified influencing factors, are suggestions on how you might manage their effect on the experiment.

> ✔ **Flow rate of the caustic solution through the filter:** Block the effect of this variable by setting and controlling the flow rate to a single value for all experiment runs.
>
> ✔ **Pressure differential measurement system being used:** Randomize the order of the experiment runs to spread out possible variation from the pressure differential measurement system.
>
> ✔ **Length of time since the last caustic cleaning of the filters:** Block the effect of this variable by conducting each experiment run after a set length of time since the last cleaning.
>
> ✔ **Shelf life of caustic chemicals:** Randomize which experiment runs get which caustic chemical dates.

7 What should you always do to mitigate the effect of unknown variable influences?

Always randomize the order of the runs of every experiment you perform.

Randomizing each experiment may seem trivial and may seem like a lot of extra work, but in the end it helps your experiment stay free of bias from outside influences. It always pays to randomize.

8 An investigator of car quality decides to test four newly manufactured cars. What are some of the blocking and randomizing strategies the investigator could use to make sure his selection of newly manufactured cars is valid?

Imagine if one of the four selected cars was manufactured on a Monday, but all the others were manufactured on Tuesday, Wednesday, or Thursday. The possible lower quality associated with a Monday-built car (due to the weekend layoff) would have an effect on the new car quality investigations. To correct this, you could block for this factor by selecting study cars all coming from the same day of production.

9 An engineer has set up a 2^2 factorial experiment to study the effects of supplier and heat treatment temperature on the yield strength of a material. See the original question earlier in this chapter for his results. Plot and calculate the main effect for the X_1 supplier factor.

The plot for the main effect for X_1 is found by drawing a line between the average of the runs with X_1 at its "high" (+1) value and the average of the runs with X_1 at its "low" (–1) value. Looking back at the coded design matrix for this example, the average for the "high" runs is:

$$\frac{y_2 + y_4}{2} = \frac{28,740 + 31,240}{2} = \frac{59,580}{2} = 29,990$$

The average for the "low" runs is:

$$\frac{y_1 + y_3}{2} = \frac{27,800 + 32,150}{2} = 29,975$$

Plotting these two points creates the plot for the X_1 main effect (next figure).

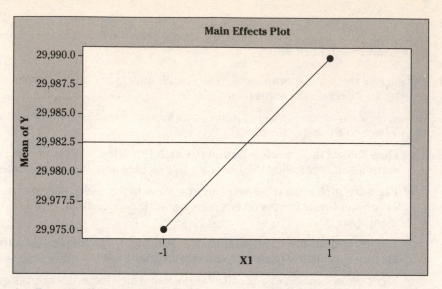

Calculating the E_1 main effect is straightforward. You just look back at the coded design matrix and plug the values into this formula:

$$E_1 = \frac{1}{2^{k-1}} \sum_{j=1}^{2^k} c_{1,j} y_j = \frac{1}{2^{k-1}} \left[c_{1,1} y_1 + c_{1,2} y_2 + c_{1,3} y_3 + c_{1,4} y_4 \right]$$

$$= \frac{1}{2^{2-1}} \left[(-1) 27{,}800 + (+1) 28{,}740 + (-1) 32{,}150 + (+1) 31{,}240 \right]$$

$$E_1 = \frac{1}{2^1} \left[-27{,}800 + 28{,}740 - 32{,}150 + 31{,}240 \right] = \frac{1}{2} [30] = 15$$

10 Using the information from the experiment in Problem 9, plot and calculate the main effect for the X_2 heat treatment temperature factor.

The plot for the main effect for X_2 is found by drawing a line between the average of the runs with X_2 at its "high" (+1) value and the average of the runs with X_2 at its "low" (−1) value. Referring to the coded design matrix, the average for the "high" runs is:

$$\frac{y_3 + y_4}{2} = \frac{32{,}150 + 31{,}240}{2} = \frac{63{,}390}{2} = 31{,}695$$

The average for the low runs is:

$$\frac{y_1 + y_2}{2} = \frac{27{,}800 + 28{,}740}{2} = \frac{56{,}540}{2} = 28{,}270$$

Plotting these two points creates the plot for the X_2 main effect. See the following figure.

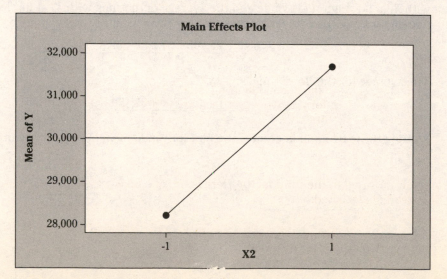

Calculating the E_2 main effect is easy. Just plug the values from the coded design matrix into the following equation:

$$E_2 = \frac{1}{2^{k-1}} \sum_{j=1}^{2^k} c_{2,j} y_j = \frac{1}{2^{k-1}} \left[c_{2,1} y_1 + c_{2,2} y_2 + c_{2,3} y_3 + c_{2,4} y_4 \right]$$

$$= \frac{1}{2^{2-1}} \left[(-1) 27{,}800 + (-1) 28{,}740 + (+1) 32{,}150 + (+1) 31{,}240 \right]$$

$$E_2 = \frac{1}{2^2} \left[-27{,}800 - 28{,}740 + 32{,}150 + 31{,}240 \right] = \frac{1}{2} \left[6{,}850 \right] = 3{,}425$$

11 Using the information from Problems 9 and 10, create a side-by-side main effects plot for X_1 and X_2 and compare the relative strengths of the two.

If you put both main effects on the same vertical scale, you get a plot that looks like the one in the next figure.

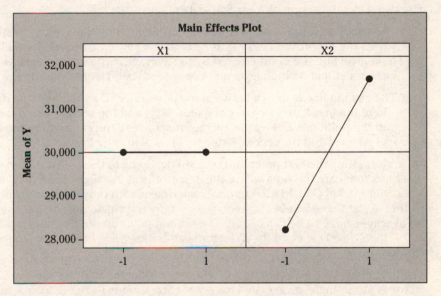

The plot of both main effects shows X_2 having a steep slope, whereas the slope for X_1 is virtually flat, which tells you that X_2 has a much stronger main effect than X_1.

12 List all of the possible interaction effects for a 2^4 factorial experiment.

To find all of the interactions, you have to carefully go through all of the possibilities. Start with the first factor and then list all the other factors the first factor could combine with to form a two-way effect. In this 4-factor case, the first factor interactions are:

- ✔ E_{12}
- ✔ E_{13}
- ✔ E_{14}

Then move on to the second factor. List all of the other factors that the second factor could combine with to form a two-way effect. Skip the two-way effects that you've already listed. Here are the factors:

- ✔ E_{23}
- ✔ E_{24}

Now move on to the third factor. Here is the one possible two-way interaction that hasn't already been listed:

- ✔ E_{34}

You use a similar process to go through and list all of the three-way effects. Here are the three-way effects:

- E_{123}
- E_{124}
- E_{134}
- E_{234}

Finally, you list the only possible four-way interaction:

- E_{1234}

13 Create a two-way interaction plot for the 2^2 factorial experiment from Problem 9. After you create the plot, calculate the E_{12} value for this interaction effect.

The two-way interaction plot for E_{12} has two lines:

- The first line is drawn between the point created by the average response of the runs where the first-listed factor is at its high level and the second-listed factor is also at its high level and the point created by the average response of the runs where the first-listed factor is still at its high level and the second-listed factor is at its low level.

- The second line is drawn between the point created by the average response of the runs where the first-listed factor is at its low level and the second-listed factor is at its high level and the point created by the average response of the runs where the first-listed factor is at its low level and the second-listed factor is also at its low level.

Start by creating the first point for the first line. Going to the coded design matrix for Problem 9, you have to locate the runs where the X_1 factor is at its "high" level (+1) and the X_2 factor is also at its "high" level (+1). In a 2^2 factorial experiment with only one run (Number 4) where the two factors are at these levels, the average is simply the single outcome result for that run: 31,240. No averages have to be calculated! The second point on the first line is where the X_1 factor is at its "high" level (+1) and the X_2 factor is at its "low" level (–1). The single outcome of run 2 is 28,740.

The first point on the second line is where the X_1 factor is at its "low" level (–1) and the X_2 factor is at its "high" level (+1). This point corresponds to run 3, with a value of 32,150. The second point on the second line is where the X_1 factor is at its "low" level (–1) and the X_2 factor is also at its "low" level (–1). These levels appear on run 1, giving an output value of 27,800.

You draw the two-way plot by drawing the lines for these points, as shown in the following figure.

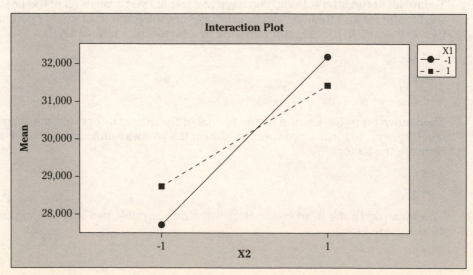

The slopes of these lines are different, which means you have an interaction effect.

The last step is to calculate the E_{12} value. To calculate this value, you use the following formula and plug in the values from the coded design matrix, as shown here:

$$E_{12} = \frac{1}{2^{k-1}} \sum_{j=1}^{2^k} c_{1,j} c_{2,j} y_j = \frac{1}{2^{k-1}} \left[c_{1,1} c_{2,1} y_1 + c_{1,2} c_{2,2} y_2 + c_{1,j} c_2 + c_{1,4} c_{3,4} y_4 \right]$$

$$E_{12} = \frac{1}{2^{2-1}} \left[(-1)(-1)\,27,800 + (+1)(-1)\,28,740 + (-1)(+1)\,32,150 + (+1)(+131,240) \right]$$

$$E_{12} = \frac{1}{2^1} \left[27,800 - 28,740 - 32,150 + 31,240 \right]$$

$$E_{12} = \frac{1}{2} \left[-1,850 \right] = -925$$

14 Of the two-way plots shown in the original question earlier in the chapter, which ones display evidence of an interaction effect?

Two-way interaction plots that show lines with different slopes indicate a strong interaction effect. For this set of two-way plots, only the X_1-X_2 interaction has lines with different slopes. The X_1-X_2 interaction is the only interaction effect among these variables.

15 In the normal probability plot for the effects shown in the original question earlier in the chapter, circle which effects appear significant.

When plotted as a normal probability plot, the effects that are far off the line created by the rest of the points are the ones that are significant. The four points on the left side of the plot create a line. The three effects plotted off the line are the ones that are significant (see the next figure).

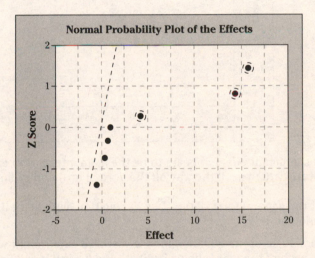

16 Plot the normal probabilities for the 2^2 factorial experiment in Problem 9. Indicate which effects are significant.

The first step is to rank order all of the calculated effects for Problem 9:

Effect	Calculated Value	Rank(i)
E_{12}	–925	1
E_1	15	2
E_2	3,425	3

Next you calculate the probability P_i for each rank ordered effect using this formula:

$$P_i = \frac{i - 0.5}{2^k - 1} = \frac{i - 0.5}{2^2 - 1} = \frac{i - 0.5}{4 - 1} = \frac{i - 1}{3}$$

Effect	Calcuated Value	Rank(i)	P_i
E_{12}	−925	1	0.1667
E_1	15	2	0
E_2	3,425	3	0.8333

Now you have to look up the Z value for each probability in the Standard Normal Distribution Table at www.dummies.com/go/sixsigmaworkbook. Remember to use the rules of table symmetry shown in this chapter to get all the right values, which are shown here:

Effect	Calcuated Value	Rank(i)	P_i	Z_i
E_{12}	−925	1	0.1667	−0.9674
E_1	15	2	0.5000	0
E_2	3,425	3	0.8333	0.9674

Now you plot each calculated effect versus its Z value, as shown in the following figure.

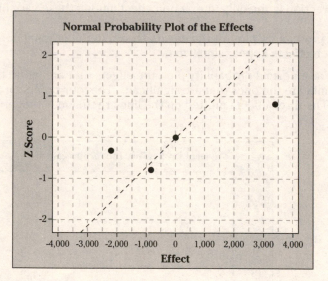

The only significant effect appears to be the main interaction effect of X_2: Heat Treatment Temperature, which is all the way off the normal probability line at 3,425.

17 Write out the general form of the $Y = f(X)$ equation, with all of its potential terms, for a 2^4 factorial experiment.

The general form of the equation for a 2^4 factorial experiment will have an overall offset term β_0, terms for each of the main effects β_1, β_2, β_3, and β_4, and it will have all the interaction effects listed in Problem 11. Your equation should look like this:

$$Y = \beta_0 + \beta_1 X_1 + \beta_2 X_2 + \beta_3 X_3 + \beta_4 X_4 + \beta_{12} X_1 X_2 + \beta_{13} X_1 X_3 + \beta_{14} X_1 X_4 + \beta_{23} X_2 X_3 + \beta_{24} X_2 X_4 + \beta_{34} X_3 X_4 +$$
$$\beta_{123} X_1 X_2 X_3 + \beta_{124} X_1 X_2 X_4 + \beta_{134} X_1 X_3 X_4 + \beta_{234} X_2 X_3 X_4 + \beta_{1234} X_1 X_2 X_3 X_4$$

18 For the experiment in Problem 9, write out the general form of the equation, including all of its potential terms.

Problem 9 is a 2^2 factorial experiment, which means that it will have an overall offset term β_0, terms for each of the two main effects, and a term for the two-way interaction effect. Here's what your equation should look like:

$$Y = \beta_0 + \beta_1 X_1 + \beta_2 X_2 + \beta_{12} X_1 X_2$$

19 For the experiment in Problem 9, write out the specific form of the equation using only the significant terms.

The only significant effect in Problem 9 is the main effect for the X_2 heat treatment temperature factor. Because you only have one significant effect, the general equation reduces down to this:

$$Y = \beta_0 + \beta_2 X_2$$

The value of the β_0 coefficient is just the average of all the experimental runs, which is calculated like this:

$$\beta_0 = \overline{y} = \frac{y_1 + y_2 + y_3 + y_4}{4} = \frac{27,800 + 28,740 + 32,150 + 31,240}{4} = \frac{119,930}{4} = 29,983$$

β_2, which is calculated here, is just one-half of the effect calculated for this factor:

$$\beta_2 = \frac{1}{2} E_2 = \frac{1}{2}(3,425) = 1,713$$

If you plug these values back into the reduced equation, you get the following:

$$Y = 29,983 + 1,713 X_2$$

Chapter 15

Constructing Control Plans and Charts

In This Chapter

▶ Avoiding mistakes with Poka-Yoke

▶ Maintaining your performance with control plans

▶ Selecting and interpreting control charts

▶ Creating (*I-MR*), ($\overline{X}$-*R*), *p*, and *u* charts

---

$\mathbf{A}$fter you've finished defining, measuring, analyzing, and improving your process or product, you still have to do more: You have to figure out how to maintain your efforts. Think of the scientific term *entropy* — the inevitable and steady deterioration of a system toward a state of inert uniformity. Or, think of how long it takes to clean up your home for company when you have young children — and then how quickly the kids can trash the place if you don't implement some controls, or in this case, rules. Many process improvements in the past have suffered a similar fate. Hard-earned gains and improvements are quickly lost when things revert to "business as usual." All of the improvements in the world will quickly evaporate without a plan to hold the achieved gains in place. This last step in the Six Sigma process is the *control phase*.

Make sure you reserve enough time and energy to make it all the way through the control phase.

Doing the Poka-Yoke: Mistake-Proofing Products or Processes

Poka-Yoke is the transliteration of a Japanese phrase meaning "to make mistakes impossible." Poka-Yoke's purpose is to arrange and structure work so that mistakes can't be made or, when they are made, to make them immediately obvious so they can be contained and fixed.

Common Poka-Yoke implementations include:

✔ Physical features or geometry, such as guide pins or stops, that make incorrect assembly or work impossible

✔ Automated processing, assembly, or inspection systems

✔ Limiting controls that don't allow the process to be operated at unacceptable levels

The following are some changes that aren't considered good Poka-Yoke implementations:

- Retraining of personnel or operators
- Threats of disciplinary actions on workers or operators who make mistakes
- Written work procedures or instructions
- Relying on increased attentiveness of workers

Q. List all the good Poka-Yokes on a modern automobile that prevent or detect mistakes.

A. Today's cars incorporate Poka-Yoke after Poka-Yoke to keep drivers from making initial mistakes and in identifying dangerous situations. Here's a list of just a few:

- Automatic transmission can't be taken out of park unless the driver has the brake pedal applied

- Passenger airbag is automatically turned off when the passenger seat isn't occupied by a person who exceeds a safe weight limit

- Seat belt reminder alarms go off until seat belts are buckled

- Headlights automatically switch off after the vehicle is parked and turned off

---

1. List four additional Poka-Yokes used in automobiles that aren't listed in the previous example.

Solve It

2. The largest source of defects in an order fulfillment process is typos in the part of the process where the person taking the order from the customer writes down the customer's name and address. When these errors happen, order shipments get mixed up and customers complain. Think of several good Poka-Yokes that will prevent typos from ever happening or that will raise an alert when a typo needs to be fixed.

Solve It

3. Using the order-taking process from Problem 2, list some Poka-Yokes you could implement that don't require computers or technology.

4. Why don't disciplinary threats or relying on improved attentiveness from workers count as good Poka-Yokes?

Solve It

Forming Control Plans to Maintain Your Improvements

After your improvements are in place, you need to have an organized plan for controlling and maintaining your performance. Many acceptable ways exist to manage the control phase, but before you choose one, make sure that every plan you're considering measures and tracks the following:

- ✔ **The output Ys that were found to be critical from your previous Define-Measure-Analyze-Improve work.** Knowing that the critical outputs are performing to required levels and variation limits assures you that the important input Xs that determine process outputs are being controlled to their individual requirements. A *process management summary* is used to list and track critical output Ys.

- ✔ **The critical input Xs that were determined from your previous Define-Measure-Analyze-Improve work.** The action lies in the critical X realm: When output Ys get off track, the input Xs must be addressed. And, by monitoring the input Xs, you can change people, equipment, materials, and production rates without losing the quality performance of the process. A *process input control plan* is used to list and track the critical input Xs.

Use the process management summary and the process input control plan templates provided in Figures 15-1 and 15-2 to set up and maintain a control plan for your process.

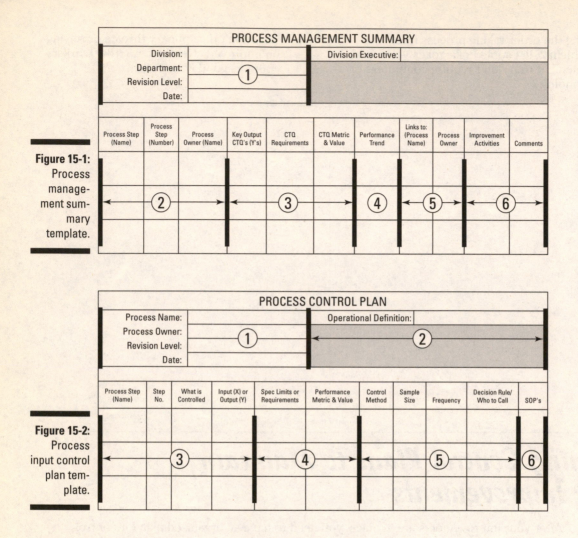

Figure 15-1: Process management summary template.

Figure 15-2: Process input control plan template.

Selecting the Right Control Chart for Your Situation

Your process control plan requires you to track and monitor your critical inputs and outputs. A primary tool you can use for tracking is a *statistical process control chart* (which is also known as a control chart).

Control charts use statistics to monitor and control the variation in processes, and they display the results in easy-to-use graphical formats. Each chart is designed for a different type of data or situation. Using the wrong chart can be very costly!

Use the decision tree in Figure 15-3 to determine which type of control chart to use for your specific situation.

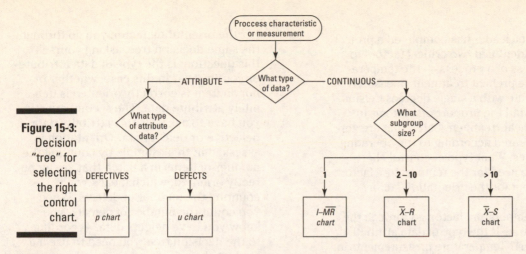

Figure 15-3:
Decision "tree" for selecting the right control chart.

REMEMBER

As you go through the decision process outlined in the tree, ask yourself what type of data you're working with: *attribute data* or *continuous data* (see Chapter 7). Use the following guidelines to figure out which chart to use with each type of data:

✔ If you have attribute data, decide whether your data is for defectives or for defects:

- *Defectives* refers to products or processes that are unacceptable due to one or more errors (defects) that make the entire product or process bad. An example of a system that tracks defectives is a loan approval process. The outcome is either "approve" or "deny." However, denials have one or more various disqualifying reasons (defects) — poor credit score, loan-to-value ratio, employment verification, and so on. Whatever the reason, when you track defectives you don't track the reasons, you just track whether the product or process ends up in one of two categories — "good" or "bad." If you have this type of data, you need to use a *p* chart.

- *Defects* refers to tracking the actual number of problems occurring on an item. An example of tracking defects is counting the number of scratches on a door panel at final inspection. The result may be 0, 5, 17, or 3. You keep track of the number and then you create a percentage or a ratio of the number of defects that occur on the item out of a total number of opportunities, such as 0 out of 20, 5 out of 20, 17 out of 20, or 3 out of 20. (The number of opportunities doesn't need to be identical in every tracked measurement. You may have 0 out of 10, 5 out of 23, 17 out of 19, or 3 out of 15. This still fits into the defects category.) Defect measurements are tracked with *u* charts.

✔ If you have continuous data, you have to ask yourself what size your measurement sample, or *subgroup,* is. Follow these guidelines:

- If your measurement samples consist of a single point, you need to use an individuals and moving range (*I-MR*) control chart.

- If your measurement samples contain between two and ten data points each, you need to use an averages and ranges ($\overline{X}$-*R*) control chart.

- If your measurement samples have more than ten data points each, you need to use an averages and standard deviations ($\overline{X}$-*S*) control chart.

We discuss how to create each of the preceding charts later in the chapter.

Q. A Six Sigma leader has completed a project that has identified two critical factors to the success of a process — the temperature of the preheat treatment (measured each minute with a single degrees Celsius reading) and the proportion of items in each preheat treatment batch that are correctly oriented according to the operating procedures. What type of control chart should be used for the temperature factor? What about for the orientation factor?

A. For the temperature factor, go through the decision tree: Is the type of data attribute or continuous? Temperature measurements in degrees Celsius are considered continuous data. Now ask yourself the follow-up question: What subgroup size is each of the temperature measurements? In this case, the answer is one, which tells you that you need to use an *I-MR* control chart.

For the orientation factor, you go through the same decision tree, asking yourself this question: Is the type of data attribute or continuous? In this case, whether or not an item is correctly oriented is definitely attribute data. The second question you have to ask is: Is this attribute data defective or defect data? Orientation is assessed in this example by counting the number of items in a batch that are incorrectly oriented, which means you're counting the number of defects. When you count the number of defects, you know you have defects data. According to the decision tree, you need to use a *u* control chart.

5. A critical process output for a hotel is the accuracy of room reservations. A recent Six Sigma project set up a measurement system to record the number of reservations made each day that contain one or more problems. What type of control chart should you use to track the performance of this process output?

6. The pressure of a plastic injection mold machine is measured by capturing a five-point sample at the start of each hour's production. Select the right control chart for this metric.

Solve It

7. Shipments of washers for a pump assembly process come in deliveries of 10,000 items. When each shipment is received, a sample of 100 washers is measured for thickness. What type of control chart should you use to track the ongoing thickness of the washers?

Solve It

8. At the end of a cellphone manufacturing process, each phone is put through a final functional test. The unit either "passes" or "fails." The number of total units produced and the number passing the final test are recorded each hour. Select the right type of control chart for tracking each hour's production performance.

Solve It

Interpreting Your Control Charts

Selecting and creating the right control chart is only a start. After creating the chart, the real point is to correctly interpret it. What you're looking for is the evidence of *special causes,* which are the out-of-the-ordinary events that throw performance off its normal level.

To interpret a control chart, the plotted sequence of points on the chart is compared to the calculated control limits (more on calculating control limits later in this chapter). When the position or sequence of the points, in relation to each other or to the control limits, follows a non-normal pattern, you know that a special cause has occurred.

Table 15-1 provides a summary of the non-normal patterns to look for in control charts.

Table 15-1	Tests for Special Causes for Rules 1 through 6			
Chart	**Description**	**Example 1**	**Example 2**	**Interpretation**
Stable and predictable	Chart points don't form a particular pattern and they lie within the upper and lower control limits.			The process is stable, not changing. Only common-cause variation is affecting the process.

(continued)

Table 15-1 (continued)

Chart	Description	Example 1	Example 2	Interpretation
Beyond control limits	One or more chart points lie beyond the upper and lower control limits.			Alerts you that a special cause has affected the process. Investigate to determine the source of the special cause.
Run	Chart points are on one side of the center line. The number of consecutive points on one side is the "length" of the run.			Suggests that the process has undergone a permanent change. May require you to compute new control limits for the shifted process.
Trend	A continued rise or fall in a series of chart points. (Seven or more consecutive points in the same direction.)			Indicates a special cause with a gradual, cumulative effect. Investigate possible special cause sources.
Cycle	Chart points show the same pattern changes (for example, rise or fall) over equal periods of time.			Indicates a special cause with a cyclical, repetitive effect. Investigate possible special cause sources.
Hugging	Chart points are close to the center line or to a control limit line.			Suggests a possible error in data sub-grouping or selection. Verify validity of sampling plan and/or investigate possible special cause sources.

To be more specific and clinical in finding evidence of special cause sources, you also divide the distance between the central line of the control chart and each calculated control limit into thirds, as shown in Figure 15-4.

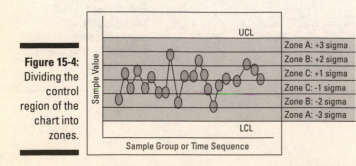

Figure 15-4: Dividing the control region of the chart into zones.

The distance above and the distance below the central limit, the third closest to the central line, is called Zone C. The middle third is called Zone B and the third farthest from the central line is called Zone A. Here are eight specific rules, based on the three zones, that indicate special causes:

1. Any point beyond either control limit

2. Nine points in a row on the same side of the center line

3. Six points in a row, all increasing or all decreasing

4. Fourteen points in a row alternating up and down

5. Two out of any three consecutive points in Zone A and all three on the same side of the central average

6. Four out of any five consecutive points in Zone B or A, and all five on the same side of the central average

7. Fifteen points in a row in Zone C, on either side of the central average line

8. Eight points in a row without a point in Zone C, on either side of the center line.

Checking all of these rules manually for each point on the control chart is tedious work. We will do it here in theses examples to illustrate the concepts, but in practice, usually your computer software will compute the control limits for you from the sample data and check for these rules automatically.

Q. For the control chart shown in the following figure, identify any evidence of special causes. State which rule from the eight-point list applies.

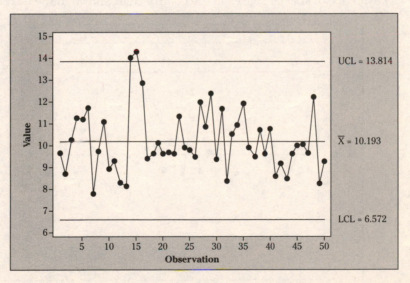

A. The obvious evidence of the presence of a special cause is the two points at observation numbers 14 and 15 that are beyond the upper control limit, which is based on the first rule in the list of eight. Going through all of the other seven rules is a bit tedious, but you'll find one other rule providing evidence of a special cause — number 5. Observations 14, 15, and 16 are all in Zone A or beyond, which fits the bill for rule number 5. Clearly something out of the ordinary happened in the process at this time.

9. Identify any evidence of special causes in the control chart shown in the next figure.

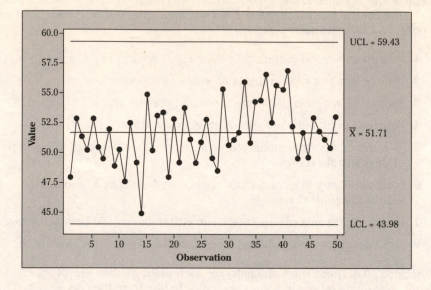

Solve It

10. Identify any evidence of special causes in the control chart shown in the next figure.

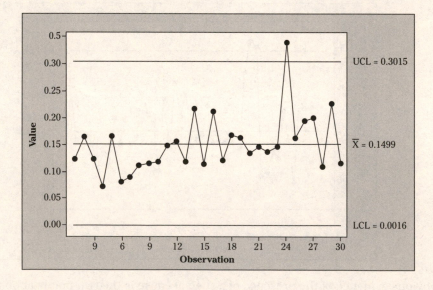

Solve It

Constructing an Individuals and Moving Range (I-MR) Chart

The *individuals and moving range chart* is probably the most widely used control chart because it requires only a sequence of individual numerical measurements. A daily recording of minimum temperature, a sequential accounting of sales figures, or an ordered history of length measurements — all of these measurements can be readily charted using an *I-MR* chart.

As with all of the control charts for continuous data types, an *I-MR* chart is a *dual chart,* which means you create a chart for the individuals and another chart with the same horizontal time axis for the moving range of the data. Having a second chart to track the range between the sequential points allows you even greater resolution at detecting special causes: If any of the test rules is broken for either the individuals or for the moving range chart, you have evidence of a special cause.

In a pinch, you can quickly create just the individuals part of the *I-MR* chart. However, you should create both parts whenever you can.

You create the moving range part (*MR*) of the *I-MR* chart by plotting the moving range (*MR$_i$*) between each of the sequential observations in your data. With the plotted moving ranges you draw a calculated central average line ($\overline{MR}$). You also calculate and draw an upper control limit (*UCL$_{MR}$*) and a lower control limit (*LCL$_{MR}$*) around the moving range data. You calculate these values from the following formulas:

$$MR_i = \left| x_i - x_{i-1} \right|$$

$$\overline{MR} = \frac{1}{k-1}\left(MR_2 + MR_3 + \ldots + MR_k \right) \text{ where } k \text{ is the number of points you are charting}$$

$$UCL_{MR} = 3.267\overline{MR}$$

$$LCL_{MR} = 0$$

You create the individuals part (*I*) of the *I-MR* chart by plotting the individual sequential measurements (*x$_i$*). You include a calculated center average line designated as $\overline{X}$. You also calculate and draw an upper control limit (*UCL$_x$*) and a lower control limit (*LCL$_x$*).

$$\overline{X} = \frac{1}{k}\left(x_1 + x_2 + \ldots + x_k \right) \text{ where } k \text{ is the number of points you are charting}$$

$$UCL_x = \overline{X} + 2.659\overline{MR}$$

$$LCL_x = \overline{X} - 2.659\overline{MR}$$

Q. Create an *I-MR* chart for the following monthly sales data collected over the last two years. Note any signs of special causes:

Month Number	Sales ($)	Month Number	Sales ($)	Month Number	Sales ($)
1	$1,030,821	9	$1,053,196	17	$930,029
2	$991,989	10	$994,710	18	$990,836
3	$1,001,260	11	$1,027,961	19	$994,533
4	$955,303	12	$988,566	20	$996,449
5	$1,009,530	13	$1,003,554	21	$1,025,286
6	$978,663	14	$968,384	22	$1,151,151
7	$963,531	15	$937,275	23	$981,045
8	$1,015,794	16	$1,097,691	24	$992,442

A. A calculation table will help solve this problem. Create a table with a row for each month's sales dollars. In a new column, calculate the moving range between each of the sequential data points. Your table will look like this:

Month Number	Sales ($)	MR	Month Number	Sales ($)	MR
1	$1,030,821	XXX	13	$1,003,554	$14,988
2	$991,989	$38,832	14	$968,384	$35,171
3	$1,001,260	$9,272	15	$937,275	$31,109
4	$955,303	$45,958	16	$1,097,691	$160,416
5	$1,009,530	$54,227	17	$930,029	$167,662
6	$978,663	$30,866	18	$990,836	$60,807
7	$963,531	$15,132	19	$994,533	$3,697
8	$1,015,794	$52,262	20	$996,449	$1,917
9	$1,053,196	$37,403	21	$1,025,286	$28,836
10	$994,710	$58,487	22	$1,181,430	$156,144
11	$1,027,961	$33,252	23	$981,045	$200,385
12	$988,566	$39,395	24	$992,442	$11,397

Now you simply plug the table values into the formulas to generate all the data for the *I-MR* chart. Here are the calculations:

$$\overline{MR} = \frac{1}{k-1}\left(MR_2 + MR_3 + \ldots + MR_k\right) = \frac{1}{24-1}\left(\$38,832 + \$9,272 + \ldots + \$11,397\right) = \$55,983$$

$$UCL_{MR} = 3.267\overline{MR} = 3.267 \cdot \$55,983 = \$182,897$$

$$LCL_{MR} = 0$$

$$\overline{X} = \frac{1}{k}\left(x_1 + x_2 + \ldots + x_k\right) = \frac{1}{24}\left(\$1,030,821 + \$991,989 + \ldots + \$992,442\right) = \$1,004,595$$

$$UCL_x = \overline{X} + 2.659\overline{MR} = \$1,004,595 + 2.659 \cdot \$55,983 = \$1,153,454$$

$$LCL_x = \overline{X} - 2.659\overline{MR} = \$1,004,595 - 2.659 \cdot \$55,983 = \$855,376$$

With these values calculated, you can draw your *I-MR* chart. Plot the points and add the center and control limit lines for each part of the dual chart (next figure).

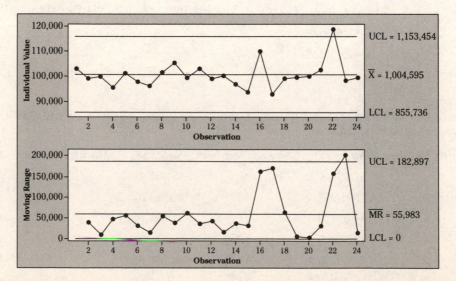

When reviewing the chart for evidence of special causes, you'll find that only the 22nd month, with its individual value and the corresponding moving range (MR_{23}), sends up a flag for violation of the rules. So, you know that something out of the ordinary must have occurred in the 22nd month.

11. Construct an *I-MR* chart for the following production line yield data. Review your finished chart for evidence of special causes, and get some scrap paper handy.

Production Date Order	Yield
1	0.80
2	0.81
3	0.76
4	0.79
5	0.80
6	0.78
7	0.82
8	0.79
9	0.78
10	0.83
11	0.78
12	0.79
13	0.83
14	0.77
15	0.75
16	0.79
17	0.82
18	0.80
19	0.80
20	0.83
21	0.75
22	0.85
23	0.78
24	0.77
25	0.76
26	0.76
27	0.81
28	0.79
29	0.84
30	0.77
31	0.79
32	0.80

Solve It

12. An airport administrator found some historical data that gives the number of aircraft landings per week at his airport. During the period of this found data, the administrator's peers believe that a drop in aircraft traffic occurred. Create an *I-MR* chart of the data and determine whether there is indeed any evidence of a significant drop in traffic.

Week	Landings
1	158
2	151
3	150
4	169
5	149
6	150
7	143
8	149
9	143
10	158
11	145
12	149
13	132
14	140
15	171
16	129
17	126
18	136
19	136
20	140
21	128
22	136
23	124
24	128
25	126
26	123

Solve It

Raising the Bar for Small Samples: Averages and Ranges ($\overline{X}$-R) Charts

When you have continuous data with each sample consisting of a small sample size of 2 to 10 measurements, pick the $\overline{X}$-R chart. Like the I-MR chart, the $\overline{X}$-R chart is a dual chart. In the top half, you plot the average, or $\overline{X}$, for each sample. In the bottom half, you plot the range (R) for each sample subgroup.

The central line and the control limits for the R half of the chart are calculated from these formulas:

$$R_i = \max(x_1, x_2, \ldots x_n) - \min(x_1, x_2, \ldots x_n)$$

$\overline{R} = \frac{1}{k}(R_1 + R_2 + \ldots + R_k)$ where k is the number of subgroups you're charting

$$UCL_R = D_4\overline{R}$$
$$LCL_R = D_3\overline{R}$$

The central line and the control limits for the $\overline{X}$ half of the chart are calculated from these formulas:

$\overline{X}_i = \frac{1}{n}(x_1 + x_2 + \ldots + x_n)$ where n is the number of measurements in each sample subgroup

$\overline{\overline{X}} = \frac{1}{k}(\overline{X}_1 + \overline{X}_2 + \ldots + \overline{X}_k)$ where k is the number of subgroups you are charting

$$UCL_x = \overline{\overline{X}} + A_2\overline{R}$$
$$LCL_x = \overline{\overline{X}} - A_2\overline{R}$$

Where the parameters A_2, D_3, and D_4 are in the above formulas depend on the size of your sample subgroup (n). Use the following table to determine which values you should use for these parameters:

Subgroup Size (n)	A_2	D_3	D_4
2	1.880	0	3.267
3	1.023	0	2.574
4	0.729	0	2.282
5	0.577	0	2.114
6	0.483	0	2.004
7	0.419	0.076	1.924
8	0.373	0.136	1.864
9	0.337	0.184	1.816
10	0.308	0.223	1.777

EXAMPLE

Q. Each hour of production, an engineer takes five samples from the light bulb production line. Each of the five samples is destructively tested to find its maximum voltage. The last 28 hourly sample measurements are listed below:

Hour	X₁	X₂	X₃	X₄	X₅
1	131.3	130.8	130.2	130.9	130.6
2	126.8	128.1	129.1	132.1	130.0
3	131.4	126.3	130.9	127.8	130.5
4	127.9	131.3	130.4	131.0	131.1
5	130.1	128.5	132.2	129.8	128.9
6	133.4	133.4	128.2	130.4	129.3
7	126.1	130.1	129.8	130.3	129.1
8	131.1	130.9	129.9	128.1	130.4
9	131.5	132.2	129.9	131.4	130.2
10	132.2	131.9	131.7	131.5	128.6
11	127.2	128.1	129.7	129.5	129.7
12	130.5	131.6	133.2	131.3	132.8
13	132.6	128.8	126.9	131.5	130.9
14	131.0	129.0	129.8	130.3	130.0
15	127.3	127.8	131.8	132.5	128.2
16	131.4	128.0	131.7	128.2	132.5
17	126.6	130.0	131.1	132.7	130.9
18	129.5	128.9	130.3	133.7	130.1
19	132.2	129.6	130.3	128.7	131.3
20	130.0	127.9	124.5	132.5	126.8
21	127.2	133.3	130.4	128.2	130.6
22	132.4	128.0	129.1	131.8	128.7
23	132.9	132.8	129.2	128.8	127.2
24	130.7	128.7	129.0	130.0	129.3
25	136.6	129.7	128.8	127.5	130.6
26	129.1	128.5	130.2	130.9	129.3
27	131.0	131.8	130.4	127.6	127.8
28	130.4	132.2	127.2	135.8	133.0

Create an $\overline{X}$-R control chart for the voltage data and identify any evidence of special causes.

A. For each hourly sample of $n = 5$ points, calculate the sample average $\overline{X}$ and the range R and include these values on your table. Your table should now look like this:

Hour	X₁	X₂	X₃	X₄	X₅	$\overline{X}$	R
1	131.3	130.8	130.2	130.9	130.6	130.8	1.2
2	126.8	128.1	129.1	132.1	130.0	129.2	5.2
3	131.4	126.3	130.9	127.8	130.5	129.4	5.1
4	127.9	131.3	130.4	131.0	131.1	130.3	3.4
5	130.1	128.5	132.2	129.8	128.9	129.9	3.7
6	133.4	133.4	128.2	130.4	129.3	130.9	5.3
7	126.1	130.1	129.8	130.3	129.1	129.1	4.2
8	131.1	130.9	129.9	128.1	130.4	130.1	3.0
9	131.5	132.2	129.9	131.4	130.2	131.0	2.3
10	132.2	131.9	131.7	131.5	128.6	131.2	3.6

Hour	X_1	X_2	X_3	X_4	X_5	$\overline{X}$	R
11	127.2	128.1	129.7	129.5	129.7	128.8	2.6
12	130.5	131.6	133.2	131.3	132.8	131.9	2.7
13	132.6	128.8	126.9	131.5	130.9	130.2	5.7
14	131.0	129.0	129.8	130.3	130.0	130.0	1.9
15	127.3	127.8	131.8	132.5	128.2	129.5	5.2
16	131.4	128.0	131.7	128.2	132.5	130.4	4.6
17	126.6	130.0	131.1	132.7	130.9	130.3	6.1
18	129.5	128.9	130.3	133.7	130.1	130.5	4.8
19	132.2	129.6	130.3	128.7	131.3	130.4	3.5
20	130.0	127.9	124.5	132.5	126.8	128.4	7.9
21	127.2	133.3	130.4	128.2	130.6	129.9	6.1
22	132.4	128.0	129.1	131.8	128.7	130.0	4.5
23	132.9	132.8	129.2	128.8	127.2	130.2	5.7
24	130.7	128.7	129.0	130.0	129.3	129.5	2.0
25	136.6	129.7	128.8	127.5	130.6	130.6	9.0
26	129.1	128.5	130.2	130.9	129.3	129.6	2.4
27	131.0	131.8	130.4	127.6	127.8	129.7	4.3
28	130.4	132.2	127.2	135.8	133.0	131.7	8.7

With the $\overline{X}$s and the Rs calculated, you can follow the formulas to calculate the center lines and the control limits for each dual part of the $\overline{X}$-R chart:

$$\overline{R} = \frac{1}{k}\left(R_1 + R_2 + \ldots + R_k\right) = \frac{1}{28}\left(1.2 + 5.2 + \ldots + 8.7\right) = \frac{1}{28}124.4 = 4.4$$

$$UCL_R = D_4\overline{R} = 2.114 \cdot 4.4 = 9.4$$

$$LCL_R = D_3\overline{R} = 0 \cdot 4.4 = 0$$

$$\overline{\overline{X}} = \frac{1}{k}\left(\overline{X}_1 + \overline{X}_2 + \ldots + \overline{X}_k\right) = \frac{1}{28}\left(130.8 + 129.2 + \ldots + 131.7\right) = \frac{1}{28}3{,}643.6 = 130.1$$

$$UCL_X = \overline{\overline{X}} + A_2\overline{R} = 130.1 + 0.577(4.4) = 132.7$$

$$LCL_X = \overline{\overline{X}} - A_2\overline{R} = 130.1 - 0.577(4.4) = 127.6$$

With these values calculated, you can draw your $\overline{X}$-R chart. Plot the calculated $\overline{X}_i$ points and the R_i points, and then add the center and control limit lines for each part of the dual chart (see the next figure).

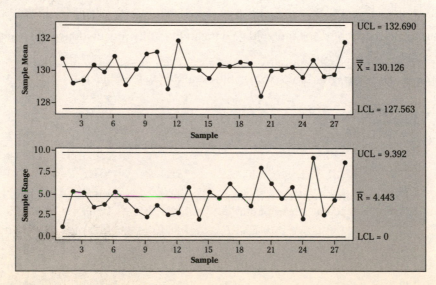

When you go through all the rules looking for special causes, no evidence can be found indicating the presence of any special causes. The voltage produced by the bulb manufacturing process is therefore stable.

13. As an in-process check, a fruit juice bottler takes a three-item sample of caps every ten minutes and measures their height. (If the height of the caps varies too much, the cap feed machines have to be adjusted.) Here's a sequence of 30 three-item samples of cap height measurements:

Sample	X_1	X_2	X_3	Sample	X_1	X_2	X_3
1	19.86	19.74	20.07	16	19.83	19.79	19.79
2	19.98	20.07	19.94	17	19.91	19.91	19.95
3	20.02	19.99	20.06	18	20.05	20.03	19.95
4	19.95	19.80	20.00	19	20.08	20.25	19.96
5	20.02	19.96	19.83	20	20.06	20.01	19.99
6	20.15	20.06	20.13	21	19.87	20.19	20.01
7	19.79	20.01	20.08	22	19.85	19.96	19.95
8	19.80	19.85	20.00	23	19.91	19.95	20.04
9	20.22	19.98	19.94	24	19.85	20.06	19.77
10	20.11	20.03	20.09	25	20.04	19.89	20.12
11	19.97	20.11	20.14	26	19.84	20.13	19.95
12	19.96	20.22	19.94	27	20.13	19.91	19.90
13	20.15	19.90	20.05	28	19.85	19.89	19.86
14	20.02	20.03	19.97	29	20.04	19.98	19.82
15	20.16	20.05	19.77	30	19.83	19.94	20.08

Create an $\overline{X}$-R control chart for the cap height data and investigate whether any special causes are present. Keep your scrap paper on hand.

Solve It

14. Part deliveries from a supplier are sampled upon arrival. Four parts from each shipment are inspected. The sample data for the last 20 shipments is shown here:

Sample	X_1	X_2	X_3	X_4	Sample	X_1	X_2	X_3	X_4
1	80	79	80	81	11	79	79	78	80
2	81	82	78	80	12	80	80	80	82
3	81	79	79	78	13	78	79	77	81
4	78	79	79	78	14	79	79	81	80
5	79	80	80	80	15	81	81	79	79
6	80	80	81	80	16	81	80	79	80
7	80	79	82	81	17	80	81	80	79
8	82	79	82	78	18	82	80	80	81
9	81	81	82	80	19	81	79	79	81
10	79	81	80	81	20	79	78	81	81

Create an $\overline{X}$-R control chart for the part inspection data and investigate whether any special causes are present. Keep that scrap paper handy!

Making a p Chart for Your Attribute Data

The "p" in p chart stands for "proportion defective." When you're tracking data that consists of a count of how many items in your sample are defective, you use a p chart. You create a p chart by plotting the sequence of values representing the proportion of each sample that's defective (p_i). Here's the equation you use:

$$p_i = \frac{d_i}{n_i}$$

where d_i is the number of inspected items found to be defective. The number of items inspected, which is designated as n_i, doesn't have to be the same for each sample. The horizontal centerline ($\overline{p}$) for the p chart is the total number of defectives found divided by the total number of items inspected. Here's the formula:

$$\overline{p} = \frac{d_1 + d_2 + \ldots + d_k}{n_1 + n_2 + \ldots + n_k}$$

The control limits for the p chart are only constant if the size of all k samples is the same. If the size isn't the same from sample to sample, the control limit envelope will expand and contract as the size of the samples change. No matter what the sample size, the following formulas allow you to calculate the control limits:

$$UCL_i = \overline{p} + 3\sqrt{\frac{\overline{p}(1-\overline{p})}{n_i}}$$

$$LCL_i = \overline{p} - 3\sqrt{\frac{\overline{p}(1-\overline{p})}{n_i}}$$

Proportions can never be less than 0 or greater than 1. If your calculated LCL_i ends up being less than 0, simply set it instead to 0. Or, if your calculated UCL_i is greater than 1, just set it to a value of 1.

Q. Each day, a restaurant manager surveys four to six patrons by asking them whether they will recommend the restaurant to their friends. Being trained in Six Sigma, the manager has recorded the last month's worth of data:

Day	No. Surveyed	No. Saying "No"	Day	No. Surveyed	No. Saying "No"
1	5	0	11	5	0
2	4	1	12	4	1
3	6	0	13	4	0
4	6	0	14	5	0
5	6	0	15	4	1
6	4	4	16	5	0
7	6	0	17	4	4
8	5	0	18	5	0
9	5	0	19	6	2
10	5	1	20	4	1

Day	No. Surveyed	No. Saying "No"	Day	No. Surveyed	No. Saying "No"
21	6	0	27	6	0
22	6	0	28	4	2
23	4	1	29	5	2
24	6	0	30	5	3
25	4	0	31	6	0
26	5	2			

Create a *p* chart for the survey data and investigate whether the restaurant experienced special causes on any of the days.

A. The overall proportion defective is simply the total number of those patrons saying "no, I wouldn't recommend the restaurant" divided by the total number of patrons surveyed. The calculations look like this:

$$\overline{p} = \frac{d_1 + d_2 + \ldots + d_k}{n_1 + n_2 + \ldots + n_k} = \frac{0 + 1 + \ldots + 0}{5 + 4 + \ldots + 6} = \frac{25}{155} = 0.161$$

The next step is to calculate the proportion defective for each sample and include them on your chart. You chart will resemble the following:

Day	No. Surveyed	No. saying "No"	p_i	Day	No. Surveyed	No. saying "No"	p_i
1	5	0	0.00	17	4	4	1.00
2	4	1	0.25	18	5	0	0.00
3	6	0	0.00	19	6	2	0.33
4	6	0	0.00	20	4	1	0.25
5	6	0	0.00	21	6	0	0.00
6	4	4	1.00	22	6	0	0.00
7	6	0	0.00	23	4	1	0.25
8	5	0	0.00	24	6	0	0.00
9	5	0	0.00	25	4	0	0.00
10	5	1	0.20	26	5	2	0.40
11	5	0	0.00	27	6	0	0.00
12	4	1	0.25	28	4	2	0.50
13	4	0	0.00	29	5	2	0.40
14	5	0	0.00	30	5	3	0.60
15	4	1	0.25	31	6	0	0.00
16	5	0	0.00				

For each of the 31 samples, you have to calculate an upper and lower control limit.

These limits will vary because the size of each day's sample also varies. As an example, the first sample's upper control limit is calculated as:

$$UCL_1 = \overline{p} + 3\sqrt{\frac{\overline{p}(1-\overline{p})}{n_1}} = 0.161 + 3\sqrt{\frac{0.161(1-0.161)}{5}} = 0.655$$

The lower control limit of the first sample is calculated as:

$$LCL_1 = \overline{p} - 3\sqrt{\frac{\overline{p}(1-\overline{p})}{n_1}} = 0.161 - 3\sqrt{\frac{0.161(1-0.161)}{5}} = -0.332$$

Because the calculated value is less than 0, you just use the theoretical limit of "0" instead:

$$LCL_1 = 0$$

You do these same upper and lower control limit calculations for each of the 31 samples and complete your table as shown here:

Day	Surveyed	"No"s	p_i	UCL_i	LCL_i
1	5	0	0.00	0.655	0
2	4	1	0.25	0.713	0
3	6	0	0.00	0.612	0
4	6	0	0.00	0.612	0
5	6	0	0.00	0.612	0
6	4	4	1.00	0.713	0
7	6	0	0.00	0.612	0
8	5	0	0.00	0.655	0
9	5	0	0.00	0.655	0
10	5	1	0.20	0.655	0
11	5	0	0.00	0.655	0
12	4	1	0.25	0.713	0
13	4	0	0.00	0.713	0
14	5	0	0.00	0.655	0
15	4	1	0.25	0.713	0
16	5	0	0.00	0.655	0
17	4	4	1.00	0.713	0
18	5	0	0.00	0.655	0
19	6	2	0.33	0.612	0
20	4	1	0.25	0.713	0
21	6	0	0.00	0.612	0
22	6	0	0.00	0.612	0
23	4	1	0.25	0.713	0
24	6	0	0.00	0.612	0
25	4	0	0.00	0.713	0
26	5	2	0.40	0.655	0
27	6	0	0.00	0.612	0
28	4	2	0.50	0.713	0
29	5	2	0.40	0.655	0
30	5	3	0.60	0.655	0
31	6	0	0.00	0.612	0

With the p_i, UCL_i, and LCL_i values all calculated for each sample, you're ready to draw the p chart. Plot the p_i points. Use the calculated value of $\overline{p}$ as the center line. Then, for each sample, draw the upper and lower control limits. Remember that these control limits will vary if the sizes of the samples vary, which they do in this case. The finished chart looks like the one in the following figure.

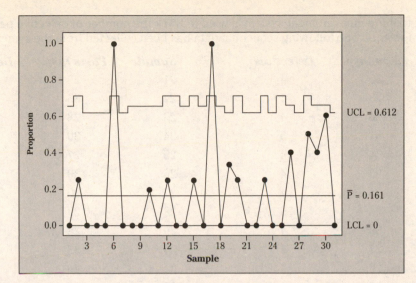

Something out of the ordinary definitely happened on the days of the 6th and 17th samples. The restaurant manager should begin looking on these dates for specific causes of the problems.

15. The final inspection of a washer manufacturing plant consists of a go/no-go gauge measurement of 100 parts. Here's a list of past final inspection performance values:

Sample	Size (n)	Defectives (d)	Sample	Size (n)	Defectives (d)
1	100	0	14	100	4
2	100	1	15	100	4
3	100	1	16	100	6
4	100	3	17	100	7
5	100	2	18	100	2
6	100	0	19	100	1
7	100	2	20	100	1
8	100	2	21	100	2
9	100	2	22	100	3
10	100	3	23	100	3
11	100	1	24	100	0
12	100	2	25	100	4
13	100	3			

Create a *p* chart and indicate whether any evidence of special causes is present.

Solve It

16. A pass-fail attribute measurement system is used to track the number of defective parts found in outgoing shipments. The following sequential data has been collected from the system:

Sample	Parts Insp.	Defectives	Sample	Parts Insp.	Defectives
1	32	4	21	25	3
2	28	4	22	35	4
3	36	4	23	28	4
4	31	5	24	30	4
5	34	4	25	27	4
6	23	4	26	30	4
7	35	4	27	30	5
8	26	5	28	29	4
9	30	4	29	28	4
10	27	4	30	33	4
11	25	4	31	26	4
12	30	4	32	29	5
13	26	4	33	31	4
14	37	3	34	29	4
15	29	4	35	34	4
16	32	4	36	34	4
17	35	4	37	27	5
18	30	4	38	26	4
19	30	3	39	28	3
20	33	4	40	28	4

Create a *p* chart and look for evidence of special causes. Make sure you have scrap paper handy!

Solve It

Creating a u Chart for Your Attribute Data

A *u chart* monitors defects per unit. A *unit* can be anything that provides a consistent opportunity for defects to occur — for example a physical assembly, a paper process, a transaction, a patient in a hospital, a day's worth of sales, or a warehouse. As long as the concept of a unit is consistently defined and applied, a *u* chart works.

You create a *u* chart by plotting the sequence of values representing the defects per unit of each sample, u_i. Use the following equation:

$$u_i = \frac{D_i}{n_i}$$

where D_i is the number of defects found in the inspection of the units in the sample. The number of units inspected (n_i) doesn't have to be the same for each sample.

The horizontal center line ($\bar{u}$) for the *u* chart is the total number of defects found in all of the samples divided by the total number of units inspected. Here's the formula:

$$\bar{u} = \frac{D_1 + D_2 + \ldots + D_k}{n_1 + n_2 + \ldots + n_k}$$

The control limits for the u chart are constant only if the number of units in all k samples is the same. If the number of units isn't the same, the control limit envelope will expand and contract as the number of units in each sample changes. No matter what the sample size, the following formulas allow you to calculate the control limits:

$$UCL_i = \bar{u} + 3\sqrt{\frac{\bar{u}}{n_i}}$$

$$LCL_i = \bar{p} - 3\sqrt{\frac{\bar{u}}{n_i}}$$

REMEMBER

The number of defects per unit can never be less than 0. If your calculated LCL_i ends up being less than 0, simply set it to "0" instead.

EXAMPLE

Q. The sequential records from an inspection point in an automobile assembly line are listed below:

Sample	Units	Defects	Sample	Units	Defects
1	8	14	16	8	16
2	7	14	17	6	15
3	7	13	18	6	10
4	6	13	19	7	12
5	8	16	20	5	15
6	8	17	21	6	17
7	6	8	22	7	13
8	7	12	23	7	12
9	7	14	24	4	13
10	6	16	25	7	14
11	8	13	26	6	13
12	6	17	27	9	13
13	5	12	28	6	14
14	6	13	29	8	17
15	7	17	30	6	14

Create a u chart for the data and identify any evidence of special causes.

A. Begin by calculating the overall, average defects per unit for the chart center line:

$$\bar{u} = \frac{D_1 + D_2 + \ldots + D_k}{n_1 + n_2 + \ldots + n_k} = \frac{14 + 14 + \ldots 14}{8 + 7 + \ldots + 6} = \frac{417}{200} = 2.085$$

The individual defects per unit (u_i) points for the chart are calculated by dividing the number of defects found (D_i) by the number of units inspected (n_i) for each sample. For example, the u_i for the first sample is calculated like this:

$$u_1 = \frac{D_1}{n_1} = \frac{14}{8} = 1.75$$

Calculate this value for all 30 samples and include them in your table, which should look like this:

Sample	Units	Defects	u_i		Sample	Units	Defects	u_i
1	8	14	1.750		16	8	16	2.000
2	7	14	2.000		17	6	15	2.500
3	7	13	1.857		18	6	10	1.667
4	6	13	2.167		19	7	12	1.714
5	8	16	2.000		20	5	15	3.000
6	8	17	2.125		21	6	17	2.833
7	6	8	1.333		22	7	13	1.857
8	7	12	1.714		23	7	12	1.714
9	7	14	2.000		24	4	13	3.250
10	6	16	2.667		25	7	14	2.000
11	8	13	1.625		26	6	13	2.167
12	6	17	2.833		27	9	13	1.444
13	5	12	2.400		28	6	14	2.333
14	6	13	2.167		29	8	17	2.125
15	7	17	2.429		30	6	14	2.333

For each of the 30 samples, you have to calculate an upper and lower control limit. These values will vary since the number of units in each sample will also vary. Remember that if the calculated lower control limit is less than 0, you need to use the theoretical limit of "0" instead. As an example, the upper control limit for the first sample is calculated as follows:

$$UCL_1 = \bar{u} + 3\sqrt{\frac{\bar{u}}{n_1}} = 2.085 + 3\sqrt{\frac{2.085}{8}} = 3.617$$

The lower control limit for the first sample is calculated like this:

$$LCL_1 = \bar{u} - 3\sqrt{\frac{\bar{u}}{n_1}} = 2.085 - 3\sqrt{\frac{2.085}{8}} = 0.682$$

Repeat the same control limit calculations for the rest of the samples and include them on your table, which should look like this:

Sample	Units	Defects	u_i	UCL_i	LCL_i
1	8	14	1.750	3.617	0.682
2	7	14	2.000	3.722	0.585
3	7	13	1.857	3.722	0.585
4	6	13	2.167	3.853	0.465
5	8	16	2.000	3.617	0.682
6	8	17	2.125	3.617	0.682
7	6	8	1.333	3.853	0.465
8	7	12	1.714	3.722	0.585
9	7	14	2.000	3.722	0.585
10	6	16	2.667	3.853	0.465
11	8	13	1.625	3.617	0.682

Sample	Units	Defects	u_i	UCL_i	LCL_i
12	6	17	2.833	3.853	0.465
13	5	12	2.400	4.022	0.310
14	6	13	2.167	3.853	0.465
15	7	17	2.429	3.722	0.585
16	8	16	2.000	3.617	0.682
17	6	15	2.500	3.853	0.465
18	6	10	1.667	3.853	0.465
19	7	12	1.714	3.722	0.585
20	5	15	3.000	4.022	0.310
21	6	17	2.833	3.853	0.465
22	7	13	1.857	3.722	0.585
23	7	12	1.714	3.722	0.585
24	4	13	3.250	4.251	0.101
25	7	14	2.000	3.722	0.585
26	6	13	2.167	3.853	0.465
27	9	13	1.444	3.529	0.762
28	6	14	2.333	3.853	0.465
29	8	17	2.125	3.617	0.682
30	6	14	2.333	3.853	0.465

You're now ready to create the u chart. Plot the calculated u_i values. Create a horizontal center line at $\bar{u}$, and draw the moving control limits at the calculated values of UCL_i and LCL_i. When you're finished the chart will look like the one in the following figure.

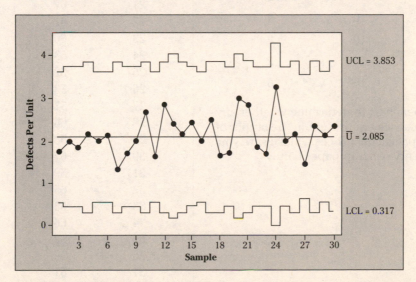

The figure shows that the defect per unit performance of the automobile assembly line is stable, with no evidence of special causes.

17. As an audit of outgoing quality, an egg company checks 10 cartons of its packaged eggs each day. The company checks each carton's eggs for correct size, for cracks or damage, and for cleanliness. A carton is considered a unit. Here are the results for the last 20 days' inspections:

Sample	Cartons	Defects
1	10	2
2	10	3
3	10	5
4	10	3
5	10	2
6	10	4
7	10	4
8	10	4
9	10	4
10	10	6
11	10	2
12	10	2
13	10	6
14	10	5
15	10	6
16	10	1
17	10	4
18	10	3
19	10	2
20	10	6

Create a u chart to determine whether any special causes are present in the output of the egg packaging process. Make sure you have plenty of scrap paper handy.

Solve It

18. A hospital's trying to improve the accuracy of its insurance claim process. To get a base line of where it's currently at, its continuous improvement leader reviews each day's claim forms for any type of error. He's done this for the last 38 days and has recorded the following results:

Day	Forms	Defects
1	61	16
2	58	8
3	59	13
4	64	6
5	61	9
6	59	18
7	60	24
8	61	1
9	58	10
10	57	16
11	67	15
12	58	11
13	49	8
14	59	10
15	58	13
16	68	18
17	63	8
18	61	13
19	62	15
20	64	15
21	57	12
22	61	10
23	60	11
24	63	12
25	62	13
26	53	13
27	57	16
28	60	19
29	58	30
30	67	20
31	59	10
32	65	17
33	63	14
34	66	9
35	62	10
36	56	8
37	61	10
38	56	16

Use a u chart to investigate the current base line performance at the hospital. Check to see whether any special causes are present.

Solve It

Solutions to Control Plan and Chart Problems

1 List four additional Poka-Yokes used in automobiles that aren't listed in the previous example.

Here are some of the many other Poka-Yokes used in modern automobiles:

- Dashboard oil light comes on when oil is low, warning the driver of the potential for serious engine damage

- Fuel gauge warning light reminds driver to look at the low fuel tank level

- Sizing of the gas tank opening prevents the driver from putting in the wrong type of fuel (diesel versus unleaded)

- Secondary release on hood prevents the driver from accidentally opening the hood while driving

- Keys are two-sided and symmetrical so there is no wrong way to insert them into the ignition

- Minivan sliding door won't open when the fuel door on the same side is already open — preventing the door from "running over" the open fuel door

- Automatic windows go completely down with a single click or push of the control, but they require constant actuation to roll the windows up, which prevents someone's arm or head from getting pinched in the window

- Ignition on a standard transmission vehicle won't work until the clutch pedal is applied

Did you think of any others?

2 The largest source of defects in an order fulfillment process is typos in the part of the process where the person taking the order from the customer writes down the customer's name and address. When these errors happen, order shipments get mixed up and customers complain. Think of several good Poka-Yokes that will prevent typos from ever happening or that will raise an alert when a typo needs to be fixed.

Here are several Poka-Yokes that help reduce typos:

- Automatically pulling the customer's address information from a database of previous customers

- Automatically checking the entered addresses against a computer database of valid city addresses

- Automatically pulling the customer's address from their billing information

What others did you think of?

3 Using the order-taking process from Problem 2, list some Poka-Yokes you could implement that don't require computers or technology.

Pulling information from billing records or from customer databases requires computers and information technology. Here are some more Poka-Yoke ideas that don't require electricity:

- Using an order form with individual blocks for each letter of the address

- Adding a customer confirmation step in the order-taking process by having the customer review the transcribed address details at the conclusion of the order call

- Having the customer enter in his or her own name and address rather than having the order clerk transcribe it

Did you think of other non-technology ways to mistake-proof the process?

4 Why don't disciplinary threats or relying on improved attentiveness from workers count as good Poka-Yokes?

The whole point of Poka-Yokes is to take the burden of mistakes off the person and to provide the person with a system that naturally prevents mistakes from ever happening. Requiring the operator to increase his attentiveness does the opposite of what a good Poka-Yoke is supposed to do: It increases the role of the operator in preventing mistakes. Along the same lines, threatening disciplinary action to reduce mistakes is completely counterproductive.

REMEMBER

Your job in Six Sigma is to reconfigure the system so that opportunities for making mistakes are eliminated. Make it virtually impossible for an operator to make mistakes and no disciplinary action will ever be required.

5 A critical process output for a hotel is the accuracy of room reservations. A recent Six Sigma project set up a measurement system to record the number of reservations made each day that contain one or more problems. What type of control chart should you use to track the performance of this process output?

A problem with a reservation is counted as a defect. And there can be more than one type of problem for a reservation. Using the decision tree provided in Figure 15-3, you follow the attribute data path and then the defects branch. The result: You should use a u chart to track room reservation performance.

6 The pressure of a plastic injection mold machine is measured by capturing a five-point sample at the start of each hour's production. Select the right control chart for this metric.

Pressure readings are continuous data, so follow that branch in the decision tree. Next decide how big the sample size is. A sample size of $n = 5$, as is the case here, means that you should select an $\overline{X}$-R chart.

7 Shipments of washers for a pump assembly process come in deliveries of 10,000 items. When each shipment is received, a sample of 100 washers is measured for thickness. What type of control chart should you use to track the ongoing thickness of the washers?

Thickness measurements are continuous data. Following that branch in the decision tree, you next ask, "How big is my sample?" A 100-washer sample is large, so you use an $\overline{X}$-S control chart in this situation.

8 At the end of a cellphone manufacturing process, each phone is put through a final functional test. The unit either "passes" or "fails." The number of total units produced and the number passing the final test are recorded each hour. Select the right type of control chart for tracking each hour's production performance.

Pass-fail data is attribute data about defectives. The choice here is a p chart.

9 Identify any evidence of special causes in the control chart shown in the figure from the original question earlier in the chapter.

Going through the numbered rules for interpreting control charts, you can find problems with the number six rule for this chart: Four out of five points are in Zone B or beyond, starting with observation number 37. These points are highlighted in the plot of the next figure.

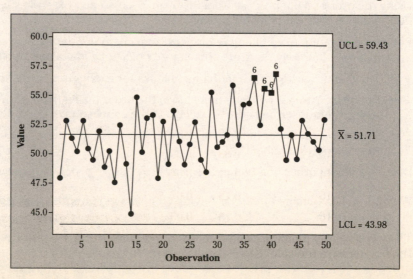

10 Identify any evidence of special causes in the control chart shown in the figure from the original question earlier in this chapter.

Going carefully through all the numbered rules for each of the points in the chart, you find that observation 12 concludes a trend of six points in a row increasing, which is a sign of a special cause. Also, at observation 24, the charted point is beyond the control limits. This is another indicator of special cause variation. These indicators are highlighted in the version of the control chart in the next figure.

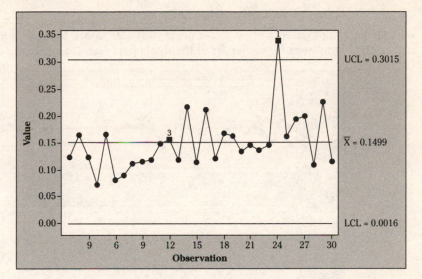

11 Construct an *I-MR* chart for the production line yield data shown in the original question earlier in this chapter. Review your finished chart for evidence of special causes.

A calculation table helps solve this problem. In a new column, calculate the moving range between each of the sequential data points. Your table should look like this:

Production Date Order	Yield	MR	Production Date Order	Yield	MR
1	0.80		17	0.82	0.04
2	0.81	0.01	18	0.80	0.02
3	0.76	0.05	19	0.80	0.00
4	0.79	0.03	20	0.83	0.03
5	0.80	0.00	21	0.75	0.08
6	0.78	0.02	22	0.85	0.10
7	0.82	0.04	23	0.78	0.07
8	0.79	0.03	24	0.77	0.01
9	0.78	0.01	25	0.76	0.01
10	0.83	0.05	26	0.76	0.00
11	0.78	0.04	27	0.81	0.05
12	0.79	0.00	28	0.79	0.02
13	0.83	0.04	29	0.84	0.05
14	0.77	0.06	30	0.77	0.07
15	0.75	0.02	31	0.79	0.02
16	0.79	0.03	32	0.80	0.01

Now you simply plug the table values into the formulas to generate all the data for the *I-MR* chart. Here are the calculations:

$$\overline{MR} = \frac{1}{k-1}\left(MR_2 + MR_3 + \ldots + MR_k\right) = \frac{1}{32-1}(0.01 + 0.05 + \ldots + 0.01) = 0.03$$

$$UCL_{MR} = 3.267\overline{MR} = 3.267 \cdot 0.03 = 0.11$$

$$LCL_{MR} = 0$$

$$\overline{X} = \frac{1}{k}\left(x_1 + x_2 + \ldots + x_k\right) = \frac{1}{32}(0.80 + 0.81 + \ldots + 0.80) = 0.79$$

$$UCL_x = \overline{X} + 2.659\overline{MR} = 0.79 + 2.659 \cdot 0.03 = 0.88$$

$$LCL_x = \overline{X} - 2.659\overline{MR} = 0.79 - 2.659 \cdot 0.03 = 0.71$$

With these values calculated, you can draw your *I-MR* chart. Plot the points and add the center and control limit lines for each part of the dual chart (see the next figure).

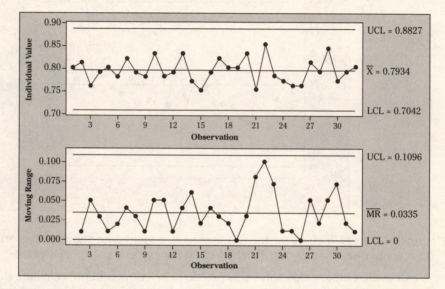

When reviewing the chart for evidence of special causes, note that everything looks good: You have no runs, trends, or points beyond the control limits.

12 An airport administrator found some historical data that gives the number of aircraft landings per week at his airport. During the period of this found data, the administrator's peers believe that a drop in aircraft traffic occurred. Create an *I-MR* chart of the data (flip to the original question shown earlier in the chapter to see the data) and determine whether there is indeed any evidence of a significant drop in traffic.

A calculation table helps solve this problem. In a new column, calculate the moving range between each of the sequential data points. Here's what your table should look like:

Week	Landings	MR	Week	Landings	MR
1	158	.	14	140	8
2	151	7	15	171	31
3	150	1	16	129	42
4	169	19	17	126	3
5	149	20	18	136	10
6	150	1	19	136	0
7	143	7	20	140	4
8	149	6	21	128	12
9	143	6	22	136	8
10	158	15	23	124	12
11	145	13	24	128	4
12	149	4	25	126	2
13	132	17	26	123	3

Now you simply plug the table values into the formulas to generate all the data for the *I-MR* chart. Here are the calculations:

$$\overline{MR} = \frac{1}{k-1}\left(MR_2 + MR_3 + \dots + MR_k\right) = \frac{1}{26-1}(7 + 1 + \dots + 3) = 10.2$$

$$UCL_{MR} = 3.267\overline{MR} = 3.267 \cdot 10.2 = 33.3$$

$$LCL_{MR} = 0$$

$$\overline{X} = \frac{1}{k}\left(x_1 + x_2 + \dots + x_k\right) = \frac{1}{26}(158 + 151 + \dots + 123) = 141.9$$

$$UCL_x = \overline{X} + 2.659\overline{MR} = 141.9 + 2.659 \cdot 10.2 = 169.0$$

$$LCL_x = \overline{X} - 2.659\overline{MR} = 141.9 - 2.659 \cdot 10.2 = 114.8$$

With these values calculated, you can draw your *I-MR* chart. Plot the points and add the center and control limit lines for each part of the dual chart (see the following figure).

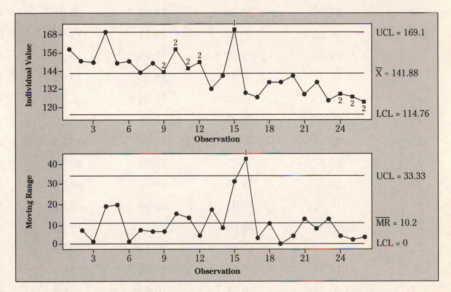

You can see by studying your *I-MR* chart that an out-of-the-ordinary change in airport traffic definitely occurred during this period. Observations 1 through 12 are all above the center line. That fits rule number two: Nine or more points in a row are along one side of the center line. The same rule is detected again starting with observation 16. But this time, the run of points are all beneath the center line. It looks like airport traffic was at a higher level — a spike in traffic occurred coincident with observation 15 and then a new, lower level of traffic emerged afterward.

13 As an in-process check, a fruit juice bottler takes a three-item sample of caps every ten minutes and measures their height. (If the height of the caps varies too much, the cap feed machines have to be adjusted.) The original question shown earlier in this chapter contains a sequence of 30 three-item samples of cap height measurements.

Create an $\overline{X}$-R control chart for the cap height data and investigate whether any special causes are present.

For each hourly sample of $n = 3$ points, calculate the sample average $\overline{X}$ and the range R. Your table will look like this:

Sample	X_1	X_2	X_3	$\overline{X}$	R
1	19.86	19.74	20.07	19.89	0.33
2	19.98	20.07	19.94	20.00	0.13
3	20.02	19.99	20.06	20.02	0.07
4	19.95	19.80	20.00	19.92	0.20

Sample	X_1	X_2	X_3	$\overline{X}$	R
5	20.02	19.96	19.83	19.94	0.19
6	20.15	20.06	20.13	20.11	0.09
7	19.79	20.01	20.08	19.96	0.29
8	19.80	19.85	20.00	19.88	0.20
9	20.22	19.98	19.94	20.05	0.28
10	20.11	20.03	20.09	20.08	0.08
11	19.97	20.11	20.14	20.07	0.17
12	19.96	20.22	19.94	20.04	0.28
13	20.15	19.90	20.05	20.03	0.25
14	20.02	20.03	19.97	20.01	0.06
15	20.16	20.05	19.77	19.99	0.39
16	19.83	19.79	19.79	19.80	0.04
17	19.91	19.91	19.95	19.92	0.04
18	20.05	20.03	19.95	20.01	0.10
19	20.08	20.25	19.96	20.10	0.29
20	20.06	20.01	19.99	20.02	0.07
21	19.87	20.19	20.01	20.02	0.32
22	19.85	19.96	19.95	19.92	0.11
23	19.91	19.95	20.04	19.97	0.13
24	19.85	20.06	19.77	19.89	0.29
25	20.04	19.89	20.12	20.02	0.23
26	19.84	20.13	19.95	19.97	0.29
27	20.13	19.91	19.90	19.98	0.23
28	19.85	19.89	19.86	19.87	0.04
29	20.04	19.98	19.82	19.95	0.22
30	19.83	19.94	20.08	19.95	0.25

With the $\overline{X}$s and the Rs calculated, you can follow the formulas and formula values for an $n = 3$ sample size to calculate the center lines and the control limits for each dual part of the $\overline{X}$-R chart. Here are the calculations:

$$\overline{R} = \frac{1}{k}\left(R_1 + R_2 + \ldots + R_k\right) = \frac{1}{30}\left(0.33 + 0.13 + \ldots + 0.25\right) = \frac{1}{30}5.66 = 0.1887$$

$$UCL_R = D_4\overline{R} = 2.574 \cdot 0.1887 = 0.4856$$

$$LCL_R = D_3\overline{R} = 0 \cdot 0.1887 = 0$$

$$\overline{\overline{X}} = \frac{1}{k}\left(\overline{X}_1 + \overline{X}_2 + \ldots + \overline{X}_k\right) = \frac{1}{30}\left(19.89 + 20.00 + \ldots + 19.95\right) = \frac{1}{30}599.38 = 19.9793$$

$$UCL_X = \overline{\overline{X}} + A_2\overline{R} = 19.9793 + 1.023\left(0.1887\right) = 20.1723$$

$$LCL_X = \overline{\overline{X}} - A_2\overline{R} = 19.9793 - 1.023\left(0.1887\right) = 19.7863$$

With these values calculated, you can draw your $\overline{X}$-R chart. Plot the calculated $\overline{X}_i$ points and the R_i points and then add the center and control limit lines for each part of the dual chart (see the next figure).

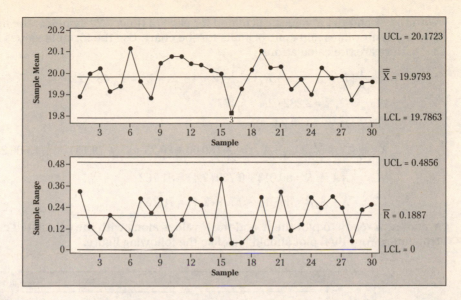

You have evidence of a special cause: Samples 10 through 16 are all decreasing, which flags rule number three. Something out of the ordinary happened with the cap height.

14   Part deliveries from a supplier are sampled upon arrival. Four parts from each shipment are inspected. The sample data for the last 20 shipments is shown in the original question earlier in this chapter.

Create an $\overline{X}$-R control chart for the part inspection data and investigate whether any special causes are present.

Start by calculating the $\overline{X}$ and the R values for each $n = 4$ sample of data. Your table will look like this:

Sample	X_1	X_2	X_3	X_4	$\overline{X}$	R
1	80	79	80	81	80.00	2
2	81	82	78	80	80.25	4
3	81	79	79	78	79.25	3
4	78	79	79	78	78.50	1
5	79	80	80	80	79.75	1
6	84	81	82	81	82.00	3
7	80	79	82	81	80.50	3
8	82	79	82	78	80.25	4
9	81	81	82	80	81.00	2
10	79	81	80	81	80.25	2
11	79	79	78	80	79.00	2
12	80	80	80	82	80.50	2
13	78	79	77	81	78.75	4
14	79	79	81	80	79.75	2
15	81	81	79	79	80.00	2
16	81	80	79	80	80.00	2
17	80	81	80	79	80.00	2
18	82	80	80	81	80.75	2
19	81	79	79	81	80.00	2
20	79	78	81	81	79.75	3

With the $\overline{X}$ and the R values calculated for each of the $k = 20$ samples, the next step is to calculate the center lines and control limits for the chart. Use the formula values for a sample size of $n = 4$. Here are the calculations:

$$\overline{R} = \frac{1}{k}\left(R_1 + R_2 + \ldots + R_k\right) = \frac{1}{20}\left(2 + 4 + \ldots + 3\right) = \frac{1}{20}\,48 = 2.4$$

$$UCL_R = D_4\overline{R} = 2.282 \cdot 2.4 = 5.477$$

$$LCL_R = D_3\overline{R} = 0 \cdot 0.24 = 0$$

$$\overline{\overline{X}} = \frac{1}{k}\left(\overline{X}_1 + \overline{X}_2 + \ldots + \overline{X}_k\right) = \frac{1}{20}\left(80.00 + 80.25 + \ldots + 79.75\right) = \frac{1}{20}\,1{,}600.25 = 80.013$$

$$UCL_X = \overline{\overline{X}} + A_2\overline{R} = 80.013 + 0.729\left(2.4\right) = 81.762$$

$$LCL_X = \overline{\overline{X}} - A_2\overline{R} = 80.013 - 0.729\left(2.4\right) = 78.263$$

You're now ready to plot the $\overline{X}$ and the R values along with the calculated center lines and control limits. Your dual plot should look like the following figure.

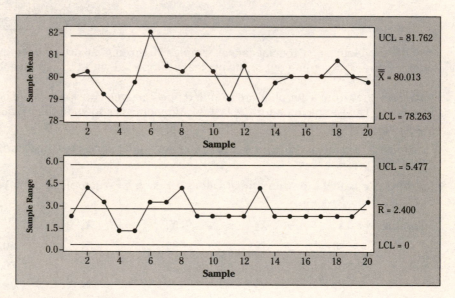

At sample number six, a special cause has occurred, leading the sample average to be outside the calculated control limits.

15 The final inspection of a washer manufacturing plant consists of a go/no-go gauge measurement of 100 parts. The original question shown earlier in this chapter contains a list of past final inspection performance values.

Create a p chart and indicate whether any evidence of special causes is present.

Start by calculating the overall proportion defectives $\overline{p}$. You calculate this value by dividing the total number of defectives by the total number of parts or items inspected. For this problem, the calculation is as follows:

$$\overline{p} = \frac{d_1 + d_2 + \ldots + d_k}{n_1 + n_2 + \ldots + n_k} = \frac{0 + 1 + \ldots + 4}{100 + 100 + \ldots + 100} = \frac{59}{2{,}500} = 0.0236$$

Then, you calculate the proportion defective for each sample. The formula is:

$$p_i = \frac{d_i}{n_i}$$

The table of samples can be updated with a new column showing the calculated proportion defectives for each sample:

Sample	Size (n)	Defectives (d)	Calculated proportion defectives	Sample	Size (n)	Defectives (d)	Calculated proportion defectives
1	100	0	0.00	14	100	4	0.04
2	100	1	0.01	15	100	4	0.04
3	100	1	0.01	16	100	6	0.06
4	100	3	0.03	17	100	7	0.07
5	100	2	0.02	18	100	2	0.02
6	100	0	0.00	19	100	1	0.01
7	100	2	0.02	20	100	1	0.01
8	100	2	0.02	21	100	2	0.02
9	100	2	0.02	22	100	3	0.03
10	100	3	0.03	23	100	3	0.03
11	100	1	0.01	24	100	0	0.00
12	100	2	0.02	25	100	4	0.04
13	100	3	0.03				

The next step is to calculate the control limits for each sample. Because each of the samples is the same size, the control limits will be the same for all samples. Here are the calculations:

$$UCL_i = \overline{p} + 3\sqrt{\frac{\overline{p}(1-\overline{p})}{n_i}} = 0.0236 + 3\sqrt{\frac{0.0236(1-0.0236)}{100}} = 0.06914$$

$$LCL_i = \overline{p} - 3\sqrt{\frac{\overline{p}(1-\overline{p})}{n_i}} = 0.0236 - 3\sqrt{\frac{0.0236(1-0.0236)}{100}} = -0.02194$$

Because no proportion can be less than 0, you need to set the lower control limit at 0 instead of the impossible negative number that was calculated.

$$LCL_i = 0$$

Now all you have to do is draw the chart. Graph the calculated p_i points and draw in the horizontal center line at $\overline{p}$ and the upper and lower control limits (see the next figure).

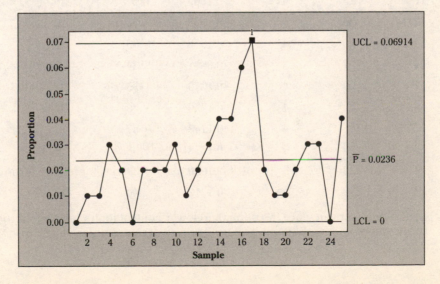

Are there any special causes evident in this graph? At the 17th sample, the proportion defective exceeds the upper control limit, which means that something non-normal has caused this increase.

16 A pass-fail attribute measurement system is used to track the number of defective parts found in outgoing shipments. Flip to the original question shown earlier in this chapter to see the sequential data that was collected from the system.

Create a *p* chart and look for evidence of special causes.

Begin by calculating the overall proportion defectives, which is equal to the total number of defective items found divided by the total number of items inspected:

$$\bar{p} = \frac{d_1 + d_2 + \ldots + d_k}{n_1 + n_2 + \ldots + n_k} = \frac{4 + 4 + \ldots + 4}{32 + 28 + \ldots + 28} = \frac{161}{1,196} = 0.1349$$

You also need to calculate the proportion defectives for each sample, which you can do by using this formula:

$$p_i = \frac{d_i}{n_i}$$

The table of the samples can be expanded to include a new column for the calculated proportion defectives. Your table will look like this:

Sample	Parts Insp.	Defectives	Calculated proportion defectives	Sample	Parts Insp.	Defectives	Calculated proportion defectives
1	32	4	0.1250	21	25	3	0.1200
2	28	4	0.1429	22	35	4	0.1143
3	36	4	0.1111	23	28	4	0.1429
4	31	5	0.1613	24	30	4	0.1333
5	34	4	0.1176	25	27	4	0.1481
6	23	4	0.1739	26	30	4	0.1333
7	35	4	0.1143	27	30	5	0.1667
8	26	5	0.1923	28	29	4	0.1379
9	30	4	0.1333	29	28	4	0.1429
10	27	4	0.1481	30	33	4	0.1212
11	25	4	0.1600	31	26	4	0.1538
12	30	4	0.1333	32	29	5	0.1724
13	26	4	0.1538	33	31	4	0.1290
14	37	3	0.0811	34	29	4	0.1379
15	29	4	0.1379	35	34	4	0.1176
16	32	4	0.1250	36	34	4	0.1176
17	35	4	0.1143	37	27	5	0.1852
18	30	4	0.1333	38	26	4	0.1538
19	30	3	0.1000	39	28	3	0.1071
20	33	4	0.1212	40	28	4	0.1429

Next, you must calculate the upper and lower control limits for each of the samples. Each of these values will be different because the size of the samples varies. Use these formulas:

$$UCL_i = \bar{p} + 3\sqrt{\frac{\bar{p}(1-\bar{p})}{n_i}}$$

$$LCL_i = \bar{p} - 3\sqrt{\frac{\bar{p}(1-\bar{p})}{n_i}}$$

Remember that a proportion can't be greater than 1 or less than 0. So, if your calculated control limit values exceed these, just set the value back to 1 or 0, respectively. The following table shows the upper and lower control limits calculated for each sample:

Sample	Parts Insp.	Defectives			
1	32	4	0.1250	0.3156	0
2	28	4	0.1429	0.3281	0
3	36	4	0.1111	0.3053	0
4	31	5	0.1613	0.3185	0
5	34	4	0.1176	0.3102	0
6	23	4	0.1739	0.3481	0
7	35	4	0.1143	0.3077	0
8	26	5	0.1923	0.3354	0
9	30	4	0.1333	0.3216	0
10	27	4	0.1481	0.3317	0
11	25	4	0.1600	0.3394	0
12	30	4	0.1333	0.3216	0
13	26	4	0.1538	0.3354	0
14	37	3	0.0811	0.3029	0
15	29	4	0.1379	0.3248	0
16	32	4	0.1250	0.3156	0
17	35	4	0.1143	0.3077	0
18	30	4	0.1333	0.3216	0
19	30	3	0.1000	0.3216	0
20	33	4	0.1212	0.3129	0
21	25	3	0.1200	0.3394	0
22	35	4	0.1143	0.3077	0
23	28	4	0.1429	0.3281	0
24	30	4	0.1333	0.3216	0
25	27	4	0.1481	0.3317	0
26	30	4	0.1333	0.3216	0
27	30	5	0.1667	0.3216	0
28	29	4	0.1379	0.3248	0
29	28	4	0.1429	0.3281	0
30	33	4	0.1212	0.3129	0
31	26	4	0.1538	0.3354	0
32	29	5	0.1724	0.3248	0
33	31	4	0.1290	0.3185	0
34	29	4	0.1379	0.3248	0
35	34	4	0.1176	0.3102	0
36	34	4	0.1176	0.3102	0
37	27	5	0.1852	0.3317	0
38	26	4	0.1538	0.3354	0
39	28	3	0.1071	0.3281	0
40	28	4	0.1429	0.3281	0

The last step is to draw out the p chart with the points for the p_i values and the varying limits for the upper and lower control limits (see the following figure).

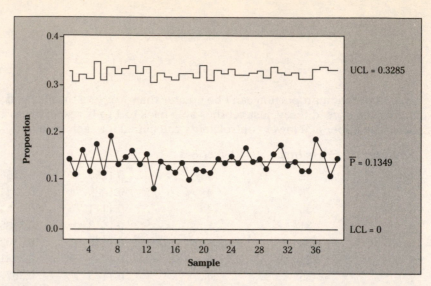

By looking at the chart, you can see that everything is normal, with no evidence of any special causes.

17 As an audit of outgoing quality, an egg company checks 10 cartons of its packaged eggs each day. The company checks each carton's eggs for correct size, for cracks or damage, and for cleanliness. A carton is considered a unit. The original question earlier in this chapter shows the results for the last 20 days' inspections.

Create a *u* chart to determine whether any special causes are present in the output of the egg packaging process.

The first step is to calculate the overall defects per unit. In this problem, a unit is a 1-dozen carton of eggs. The overall defects per unit is the total number of defects observed divided by the total number of units inspected, as calculated here:

$$\bar{u} = \frac{D_1 + D_2 + \ldots + D_k}{n_1 + n_2 + \ldots n_k} = \frac{2 + 3 + \ldots + 6}{10 + 10 + \ldots + 10} = \frac{74}{200} = 0.3700$$

Now calculate the defects per unit for each sample using this formula:

$$u_i = \frac{D_i}{n_i}$$

The table of sample data values can be expanded with a new column for the calculated defects per unit, like this:

Sample	Cartons	Defects	u	Sample	Cartons	Defects	u
1	10	2	0.2	11	10	2	0.2
2	10	3	0.3	12	10	2	0.2
3	10	5	0.5	13	10	6	0.6
4	10	3	0.3	14	10	5	0.5
5	10	2	0.2	15	10	6	0.6
6	10	4	0.4	16	10	1	0.1
7	10	4	0.4	17	10	4	0.4
8	10	4	0.4	18	10	3	0.3
9	10	4	0.4	19	10	2	0.2
10	10	6	0.6	20	10	6	0.6

Now you need to calculate the upper and lower control limits for each of the samples. Because the number of units inspected is identical for each sample, the control limits will be constant. The formula and calculations are:

$$UCL_u = \bar{u} + 3\sqrt{\frac{\bar{u}}{n_i}} = 0.3700 + 3\sqrt{\frac{0.3700}{10}} = 0.9471$$

$$LCL_u = \bar{u} - 3\sqrt{\frac{\bar{u}}{n_i}} = 0.3700 - 3\sqrt{\frac{0.3700}{10}} = -0.2071$$

However, because the lower control limit is less than 0, you have to set its value back to the theoretical limit of 0.

Now you're ready to draw the u chart. Plot the calculated u_i points for each sample. Draw the horizontal center line at $\bar{u}$. Then draw in the constant control limits. The chart should look like the one in the next figure.

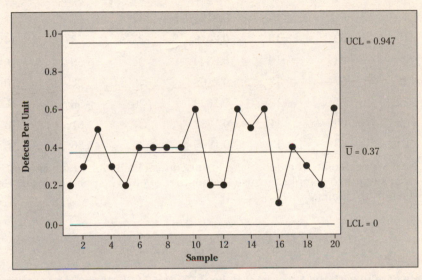

When looking at the chart, you can see that everything looks normal. You have no evidence of special causes.

18 A hospital's trying to improve the accuracy of its insurance claim process. To get a base line of where it's currently at, its continuous improvement leader reviews each day's claim forms for any type of error. He's done this for the last 38 days and recorded the results. Flip to the original question earlier in this chapter to see the results.

Use a u chart to investigate the current base line performance at the hospital. Check to see whether any special causes are present.

Start this problem out by calculating the overall defects per unit $\bar{u}$. You can calculate this value by dividing the total number of defects found in all the samples divided by the total number of units inspected. Mathematically, this value can be written like this:

$$\bar{u} = \frac{D_1 + D_2 + \ldots + D_k}{n_1 + n_2 + \ldots + n_k} = \frac{16 + 8 + \ldots + 16}{61 + 58 + \ldots + 56} = \frac{497}{2,293} = 0.2167$$

Now calculate the defects per unit for each sample with this formula:

$$u_i = \frac{D_i}{n_i}$$

You can expand the table of sample data to include a column for the calculated u_i values, which makes the table look like this:

Day	Forms	Defects	u	Day	Forms	Defects	u
1	61	16	0.2623	6	59	18	0.3051
2	58	8	0.1379	7	60	24	0.4000
3	59	13	0.2203	8	61	1	0.0164
4	64	6	0.0938	9	58	10	0.1724
5	61	9	0.1475	10	57	16	0.2807

Day	Forms	Defects	u	Day	Forms	Defects	u
11	67	15	0.2239	25	62	13	0.2097
12	58	11	0.1897	26	53	13	0.2453
13	49	8	0.1633	27	57	16	0.2807
14	59	10	0.1695	28	60	19	0.3167
15	58	13	0.2241	29	58	30	0.5172
16	68	18	0.2647	30	67	20	0.2985
17	63	8	0.1270	31	59	10	0.1695
18	61	13	0.2131	32	65	17	0.2615
19	62	15	0.2419	33	63	14	0.2222
20	64	15	0.2344	34	66	9	0.1364
21	57	12	0.2105	35	62	10	0.1613
22	61	10	0.1639	36	56	8	0.1429
23	60	11	0.1833	37	61	10	0.1639
24	63	12	0.1905	38	56	16	0.2857

Next you calculate the upper and lower control limits for each sample. These limits will vary from sample to sample because the number of units inspected varies. Here are the formulas for the control limits:

$$UCL_i = \bar{u} + 3\sqrt{\frac{\bar{u}}{n_i}}$$

$$LCL_i = \bar{u} - 3\sqrt{\frac{\bar{u}}{n_i}}$$

Be careful with the lower control limit. Theoretically, the number of defects, and hence the defects per unit value, can never drop below 0. So, if a calculated lower control limit ends up negative, just replace it with the theoretical limit of 0. You can expand the table again with a column for the upper and another column for the lower control limits, like this:

Day	Forms	Defects	u	UCL	LCL
1	61	16	0.2623	0.3956	0.0379
2	58	8	0.1379	0.4001	0.0334
3	59	13	0.2203	0.3986	0.0349
4	64	6	0.0938	0.3913	0.0422
5	61	9	0.1475	0.3956	0.0379
6	59	18	0.3051	0.3986	0.0349
7	60	24	0.4000	0.3971	0.0364
8	61	1	0.0164	0.3956	0.0379
9	58	10	0.1724	0.4001	0.0334
10	57	16	0.2807	0.4017	0.0318
11	67	15	0.2239	0.3874	0.0461
12	58	11	0.1897	0.4001	0.0334
13	49	8	0.1633	0.4163	0.0172
14	59	10	0.1695	0.3986	0.0349
15	58	13	0.2241	0.4001	0.0334
16	68	18	0.2647	0.3861	0.0474
17	63	8	0.1270	0.3927	0.0408

Day	Forms	Defects	u	UCL	LCL
18	61	13	0.2131	0.3956	0.0379
19	62	15	0.2419	0.3941	0.0394
20	64	15	0.2344	0.3913	0.0422
21	57	12	0.2105	0.4017	0.0318
22	61	10	0.1639	0.3956	0.0379
23	60	11	0.1833	0.3971	0.0364
24	63	12	0.1905	0.3927	0.0408
25	62	13	0.2097	0.3941	0.0394
26	53	13	0.2453	0.4086	0.0249
27	57	16	0.2807	0.4017	0.0318
28	60	19	0.3167	0.3971	0.0364
29	58	30	0.5172	0.4001	0.0334
30	67	20	0.2985	0.3874	0.0461
31	59	10	0.1695	0.3986	0.0349
32	65	17	0.2615	0.3900	0.0435
33	63	14	0.2222	0.3927	0.0408
34	66	9	0.1364	0.3887	0.0448
35	62	10	0.1613	0.3941	0.0394
36	56	8	0.1429	0.4034	0.0301
37	61	10	0.1639	0.3956	0.0379
38	56	16	0.2857	0.4034	0.0301

With all these values calculated, now you just need to draw the u chart. Plot the calculated u_i points for each sample. Draw the horizontal center line at $\bar{u}$. And then draw in the varying control limits. The chart should look something like the one in the following figure.

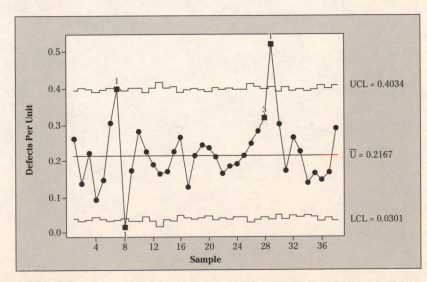

Notice the handful of suspicious points in the control chart. Samples 7, 8, and 29 have exceeded the control limits. Also, observation 28 concludes a six-point trend of defect per unit calculations that are all increasing. These artifacts are evidence that something out of the ordinary has occurred within the insurance claim process at the hospital for these days.

Part VI
The Part of Tens

The 5th Wave   By Rich Tennant

"What exactly are we saying here?"

In this part . . .

Here we give you three short lists of common mis-
steps, best practices, and interesting areas of Six
Sigma application. Chapter 16 debunks the ten most
common myths about Six Sigma. Chapter 17 gives you the
ten most critical things to do in order to complete a Six
Sigma project. Chapter 18 is a list of ten ways to use Six
Sigma and gain its breakthrough benefits outside of a
traditional Six Sigma "belt" project. And don't forget to
check out www.dummies.com/go/sixsigmaworkbook for
some useful tables and forms!

Chapter 16

Ten Implementation Myths of Six Sigma

In This Chapter
▶ Dispelling the most common myths about implementing Six Sigma
▶ Avoiding mistakes and barriers to implementation

As many times as Six Sigma has been implemented around the world, countless war stories, opinions, and myths have emerged, augmented by numerous urban legends, anecdotes, and hearsay. Misconceptions abound regarding what a Six Sigma implementation is really about.

Like most myths, the myths about Six Sigma are all rooted in some truth. With thousands of implementations and hundreds of thousands of projects completed, you know already from the normal distribution that some have gone poorly and that the failures can be notorious. Most failures are due to poor leadership, but others are due to bad management. Even worse are those projects that simply suffer bad luck. However, out of these failures — and the agendas of the people who tell them — the stories take on mythic proportion.

This chapter addresses ten of the most common myths about a Six Sigma implementation. You're likely to come across many more, but these are the biggies that you need to watch out for.

Six Sigma Is about Achieving "Six Sigma"

Based on everything you've ever read, Six Sigma is 3.4 DPMO, right? So, if you're implementing "Six Sigma," it only goes to follow that you're going to keep working at it until you achieve that Six Sigma level of performance, right?

Wrong! Six Sigma is *not* about achieving a Six Sigma level of performance. In other words, a Six Sigma implementation isn't about achieving 3.4 DPMO in every key performance metric. Instead, it's about achieving the proper, optimized level of performance of your organization — and it's very likely not to be precisely 3.4 DPMO.

 A Six Sigma initiative is about developing the capabilities to continuously improve the efficiency and effectiveness of your organization so that the performance and value of your work processes continuously increase. The precise sigma level at which any given process should operate is a matter of the process characteristics and the customer's needs. In most cases, it's below "six sigma." In other words, it's greater than 3.4 DPMO, and in some cases, it's even more than Six Sigma!

Six Sigma Will Make Us Start All Over Again with Something Different

You'll often hear Six Sigma devotees using the common refrain "You'll never do things the same again." Because of this viewpoint — and because of the natural fear of change — the myth emerged that a Six Sigma implementation causes people to abandon everything and start all over again. Of course, Six Sigma doesn't do that. You won't find a more effective way to grind an organization to a halt than to tell everyone to stop doing what he or she is doing!

In fact, Six Sigma isn't about stopping *what* you're doing; it's about changing *how* you're doing it. The Six Sigma initiative helps you do what you're doing now, but more efficiently and effectively. Incremental change is self-perpetuating because project improvements result in measurable gains in performance, which feed more improvements, and so on.

Six Sigma Stifles Creativity

One of the biggest mistaken impressions about Six Sigma is that it stifles creativity and only works for high-volume repetitive processes, such as manufacturing, where consistency is most critical. This myth emerged because of the way Motorola first applied it — in volume manufacturing. But Six Sigma, which attacks the root cause of any problem, improves outcomes by improving processes. Any processes. Creative processes such as marketing and design are processes just as manufacturing and production are processes. And so are transaction processes, such as billing or procurement. And any such process — creative processes included — can be characterized, analyzed, and improved.

Modeling Processes Is Too Complicated and Doesn't Go Anywhere

Didn't it all somehow seem easier when you scribbled process models on the back of a napkin or on a white board — all those little boxes with arrows depicting functions and information flowing between them? Your informal scribblings certainly enabled the discussion in the moment.

However, process modeling became more formalized when you started drawing the functions and flows using computer tools, such as PowerPoint or Visio. The models were shareable and the presentations looked downright spiffy. But, true process modeling requires so much more rigor than just drawing pictures, and the effort level for drawing pictures was always just too much work. So, for a long time, as important as it was, process modeling seemed too complicated, and as a result, it was rarely used.

That's all changed now. The new era of tools, such as iGrafx, enables true process modeling and is a key enabler in a core activity in Six Sigma: the definition and analysis of processes.

Six Sigma Is Another "Program of the Month"

You've heard it countless times: The initiative launched with great fanfare and then quietly died after it failed to live up to initial expectations. Quality initiatives, marketing initiatives, new product initiatives, efficiency initiatives — and the managers who announced them — all here today and gone tomorrow. Why should Six Sigma be any different?

What makes a Six Sigma initiative so different is the prescriptive nature of the deployment. Unlike many initiatives in the past, which meant well, but had little deployment fidelity, a Six Sigma initiative has a thorough script, where everyone's roles and actions in the deployment are defined and known. Not only does this help the initiative succeed on its own, but it also helps the senior managers understand what their role is and how to fuel the initiative going forward. This rigorous deployment definition is why Six Sigma initiatives in major corporations like GE and Honeywell not only began strong, but also have continued — well past the honeymoon phase and well beyond the tenure of the executives and managers who first announced them.

Six Sigma Is Just a Quick-hit, Cost-Reduction Initiative

Most companies today have committed leadership and are governed by principles and values that better balance short-term opportunities with long-term vision. As a result, most Six Sigma initiatives now create a culture of improvement that continues to produce gains and values for years. Companies like Motorola and Honeywell have Six Sigma initiatives that have lasted well over a decade and continue as strong as ever.

Six Sigma Is Too Onerous and Prescriptive

Does this sound familiar: "We're different and we have our own way of doing things — and our unique style is what makes us special and competitive in our industry. We're flexible and individualistic. Bringing in the Six Sigma standardized approach to doing things will wipe out our uniqueness. We'll be just like everyone else and lose our edge."

Some people consider the Six Sigma training onerous because of the rigorous nature of the curricula and projects. And, yes, the deployment framework is clearly prescriptive, in that it formally defines the roles and activities in the leadership and knowledge transfer. But the Six Sigma formula is a toolbox and application knowledge set. It's a language and communication framework.

You Can't Implement Six Sigma Yourself

The perpetuated myth has been that Six Sigma is too heady, too difficult, too troublesome, and too dangerous to implement by yourself. The people who want you to believe that myth want you to think that without a group of consultants to assist you at every step, performing your training and overseeing your projects, you're doomed to failure.

Given the title of this workbook, you can probably guess that this myth is wrong: You *can* implement Six Sigma yourself! First of all, Six Sigma isn't rocket science — yes, you will have to figure some statistics, to be sure, but nothing over the heads of your top staff. Second, the extensive body of experience across the industry has led to standardization and repeatability in the methods and approaches. Third, Six Sigma is now well-supported, with hundreds of books and guides, dozens of conferences and symposia, considerable online resources, standardized training curricula, and more.

The Six Sigma Approach Is Way Too Expensive and Disruptive

The training can be as inexpensive or as extensive as you want, and the implementations can be as rigorous or as informal as you like. And while these choices may be difficult, at least now you have them — Six Sigma teams never used to have the choices you do today.

On the cost front, the intellectual capital of Six Sigma can be bought and applied more inexpensively and seamlessly than ever. It need not be expensive. The training materials can be purchased from any number of providers — even on eBay! Most training can be conducted online, which eliminates the time and expense of classroom training. Trainers are prevalent and you can contract with them or even hire them outright to insource your training. Boutique mentors and facilitators can guide you through the implementation.

If You're Not Doing Black Belt Projects, You're Not Really Doing Six Sigma

We've saved one of the biggest Six Sigma myths for last. This myth is perpetuated on several fronts:

- By trainers who overtrain because they make their money based on training days
- By purists and academicians who make their mark in esoterica
- By those Black Belts who have been put on a pedestal and consider anything less to be inferior

Mostly, this myth is perpetuated on these fronts because Black Belt projects have always had their place in Six Sigma — that's simply the way it has always been done.

This notion that you have to do Black Belt projects or none at all is absurd for many reasons. Most directly, the majority of an organization's challenges simply don't require a Black Belt level of analysis to solve. (For that matter, many don't require any Belt level of analysis to solve!) Only a very small percentage of the problems are this serious. If you're solving real business problems by using Six Sigma tools and techniques at a lower level than Black Belt, you're still doing Six Sigma.

Chapter 17

Ten Tips for Finishing a Six Sigma Project Successfully

As with any type of project, managing Six Sigma projects is a balancing act: not too much and not too little; not too long and not too short; not too many cooks and not too few. As evident in the project definition phase in Chapter 4, and as with any project, much of the risk and uncertainty in Six Sigma projects comes from the setup. But, then again, you also face the long road to project completion — which isn't exactly a picnic. The project charter (see the "Charting the Entire Course" section later in this chapter) may have launched your project successfully, but you may still encounter many pitfalls before you actually complete the process. This chapter lists ten major areas of focus to avoid those pitfalls and help you finish your Six Sigma project successfully.

Properly Scoping Your Project

The most common contributor to project failure is improper scoping of the project at the outset. *Scoping* is the breadth of coverage. Typically, when projects are improperly scoped, they're scoped too broadly — in a noble but misguided attempt to address too many Ys (outputs) or too high-level Ys for improvement. Or, projects may be scoped too broadly because multiple goals, multiple process owners, and multiple organizations are involved. However, projects are sometimes scoped too narrowly — solving a problem that's too easy, already has a solution, or has an outcome that makes an insignificant impact.

A project has to be worth completing, but it also has to be achievable. As a rule, you're much better off if you define and solve a smaller problem instead of a larger one. Small projects are usually achievable, but larger ones are fraught with increased risk. So, be sure to scope your project tightly at the outset. Solve one problem at a time and don't overcommit. As the expression goes, *underpromise and overdeliver*.

Anticipating Scope Creepy-Crawlies

Even if you scope the project perfectly from the beginning, the scope will naturally tend to grow and expand as the project progresses. This unruly phenomenon, known as *scope creep*, infects all projects. You must treat scope creep as the vicious and insidious monster that it is, and you must fight unwaveringly against it! If someone wants more, don't fall prey to the seductive temptation to just take on more in an attempt to accomplish more and satisfy more people. Even if you get more time and resources to accomplish more, you risk failing in your primary objective. New or increased scope should be reserved for another project.

Charting the Entire Course

A Six Sigma project is a process too, so it deserves maps, analysis, and controls just like any other process. You must chart the course and create a SIPOC diagram for your project. You accomplish this manageability by building and maintaining the *project charter,* which contains all the ingredients you must manage to ensure that your project is successful.

The project charter is your Magna Carta. It explicitly defines the scope and grants authority to project activities. It's the basis of communications and management. You measure your accomplishments by its goals and milestones.

The project charter is a living document. Changes to the project in any form, including scope (which is bad, but sometimes necessary), schedules, or resources, should be reflected in a formal change to the project charter and should be properly communicated and authorized. In this way, your changes are explicitly managed and approved.

Making Sure the Right People Are Aboard

Set sail on your project adventure with a core team of mates and hands, and be certain that the following are true of your team:

- You have all the right roles and skills present.
- You have only the right roles and skills present.

Having the right roles and skills is critical to the success of any project. For a Six Sigma project, make sure that your skill set includes the appropriate degree of measurement, analytical, simulation, and experimental prowess needed to address the causes that affect your significant Y. The key word here is "appropriate" — not too little and not too much. If you have too little prowess, the problems overpower you, but if you have too much, you're bound to overanalyze.

Remembering That Short Is Sweet

The milestone that matters most in your Six Sigma project is the endpoint — the point where you have demonstrated the breakthrough improvement in the performance of your key metric, or significant Y. Don't waste one minute — get there as fast as you can.

Swift project completion is paramount for two reasons:

- You lose interest and support if your project drags out. Team members with short attention spans will turn away, resources will dwindle, and people will lose confidence. Conversely, success attracts support and creates positive momentum.

✔ Slow project completion delays the creation of value in the organization. The cost of delay is significant — it cheats the organization out of money it would have if the project were completed.

Setting Achievable Goals

Some Six Sigma projects have failed not because they weren't important, well-defined, or properly staffed and supported, but because the improvements simply weren't achievable. After beginning with the best intentions, team members expect the project to reel in Xs whose controls were simply beyond reach.

The solutions that affect your significant Y must be practically achievable. As you complete your analyses and realize the critical few Xs that affect the outcomes, make sure in the improvement phase that you can actually implement the changes. Keep those changes simple, practical, understandable, and controllable.

Communicating for Success

Most projects and institutions are plagued by a failure to communicate. This failure results in lost time, ineffective outcomes, frustrated participants, overrun budgets, and unmet expectations due to a lack of awareness, coordination, and participation. Project leaders must regularly plow through these barriers.

In a Six Sigma project, communications failures most often include the failure to communicate with the groups whose processes, roles, obligations, workloads, empires, behaviors, and attitudes are redefined as you modify the critical Xs that create breakthrough performance in your significant Y. Not communicating with these groups can result in your failure to fully move a critical X, and therefore not achieve breakthrough.

Satisfying the Stakeholders

For every Six Sigma project, you find key stakeholders — the individuals who really matter and whose personal or professional agendas are significantly enhanced by a successful project outcome. At the end of the day, if you're successful and the stakeholders realize it, you'll likewise be rewarded.

These stakeholders may not necessarily be visible, and they may not even be openly supportive of the project. In fact, they may feign opposition in certain circles. However, knowing who they are and understanding the value and power they represent is vitally important. The true stakeholders may be executives, managers, or rank and file — basically anyone in the organization who will benefit when your project succeeds.

Maintaining Active and Unwavering Support

Maintaining active and unwavering support from the coalition of benefactors and beneficiaries alike is vital to the success of your project. Your most direct and authoritarian support comes from the official channels of approval, but you may also receive powerful support from the stakeholders.

Remember that Six Sigma projects often alienate those who have a vested interest in maintaining the status quo of the critical Xs. The success of your project means that you must marshal and maintain the armada of support required to displace all the resistance. Keep your channels of support fully informed, enroll your supporters in the process, and make them part of the success! Ask for help when you need it. And don't forget: You're enabled on this mission to pursue breakthrough performance gains in your significant Y and empowered to change the critical Xs.

Applying Formal Project Management

Just because Six Sigma projects are different from design or development projects doesn't mean that the formal rules of project management don't apply, because in reality they do. If you want your project to be successful, you need to treat the management of your project with the respect it deserves through the application of the methods and tools of formal project management.

Such formalities include the following:

- Official project documentation library
- Formal control, release, and configuration management of project information
- Official and prompt project status reporting and communications
- Strict budget, schedule, and milestone management
- Clearly defined and communicated participants, roles, and responsibilities

Index

• F •

BUSINESS, CAREERS & PERSONAL FINANCE

0-7645-5307-0

0-7645-5331-3 *†

Also available:

- Accounting For Dummies †
  0-7645-5314-3
- Business Plans Kit For Dummies †
  0-7645-5365-8
- Cover Letters For Dummies
  0-7645-5224-4
- Frugal Living For Dummies
  0-7645-5403-4
- Leadership For Dummies
  0-7645-5176-0
- Managing For Dummies
  0-7645-1771-6

- Marketing For Dummies
  0-7645-5600-2
- Personal Finance For Dummies *
  0-7645-2590-5
- Project Management For Dummies
  0-7645-5283-X
- Resumes For Dummies †
  0-7645-5471-9
- Selling For Dummies
  0-7645-5363-1
- Small Business Kit For Dummies *†
  0-7645-5093-4

HOME & BUSINESS COMPUTER BASICS

0-7645-4074-2

0-7645-3758-X

Also available:

- ACT! 6 For Dummies
  0-7645-2645-6
- iLife '04 All-in-One Desk Reference
  For Dummies
  0-7645-7347-0
- iPAQ For Dummies
  0-7645-6769-1
- Mac OS X Panther Timesaving
  Techniques For Dummies
  0-7645-5812-9
- Macs For Dummies
  0-7645-5656-8
- Microsoft Money 2004 For Dummies
  0-7645-4195-1

- Office 2003 All-in-One Desk Reference
  For Dummies
  0-7645-3883-7
- Outlook 2003 For Dummies
  0-7645-3759-8
- PCs For Dummies
  0-7645-4074-2
- TiVo For Dummies
  0-7645-6923-6
- Upgrading and Fixing PCs For Dummies
  0-7645-1665-5
- Windows XP Timesaving Techniques
  For Dummies
  0-7645-3748-2

FOOD, HOME, GARDEN, HOBBIES, MUSIC & PETS

0-7645-5295-3

0-7645-5232-5

Also available:

- Bass Guitar For Dummies
  0-7645-2487-9
- Diabetes Cookbook For Dummies
  0-7645-5230-9
- Gardening For Dummies *
  0-7645-5130-2
- Guitar For Dummies
  0-7645-5106-X
- Holiday Decorating For Dummies
  0-7645-2570-0
- Home Improvement All-in-One
  For Dummies
  0-7645-5680-0

- Knitting For Dummies
  0-7645-5395-X
- Piano For Dummies
  0-7645-5105-1
- Puppies For Dummies
  0-7645-5255-4
- Scrapbooking For Dummies
  0-7645-7208-3
- Senior Dogs For Dummies
  0-7645-5818-8
- Singing For Dummies
  0-7645-2475-5
- 30-Minute Meals For Dummies
  0-7645-2589-1

INTERNET & DIGITAL MEDIA

0-7645-1664-7

0-7645-6924-4

Also available:

- 2005 Online Shopping Directory
  For Dummies
  0-7645-7495-7
- CD & DVD Recording For Dummies
  0-7645-5956-7
- eBay For Dummies
  0-7645-5654-1
- Fighting Spam For Dummies
  0-7645-5965-6
- Genealogy Online For Dummies
  0-7645-5964-8
- Google For Dummies
  0-7645-4420-9

- Home Recording For Musicians
  For Dummies
  0-7645-1634-5
- The Internet For Dummies
  0-7645-4173-0
- iPod & iTunes For Dummies
  0-7645-7772-7
- Preventing Identity Theft For Dummies
  0-7645-7336-5
- Pro Tools All-in-One Desk Reference
  For Dummies
  0-7645-5714-9
- Roxio Easy Media Creator For Dummies
  0-7645-7131-1

* Separate Canadian edition also available
† Separate U.K. edition also available

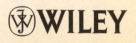

SPORTS, FITNESS, PARENTING, RELIGION & SPIRITUALITY

0-7645-5146-9

0-7645-5418-2

Also available:

- Adoption For Dummies
  0-7645-5488-3
- Basketball For Dummies
  0-7645-5248-1
- The Bible For Dummies
  0-7645-5296-1
- Buddhism For Dummies
  0-7645-5359-3
- Catholicism For Dummies
  0-7645-5391-7
- Hockey For Dummies
  0-7645-5228-7

- Judaism For Dummies
  0-7645-5299-6
- Martial Arts For Dummies
  0-7645-5358-5
- Pilates For Dummies
  0-7645-5397-6
- Religion For Dummies
  0-7645-5264-3
- Teaching Kids to Read For Dummies
  0-7645-4043-2
- Weight Training For Dummies
  0-7645-5168-X
- Yoga For Dummies
  0-7645-5117-5

TRAVEL

0-7645-5438-7

0-7645-5453-0

Also available:

- Alaska For Dummies
  0-7645-1761-9
- Arizona For Dummies
  0-7645-6938-4
- Cancún and the Yucatán For Dummies
  0-7645-2437-2
- Cruise Vacations For Dummies
  0-7645-6941-4
- Europe For Dummies
  0-7645-5456-5
- Ireland For Dummies
  0-7645-5455-7

- Las Vegas For Dummies
  0-7645-5448-4
- London For Dummies
  0-7645-4277-X
- New York City For Dummies
  0-7645-6945-7
- Paris For Dummies
  0-7645-5494-8
- RV Vacations For Dummies
  0-7645-5443-3
- Walt Disney World & Orlando For Dummies
  0-7645-6943-0

GRAPHICS, DESIGN & WEB DEVELOPMENT

0-7645-4345-8

0-7645-5589-8

Also available:

- Adobe Acrobat 6 PDF For Dummies
  0-7645-3760-1
- Building a Web Site For Dummies
  0-7645-7144-3
- Dreamweaver MX 2004 For Dummies
  0-7645-4342-3
- FrontPage 2003 For Dummies
  0-7645-3882-9
- HTML 4 For Dummies
  0-7645-1995-6
- Illustrator CS For Dummies
  0-7645-4084-X

- Macromedia Flash MX 2004 For Dummies
  0-7645-4358-X
- Photoshop 7 All-in-One Desk Reference For Dummies
  0-7645-1667-1
- Photoshop CS Timesaving Techniques For Dummies
  0-7645-6782-9
- PHP 5 For Dummies
  0-7645-4166-8
- PowerPoint 2003 For Dummies
  0-7645-3908-6
- QuarkXPress 6 For Dummies
  0-7645-2593-X

NETWORKING, SECURITY, PROGRAMMING & DATABASES

0-7645-6852-3

0-7645-5784-X

Also available:

- A+ Certification For Dummies
  0-7645-4187-0
- Access 2003 All-in-One Desk Reference For Dummies
  0-7645-3988-4
- Beginning Programming For Dummies
  0-7645-4997-9
- C For Dummies
  0-7645-7068-4
- Firewalls For Dummies
  0-7645-4048-3
- Home Networking For Dummies
  0-7645-42796

- Network Security For Dummies
  0-7645-1679-5
- Networking For Dummies
  0-7645-1677-9
- TCP/IP For Dummies
  0-7645-1760-0
- VBA For Dummies
  0-7645-3989-2
- Wireless All In-One Desk Reference For Dummies
  0-7645-7496-5
- Wireless Home Networking For Dummies
  0-7645-3910-8

HEALTH & SELF-HELP

0-7645-6820-5 *†

0-7645-2566-2

Also available:
- Alzheimer's For Dummies
  0-7645-3899-3
- Asthma For Dummies
  0-7645-4233-8
- Controlling Cholesterol For Dummies
  0-7645-5440-9
- Depression For Dummies
  0-7645-3900-0
- Dieting For Dummies
  0-7645-4149-8
- Fertility For Dummies
  0-7645-2549-2
- Fibromyalgia For Dummies
  0-7645-5441-7

- Improving Your Memory For Dummies
  0-7645-5435-2
- Pregnancy For Dummies †
  0-7645-4483-7
- Quitting Smoking For Dummies
  0-7645-2629-4
- Relationships For Dummies
  0-7645-5384-4
- Thyroid For Dummies
  0-7645-5385-2

EDUCATION, HISTORY, REFERENCE & TEST PREPARATION

0-7645-5194-9

0-7645-4186-2

Also available:
- Algebra For Dummies
  0-7645-5325-9
- British History For Dummies
  0-7645-7021-8
- Calculus For Dummies
  0-7645-2498-4
- English Grammar For Dummies
  0-7645-5322-4
- Forensics For Dummies
  0-7645-5580-4
- The GMAT For Dummies
  0-7645-5251-1
- Inglés Para Dummies
  0-7645-5427-1

- Italian For Dummies
  0-7645-5196-5
- Latin For Dummies
  0-7645-5431-X
- Lewis & Clark For Dummies
  0-7645-2545-X
- Research Papers For Dummies
  0-7645-5426-3
- The SAT I For Dummies
  0-7645-7193-1
- Science Fair Projects For Dummies
  0-7645-5460-3
- U.S. History For Dummies
  0-7645-5249-X

Get smart @ dummies.com®

- **Find a full list of Dummies titles**
- **Look into loads of FREE on-site articles**
- **Sign up for FREE eTips e-mailed to you weekly**
- **See what other products carry the Dummies name**
- **Shop directly from the Dummies bookstore**
- **Enter to win new prizes every month!**

* Separate Canadian edition also available
† Separate U.K. edition also available

Available wherever books are sold. For more information or to order direct: U.S. customers visit www.dummies.com or call 1-877-762-2974.
U.K. customers visit www.wileyeurope.com or call 0800 243407. Canadian customers visit www.wiley.ca or call 1-800-567-4797.